Reflections on Learning

Third Edition

Case Studies for Teacher Problem Solving
Second Edition

Rita Silverman
Pace University

William M. Welty
Pace University

Sally Lyon

Child Development: A Topical Approach

Diane E. Papalia

Dana Gross
Saint Olaf College

Ruth Duskin Feldman

Psychology: An Introduction
Ninth Edition

Benjamin B. Lahey
University of Chicago

Adolescence: Continuity, Change, and Diversity
Sixth Edition

Nancy Cobb
California State University-Los Angeles

Child and Adolescent Development for Educators
Third Edition

Judith L. Meece
University of North Carolina at Chapel Hill

Denise H. Daniels
California Polytechnics State University at San Luis Obispo

Educational Psychology
Third Edition

John W. Santrock
University of Texas at Dallas

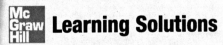

D1500809

McGraw Hill **Learning Solutions**

Boston   Burr Ridge, IL   Dubuque, IA   New York   San Francisco   St. Louis
Bangkok   Bogotá   Caracas   Lisbon   London   Madrid
Mexico City   Milan   New Delhi   Seoul   Singapore   Sydney   Taipei   Toronto

Reflections on Learning, Third Edition

This book is a McGraw-Hill Learning Solutions textbook and contains select material from the following sources:
Case Studies for Teacher Problem Solving, Second Edition by Rita Silverman, William M. Welty, Sally Lyon. Copyright © 1996 by The McGraw-Hill Companies, Inc.
Child Development: A Topical Approach by Diane E. Papalia, Dana Gross, Ruth Duskin Feldman. Copyright © 2003 by The McGraw-Hill Companies, Inc.
Psychology: An Introduction, Ninth Edition by Benjamin B Lahey. Copyright © 2007 by The McGraw-Hill Companies, Inc.
Adolescence: Continuity, Change, and Diversity, Sixth Edition by Nancy Cobb. Copyright © 2007 by The McGraw-Hill Companies, Inc.
Child and Adolescent Development for Educators, Third Edition by Judith L. Meece and Denise H. Daniels. Copyright © 2008 by The McGraw-Hill Companies, Inc.
Educational Psychology, Third Edition by John W. Santrock. Copyright © 2008 by The McGraw-Hill Companies, Inc.
All are reprinted with permission of the publisher. Many custom published texts are modified versions or adaptations of our best-selling textbooks. Some adaptations are printed in black and white to keep prices at a minimum, while others are in color.

4 5 6 7 8 9 0 QWD QWD 0 9

ISBN-13: 978-0-07-729359-8
ISBN-10: 0-07-729359-2

Learning Solutions Specialist: Kyle Zimmerman
Production Editor: Tina Hermsen
Printer/Binder: Quebecor World

Contents

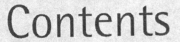

Expertise and Metacognition 101

Metacognition: A Bridge Between Cognitive Psychology and Educational Practice 115

UNIT 5

Piagetian Stages 125

Adolescent Thought 134

The Self and Gender 136

Unit 1

Chapter Outline

Learning Principles

1 DEFINITION OF LEARNING

Life is a process of continual change. From infancy to adolescence to adulthood to death, we are changing. Many factors produce those changes, but one of the most important is the process of **learning**. Through our experiences, we learn new information, new attitudes, new fears, and new skills. We also learn to understand new concepts, to solve problems in new ways, and even to develop a personality over a lifetime. And, in the course of reading textbooks, we learn new definitions for words such as *learning*. In psychology, the term *learning* refers to any relatively permanent change in behavior brought about through experience—that is, through interactions with the environment.

As the definition states, not *all* changes in behavior are the result of learning. The term is restricted to the relatively permanent, as opposed to temporary, changes that are the result of experience, rather than changes due to biological causes such as drugs, fatigue, maturation, and injury. If a baseball pitcher throws the ball differently this season because his pitching coach has demonstrated a new way to pitch, learning has occurred—a relatively permanent change in pitching due to the experience of the coach's demonstration. But if the pitcher's changed style is due to an injury, fatigue from throwing too much before each game, an arm strengthened by weight lifting, or biological maturation (if the pitcher is Little League pitcher), we would not refer to the change in pitching as learning.

The *change in behavior* is not always immediately obvious, however. If you watch a film on the proper way to hit backhands in tennis this winter, the change will not be evident until you are on the tennis court again next spring. Notice also that the definition of learning does not restrict its usage to intentionally produced changes in behavior or even to desirable changes in behavior. For instance, if you begin to loathe fish sandwiches because you got sick after eating one, learning has occurred. The new disgust for fish sandwiches is undesirable and certainly unintentional, but it's still the result of learning.

Over the years, psychologists have isolated and studied a number of ways that learning takes place. As a result, we now understand a number of different principles of learning. In the following sections, we describe these principles of learning and indicate some of the ways that they can influence us in our daily lives.

learning Any relatively permanent change in behavior brought about through experience.

Learning is any relatively permanent change in behavior brought about through experience.

2 CLASSICAL CONDITIONING: LEARNING BY ASSOCIATION

Our study of specific types of learning begins with a simple form called *classical conditioning*. The scientific study of classical conditioning began in Russia around the turn of the twentieth century with an accidental discovery made in the laboratory of Ivan Pavlov. Pavlov was a Russian physiologist who received a Nobel Prize for his work on the role of saliva in digestion. To study salivation, Pavlov surgically implanted tubes in the cheeks of his dogs. This allowed him to measure the amount of saliva produced when food was placed in their mouths (see Figure 1.1). Pavlov noticed that after a few days dogs in the experiment started salivating when the attendant entered the room with the food dish—*before* food was placed in their mouths. The sights (and probably sounds) of the attendant had come to *elicit* (evoke or produce) a reflexive response that only the food had originally elicited. This fact would have gone unnoticed had the saliva-collection tubes not been placed in the dogs' cheeks—that is the accidental part of the discovery. Noticing that a dog salivates whenever it sees the laboratory attendant who brings food may not seem like a great step forward for science at first glance. But Pavlov recognized that an inborn reflexive response to food, which was biologically "wired into" the dogs' nervous systems, had come under the control of an *arbitrary* stimulus—the sight of the attendant.

Stated in a different way, Pavlov knew he had witnessed a form of learning based on the repeated association of two stimuli. *Stimulus* is anything that can directly influence behavior or conscious experience. Because the dogs' experience of food was linked to the sight of the attendant, the dogs' behavior changed—the dogs now salivated to the stimuli of the approaching attendant. That is, the stimuli elicited a *response*. When you were born, you could respond to the outside world with only a limited repertoire of inborn reflexes, but now you are a marvelously complex product of your learning experiences. Pavlov wanted to understand this process of learning, so over his colleagues' objections, he hastily completed his studies of digestion and devoted the rest of his career to the study of learning (Watson, 1971).

Association: The Key Element in Classical Conditioning

More than 2,000 years before Pavlov, Aristotle noted that two sensations repeatedly experienced together become *associated*. For example, if you have frequently visited the seashore with a friend, visiting the seashore alone may trigger memories of that friend. If you got sick the last time you ate a hot dog, you will likely feel nauseous the next time you see one. Learning through association is a common part of our lives.

Pavlov considered classical conditioning to be a form of learning through association—the association in time of a neutral stimulus (one that originally does not elicit the response) and a stimulus that does elicit the response. Pavlov used an apparatus that was already constructed in his laboratory to measure the progress of learning, and he used food as the stimulus to elicit the response (of salivation).

FIGURE 1.1

Apparatus originally used by Pavlov to study the role of salivation in digestion, and later in his studies of classical conditioning.

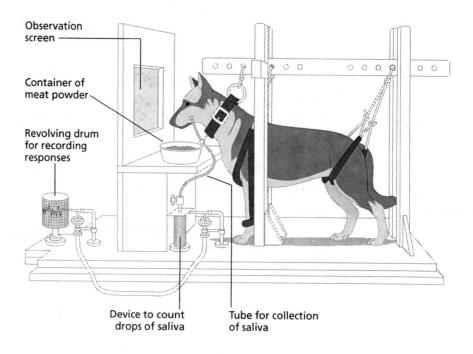

Observation screen

Container of meat powder

Revolving drum for recording responses

Device to count drops of saliva

Tube for collection of saliva

Ivan Pavlov (middle of photo) *accidentally discovered that dogs learn to associate the sounds of food being prepared with the food itself.*

Specifically, Pavlov presented (as the neutral stimulus) a clicking metronome that the dog could easily hear. After a precisely measured interval of time, he would blow a small quantity of meat powder into the dog's mouth to elicit salivation. Every 15 minutes, the same procedure was repeated, and soon the dog began salivating to the metronome when it was presented alone. By continuously measuring the amount of saliva drained through the tube in the dog's cheek, the strength of the new learning was accurately monitored throughout the process of classical conditioning.

Keep in mind that the key phrase in classical conditioning is the *association* of the two stimuli. The more frequently the metronome and the food are associated, the more often the metronome elicits salivation (see Figure 1.2). The *timing* of the association of the two stimuli is also highly important. Pavlov found, for example, that he obtained the best results when the metronome preceded the food powder by about a half a second. Longer time intervals were less effective, and almost no learning occurred when the metronome was presented at the same time as the food or when the food was presented slightly before the metronome.

Thus, Pavlov took advantage of a chance observation and began a systematic study of one aspect of the learning process. Although learning had been studied before Pavlov's time, his experiments were highly influential because of their extensiveness and precision. Perhaps his true genius lay in seeing that this simple form of learning had important implications far beyond clicking metronomes and salivating dogs. Pavlov's writings became an important part of American psychology when they came to the attention of John B. Watson, who expanded upon and popularized Pavlov's views in English.

Hank Ketcham, Dennis the Menance © North America Syndicate.

FIGURE 1.2

In Pavlov's studies, the more often the metronome was associated in time with meat powder, the more effective it was in eliciting salivation.

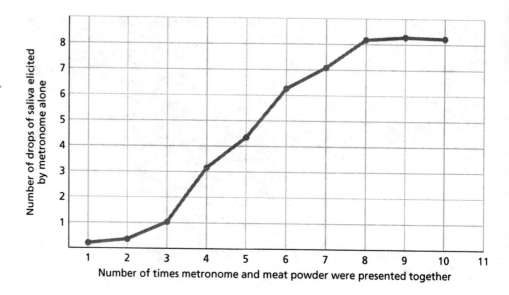

What Are Concepts?

3 DEFINITION OF COGNITION

Cognition can be defined as the intellectual processes (such as perception, memory, thinking, and language) through which information is obtained, transformed, stored, retrieved, and used. Let's analyze this complicated definition and its three primary facets:

1. *Cognition processes information.* Information is the stuff of cognition: the stuff that is obtained, transformed, kept, and used. Much of this information is dealt with in the form of categories or concepts, the subject of the next section.

2. *Cognition is active.* The information that the world gives us is actively changed, kept, and used in the process of cognition. In cognition, information is

    a) Obtained through the senses

    b) *Transformed* through the interpretive processes of perception and thinking

    c) *Stored and retrieved* through the processes of memory

    d) *Used* in problem solving and language

3. *Cognition is useful.* It serves a purpose. We think because there is something we do not understand. We use language when we need to communicate something to others. We create when we need something that does not exist. Humans use cognition to survive physically and to live in a social world.

In this chapter, we will survey problem solving, concept formation, language, and general intelligence. Other important aspects of cognition have already been discussed in the chapters on perception, consciousness, learning, and memory. And more aspects of cognition are mentioned in later chapters on development, emotion, personality, stress, abnormal behavior, and social psychology. Cognition is more than a topic in the science of psychology; it's a theme that cuts across many diverse topics.

4 CONCEPTS: THE BASIC UNITS OF THINKING

Concepts are the basic units of thinking. Concepts are general categories of things, events, and qualities that are linked by a common feature or features, in spite of their differences. About an hour ago, I went for a ride on my new bicycle. My bicycle is a specific object, but *bicycle* in general is a concept. I passed several people on bicycles as I rode—each bicycle was different in some ways from every other one, but I knew that they were all bicycles because they shared a list of characteristics (two wheels, pedals, and handlebars) that all bicycles share. I also passed a lot of things that were not bicycles (cars, trucks, and barbecue grills), but being a clever fellow, I knew in a flash that they were not bicycles because they did not have the features shared by all bicycles. Keep in mind that concepts are categories of more than just concrete things—the terms *vacation*, *romance*, and *generosity* refer to concepts as well.

cognition The intellectual processes through which information is obtained, transformed, stored, retrieved, and otherwise used.

concepts (kon´septs) Categories of things, events, and qualities that are linked together by a common feature or features in spite of their differences.

Cognition involves intellectual processes through which information is obtained, transformed, stored, retrieved, and put to use.

Adults take for granted that all these objects belong to the concept bicycle.

Nearly all productive thinking would be impossible were it not for concepts. Consider the following syllogism:

> All human beings are mortal.
> I am a human being.
> Therefore, I am mortal.

When I reason in that way, I am using the general concepts of *human beings* and *mortality*. Without concepts, we would be able to think only in terms of specific things and acts. Concepts allow us to process information in more general, efficient ways. In this way, concepts are the basic units of logical thinking.

Simple and Complex Concepts

We humans try to categorize things in simple ways and move to more complex concepts only when necessary (Feldman, 2003, Love & others, 2004). Simple concepts are based on a single common feature, such as the concept *red*. If a thing is red, it belongs to the concept *red* regardless of its other characteristics. Red apples, red balls, and red T-shirts are all examples of the concept *red*, in spite of the other ways in which these objects differ. Other concepts are more complex. **Conjunctive concepts** are defined by the simultaneous presence of two or more common characteristics. The concept of *aunt* is an example of a conjunctive concept because it has two simultaneous defining characteristics (female and sister of one of your parents). To be considered an aunt, a person must have both characteristics. **Disjunctive concepts** are defined by the presence of one common characteristic or another one, *or both*. For example, a person might be considered to be schizophrenic if he persistently has distorted perceptual experiences (such as hearing strange voices that are not there) or persistently holds distorted false beliefs (such as believing he is a king or a CIA agent), *or both*. The concept *schizophrenic person* is a disjunctive concept because it is defined by the presence of either of two characteristics or both of them.

Suppose the six cards in Figure 1.3 were presented to you in the order shown (left to right). The odd-numbered cards are members of the concept and the even-numbered cards are not. What is the concept—and is it a simple, conjunctive, or disjunctive concept?[1]

Natural Concepts

Eleanor Rosch (1973) has suggested that some concepts are easier for humans to learn than others; some are more *natural* than others. This idea is an important extension of the notion that we are biologically prepared to learn some things more readily than others. Rosch suggests that, by virtue of being born human beings, we are prepared to learn some concepts more easily than others. According to Rosch, natural concepts have two primary characteristics: They are *basic* and *prototypical*. Let's define these terms.

Natural Concepts Are Basic A *basic concept* is one that has a medium degree of *inclusiveness*. Inclusiveness simply refers to the number of members included in a concept. Three levels of inclusiveness have been distinguished by Rosch:

conjunctive concepts
(kon-junk´´tiv´) Concepts defined by the simultaneous presence of two or more common characteristics.

disjunctive concepts (dis-junk´´tiv´) Concepts defined by the presence of one of two common characteristics or both.

1. *Superordinate concepts are very inclusive.* Therefore, they contain a great many members. For example, *vehicles* is a superordinate concept that contains all of the many cars, boats, planes, wagons, and so on that carry loads (see Figure 1.4).

2. *Basic concepts are of a medium degree of inclusiveness.* Cars is an example of a basic concept because it is less inclusive than the superordinate concept *vehicles*, yet this category still includes many members.

3. *Subordinate concepts are the least inclusive level of concepts.* For example, the subordinate concept *sports car* includes far fewer members than the basic concept *cars* or the superordinate concept *vehicles*.

Rosch suggests that basic concepts are more natural and, hence, easier to learn and use. She offers an observation on the way in which young children learn concepts as evidence. Children generally learn basic concepts, such as *cars*, before they learn superordinate or subordinate concepts, such as *vehicles* or *sports cars*. Why is this so? Why are basic concepts easier to learn than either superordinate or subordinate concepts? Rosch suggests that the explanation lies in several characteristics of basic concepts that "fit" the human intellect very well (Matlin, 1983; Rosch, Mervis, Gray, Johnson, & Boyes-Braem, 1976).

1. *Basic concepts share many attributes.* For example, the members of the basic concept *screwdriver* are all used to turn screws, have a metal protrusion, have a handle, are usually 4 to 10 inches long, and so on. Members of the superordinate category of *tools* have far fewer characteristics in common. Although the members of the subordinate category of chrome-plated screwdrivers have many common characteristics, only a few of them are not also common to the basic concept of screwdrivers (Jones, 1983).

2. *Members of basic concepts share similar shapes.* All screwdrivers (a basic concept) are shaped about the same, but the same cannot be said about all tools (a superordinate concept). The shapes of all chrome-plated screwdrivers (a subordinate concept) are also similar, but they are distinguishable from other screwdrivers on the basis of only one difference—the chrome plating—that has nothing to do with shape.

3. *Members of basic concepts often share motor movements.* The motor movements associated with members of basic-level concepts are similar (turning screwdrivers), but the same cannot be said for superordinate concepts (the motor

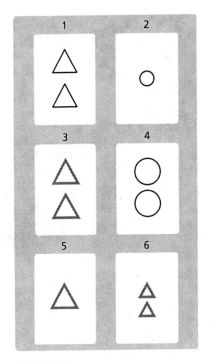

FIGURE 1.3
Cards like those used in laboratory studies of concept formation.

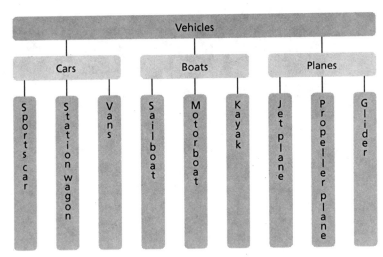

Superordinate concept	Vehicles								
Basic concepts	Cars			Boats			Planes		
Subordinate concepts	Sports car	Station wagon	Vans	Sailboat	Motorboat	Kayak	Jet plane	Propeller plane	Glider

FIGURE 1.4
Basic concepts, which include neither the most nor the least other concepts under them, are easier to learn than superordinate or subordinate concepts.

Medium-degree inclusive concepts such as cars *are called basic concepts; the broader concept of* vehicle *is a superordinate concept; and the narrower concept of* luxury sedan *is a subordinate concept.*

movements for using different kinds of tools are very different). Members of subordinate concepts like chrome-plated screwdrivers also share motor movements, but they are generally the same as or similar to the basic concept to which they belong (see Figure 1.5).

4. *Basic concepts are easily named.* If you were asked to name a half-dozen objects in your classroom, most of the words that you would use probably would refer to the basic concepts to which the objects belong. When referring to a chrome-plated screwdriver, we tend to say *screwdriver* instead of tool or chrome-plated screwdriver.

Rosch believes that these four characteristics of basic concepts make them more "natural"—easier to learn and use in the human information-processing system.

Natural Concepts Are Good Prototypes   The second defining characteristic of natural concepts is that they are good examples, or *prototypes* (Rosch, 1975). If you were asked to give the best example, or the prototype, of the superordinate concept *toy*, you might say *doll* or toy *fire truck*, but you would be unlikely to say *sandbox*. Similarly, you might think of *chair* or *sofa* as prototypes of the superordinate concept of *furniture*, but you would not think of *carpet*. Rosch suggests that natural concepts tend to be both basic and good prototypes.

In her research with the Dani tribe of New Guinea, Rosch (1973) has provided intriguing evidence to support her notion that natural concepts are good prototypes. This tribe, which possessed a very limited technology in the 1970s, has only two color concepts in its vocabulary: *mola* for light colors and *mili* for dark colors. Hence, these people were ideal individuals for research on learning new color concepts.

Rosch's Dani research participants were taught to give a label to members of a color category that corresponded to both "pure" primary colors (wavelengths that are near the middle of the range described as red or blue, for example) and intermediate

FIGURE 1.5

Members of the basic concepts like *screwdrivers* often share the same motor movements in spite of other differences.

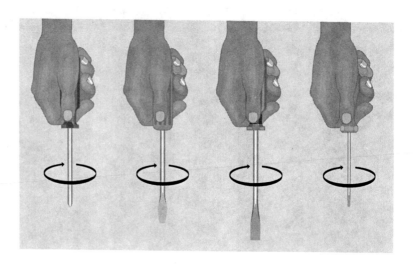

colors (such as bluish-green). Both kinds of color names are basic concepts (with the superordinate concept being *color*), but the Dani learned the names of the primary colors more easily.

The memory for details of an experience fades more rapidly than memory for the gist—the general idea. Consistent with Rosch's research, memories fade to make them consistent with basic concepts (Pansky & Koriat, 2004). Basic concepts are central to many aspects of cognition.

Review

Concepts are the basic units of thinking. They allow us to reason because they permit us to think in general categories. Concepts are categories that have one or more features in common in spite of differences among members of that concept. All red things belong to the concept of red even though apples, fire trucks, and red balls differ from one another in many ways. Some concepts are defined by a single characteristic, whereas others are defined by multiple characteristics in complex ways. Not all concepts are equally easy to learn; apparently, some concepts are more "natural" than others. These natural concepts are easy to learn because they are of a medium degree of inclusiveness and are good prototypes.

Check Your Learning

To be sure that you have learned the key points from the preceding section, cover the list of correct answers and try to answer each question. If you give an incorrect answer to any question, return to the page given next to the correct answer to see why your answer was not correct. Remember that these questions cover only some of the important information in this section; it is important that you make up your own questions to check your learning of other facts and concepts.

1. _____ are categories of things, events, or qualities that are linked by some common feature or features in spite of their differences.

2. The concept of *aunt* is an example of a _____ because it has two simultaneous defining characteristics (female and sibling of one of your parents).
   a) disjunctive concept   c) simple concept
   b) conjunctive concept   d) natural concept

3. By virtue of being born human beings, we are prepared to learn some concepts more easily than others. These concepts are termed

   _____ .

   a) simple concepts   c) natural concepts
   b) disjunctive concepts   d) conjunctive concepts

4. Which of the following statements is *not* true?
   a) Basic concepts share many attributes.
   b) Basic concepts share similar shapes.
   c) Basic concepts often share motor movements.
   d) Basic concepts are difficult to describe in words.

Thinking Critically about Psychology

There are no right or wrong answers to the following questions. They are presented to help you become an active reader and think critically about what you have just read.

1. What is your favorite kind of thing (think of a concept, not a specific thing)? Try to describe in words the prototype of that concept.
2. Recall what you learned earlier about the role of the cones in color vision. Does this suggest why primary colors are "natural" color concepts?

Correct Answers: 1. Concepts (p. 273), 2. b (p. 273), 3. c (p. 274), 4. d (p. 275).

Endnotes

1. The concept illustrated in this example is large triangles, which is a conjunctive concept.

Children's Analogical Reasoning in a Third-Grade Science Discussion

—David B. May

University System of Maryland, 3300 Metzerott Rd., Adelphi, MD 20783-1690, USA

—David Hammer

Department of Curriculum & Instruction, University of Maryland, College Park, MD 20742, USA

—Patricia Roy

Mount Rainier Elementary School, Prince George's County Public Schools, 4011 32nd St., Mount Rainier, MD 20712, USA

Preview

ABSTRACT: Expert scientific inquiry involves the generation and use of analogies. How and when students might develop this aspect of expertise has implications for understanding how and when instruction might facilitate that development. In a study of K-8 student inquiry in physical science, we are examining cases of spontaneous analogy generation. In the case we present here, a third-grader generates an analogy and modifies it to reconcile his classmates' counterarguments, allowing us to identify in these third-graders specific aspects of nascent expertise in analogy use. Promoting abilities and inclinations such as these children display requires that educators recognize and respond to them.
© 2006 Wiley Periodicals, Inc. Sci Ed 90:316–330, 2006

5 INTRODUCTION

A third-grade class is having a discussion about what causes earthquakes. One boy, Skander, gives his idea:

> You know if the ground is closed and there's lava, like, a giant rock, er a giant rock might fall into the lava and which would cause the lava to go up because it's pressing it to go up. . . . if it goes into the lava it cause it to go up and then the ground starts shaking to um open.

A minute later, Skander uses an analogy to explain his idea further:

> You know how if you fill your water up and you put like too many ice cubes in it, it can flood? That's what I mean. . . . a rock could go in, and pretend like, pretend the lava is water and the giant rock is a cube. It goes up and since it's blocked, the ground has to shake which causes it to crack open so it it'll actually like go up farther. So it's like you're actually flooding the cup of the water.

Skander is wrong about what causes earthquakes in several respects. To educators focused on conceptual change, the significance of this moment would lie there, in Skander's understanding of earthquakes. Consequently, the instructional challenge would be to elicit and confute the misconception that the ground cracks open in an earthquake and, perhaps, to guide him and his classmates toward a basic understanding of shifting tectonic plates.

We also expect that most educators would notice and appreciate Skander's analogy as an impressive bit of third-grade intelligence and expressiveness, as they might admire a child's imagination and articulateness in some everyday setting. But that observation would typically be of little technical interest, merely an informal appreciation off the point of the lesson. Science education research and methods texts offer little basis for instructional attention to children's abilities for analogical reasoning, to how Skander used an analogy to explain his reasoning or, as we recount below, to how his classmates went on to think about it.

Our purpose is twofold: (1) to contribute case-study evidence that even children without formal training have the beginnings of scientific abilities for generating and using analogies, and (2) to argue that elementary science education should pay these abilities direct instructional attention.

Research on Analogies

Over the last two decades, researchers have used carefully controlled laboratory studies to examine the cognitive mechanisms involved in analogy use (e.g., Gentner, 1983; Gick & Holyoak, 1980, 1983). Most take an analogy to consist of a target case (about which new knowledge is desired), a base case (which is generally already understood to some extent), and a relation that maps elements from one case to the other; the analogy helps learners make connections between the pre-existing base knowledge and the new target (Driver & Bell, 1986). Other accounts suggest analogies facilitate abstraction from individual cases to general schemata (Duit, 1991; Gick & Holyoak, 1983; Rumelhart & Norman, 1981) or help the learner generate new inferences about the target (Gentner, 1983). Some authors have noted that analogies can support productive conceptual change when neither the target nor base are well understood; knowledge of each case can be enriched through a process of "bootstrapping" (Duit et al., 2001; Kurtz, Miao, & Gentner, 2001). Some have investigated how analogies are used in nonexperimental settings such as political debates (Blanchette & Dunbar, 2001).

Research on analogies in science education, although done with a variety of theoretical approaches, has focused almost exclusively on their pedagogical value in materials and in teachers' explanations for promoting conceptual change in students. The use of analogies for instruction, whether initiated by the text, by the teacher, or by the students themselves, has been shown to improve conceptual learning in a variety of science contexts (Dagher, 1995a; Duit, 1991), including psychology (Mayo, 2001), mathematics (Didierjean & Cauzinille-Marmeche, 1998), biology (Baker & Lawson, 2001; Glynn & Takahashi, 1998; Kaufman, Patel, & Magder, 1996; Mason, 1994; Newby, Ertmer, & Stepich, 1995; Pittman, 1999; Swain, 2000), and physics (Chiu & Lin, 2005; Clement, 1988, 1989, 1993, 1998; Heywood & Parker, 1997; Mason & Sorzio, 1996; Stavy, 1991; Wong, 1993a, 1993b). In addition, instructional activities involving student-generated analogies may reveal student understanding better than traditional assessment (Pittman, 1999).

Most of the discussion focuses on analogies presented to students, usually in instructional materials, sometimes in teachers' spontaneous use (Dagher, 1995b). Studies that address student-generated analogies in science (e.g., Clement, 1988, 1989, 1998; Wong, 1993a, 1993b) generally maintain the emphasis on their relevance for conceptual understanding.

Mostly tacit in this literature is the understanding that the generation and use of analogies comprise an aspect of professional science. This is more prominent in studies of science, where by many accounts analogical reasoning plays a central role in scientific expertise (Dunbar & Blanchette, 2001; Hesse, 1966; Hofstadter, 2003; Leatherdale, 1974; Nersessian, 1992; Rouvray, 1994). Analogical reasoning may even be "the main engine of inventive thinking" in scientific discovery (Hofstadter, 2003). A small body of research in science education has begun to place analogical reasoning into the foreground (Clement, 1988, 1989, 1993, 1998; Else, Clement, & Ramirez, to appear; Mayo, 2001), identifying elements of expertise in older students: Students can generate analogies spontaneously, evaluate their validity and refine them accordingly, use them to create new knowledge, and use them to communicate ideas to others.

Children's Abilities

Our purpose in this article is to help extend the study of analogical reasoning to children. We argue that children show these abilities as well, or the beginnings of them, and we argue that elementary science education should pay them direct instructional attention. We are beginning work to understand analogies as students use them in science classrooms. In a study of K-8 inquiry in physical science, we have seen a variety of cases of spontaneous analogy generation at different levels of sophistication.

Below we provide a detailed example of how this third-grade student, Skander, generates and uses an analogy when engaging in inquiry in physical science with his classmates, and how his classmates respond to it. By looking closely at this episode, we attempt to identify some aspects of expertise in analogy use that can be seen among young children and therefore may be developed and encouraged by instruction.

We have chosen this episode for several reasons. First, we believe it is a clear example of early sophistication in the generation and use of analogies, a quintessential instance of what we argue instruction should promote. Second, the analogy is incorrect, and this is valuable in that it helps us focus on its value *as inquiry*, not conflated with a value for conceptual understanding. National standards (e.g., National Committee on Science Education Standards and Assessment, 1996) have argued for a shift in emphasis toward learning science as inquiry, a different emphasis from learning the content of science *by* inquiry (Hodson, 1988), but it can be difficult to distinguish these objectives. In specific moments of instruction, there is often tension between objectives of inquiry and conceptual understanding. We have chosen an instance of that tension, rather than another in which the child's analogy was in line with the intended conceptual objectives. This provides a basis for discussing what it means for instruction to focus on this aspect of sophistication in scientific inquiry as a target of instruction in its own right, rather than as an approach to the target of conceptual understanding.

To be clear, and to forestall possible confusion, we will use the word "expertise" in referring to the children's abilities. Naturally, we do not mean that they are experts as scientists! We use the term to refer to everyday reasoning abilities children have developed. By the time children are in third grade, they are "experts" at many things. Most are experts at walking, for example, and well on their way to expertise at running, using dinner table utensils, pencils, and so on. In other areas, such as throwing and catching a ball or turning cartwheels, we may expect only to see the beginnings of expertise, beginnings that if attended and developed would contribute to expertise in more refined activities of baseball or gymnastics.

To think of cognitive abilities, most children are experts at counting, at learning songs, or (in many cases) at a variety of computer games. Here we are pointing to analogical reasoning—generation, recognition, use, and critique of analogies—as a potential area of everday expertise. We will speak of the beginnings of expertise in children, beginnings that if attended and developed would contribute to expertise in the more refined activities of scientific inquiry.

The rest of this article is organized as follows. In the following section, we draw from the literature on expertise in analogical reasoning, in older students and scientists, to posit a starting framework for looking at children's analogies. We then present the case study of Skander's analogy and argue that it shows several aspects of expertise, on the part of Skander in generating and applying his analogy and on the part of his classmates in criticizing and extending it. Finally, we discuss implications and further directions for research and instruction.

6 EXPERTISE IN ANALOGICAL REASONING

The literature cited above highlights the prevalence of analogies in expert thinking and describes why and how analogy use is helpful for constructing understanding in many contexts, especially in teaching and learning science. These findings point to the need to explore students' capabilities for using analogies. Although the literature is sparse in this realm, several different elements of expertise in generating and using analogies have been identified, or at least suggested, by education and psychology researchers.

Here we cull from that literature aspects of the phenomenology of analogies in scientific reasoning. This is not to construct a model of expertise or constituent abilities; our intent here is simply to review the sorts of things older students and scientists do and from there to compare what we have observed with children. Consequently, we will not claim that Skander or his classmates are experts, only that in this episode, they display much of what we know experts consistently do when using analogies.

The most basic aspect is simply that of *generating analogies* in the course of learning, problem solving, or conducting an investigation. Clement (1988, 1989, 1998) showed that many undergraduate students and technical experts generate analogies when attempting to solve physics problems in interview settings. For example, Clement (1998) describes how one scientist generated an analogy spontaneously to help him solve the "wheel-push problem," which asks whether it takes more, less, or the same effort to push a wheel up a hill (Figure 1.6a) by pushing along the top edge (at X) rather than toward its center (at Y). In his analogy, the wheel is replaced by a heavy lever hinged to the hill (Figure 1.6b). Dunbar and Blanchette (2001) showed that spontaneous analogies tend to be structurally deeper than analogies generated by prompting, which are often based on more superficial features.

Regardless of the impetus for generating an analogy, using the analogy successfully often requires that the user establishes or confirms his or her understanding of the base case (Clement 1988, 1998; Duit, 1991; Else et al., to appear). This highlights one of the important analytic activities of experts: *validating the analogy*. Clement (1998) has identified three methods experts use to establish for themselves the validity of an analogy: (1) matching key features between cases, (2) generating a bridging case which shares features of both the target and base cases, and (3) finding a conserving transformation by using multiple bridging cases. The first of these, matching key features, may be an important skill regardless of whether analogy validation is sought. It involves mapping relationships that exist among the elements of each case (Gentner, 1983), as well as mapping the elements themselves. For example, middle-school students applying the analogy of a river delta to the human circulatory system (given to them by the teacher) successfully mapped the key relationship that vessels branch from big to small (Else et al., to appear).

Several researchers have also suggested that students should be able to *criticize* a particular analogy and determine its limitations by looking for similarities and differences between target and base (Clement, 1998; Heywood & Parker, 1997; Mayo, 2001; Wong, 1993a, 1993b). Indeed, Clement's (1998) subject noticed that unlike the hinge at the bottom of the lever, the "fulcrum" at the bottom of the wheel is not fixed in place

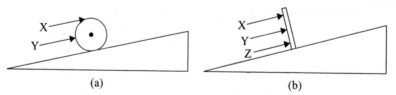

(a)   (b)

FIGURE 1.6

(a) The "Wheel-push problem" and (b) one scientist's analogy for solving it. Adapted from Clement (1998).

(Figure 1.6); this mismatch between key features caused him to question the validity of his analogy. It is also important to be able to *refine* or "re-represent" an analogy in response to criticism, something that has been seen in undergraduate physics students (Clement, 1989; Wong, 1993a, 1993b). Mayo (2001) has shown that undergraduates in psychology can deliberately make use of peer feedback for refining their analogies.

In addition to these analytic activities, analogies are used by experts for what might be considered their main purpose, *new knowledge creation*. In particular, analogies allow one to *make new inferences* about the target (Gentner, 1983; Kurtz et al., 2001). Duit et al. (2001) have observed students spontaneously testing conjectures about the base case in the target case, and vice versa, when provided with an analogy generated by the teacher. This process has been referred to elsewhere as "bootstrapping" (Kurtz et al., 2001). In addition, expert-like analogy use sometimes involves the synthesis of *abstract knowledge* or general principles, as when the student sees deeper structural similarities between the target and base rather than just surface similarities (Clement, 1989; Gick and Holyoak, 1983; Kurtz et al., 2001). In general, it is a sign of sophistication to be able to reason about phenomena for which one does not already have a well-structured understanding.

Finally, many have long known that expert scientists and teachers of science often use analogies for *communicating knowledge* to others (Duit, 1991; Hesse, 1966; Hofstadter, 2003; Leatherdale, 1974). Communication using analogies is therefore another important aspect of expertise. All of the aspects cited above are listed in Table 1.1.

TABLE 1.1

Aspects of Expert Analogy Use

Generation
Analysis
  - Understanding the base
  - Validating by matching key features
  - Criticizing
  - Determining limitations
  - Refining
Synthesis of new knowledge
  - Making new inferences about the target
  - Creating abstract generalizations
Communication

While many of these aspects of analogy use have been documented in experts and older students, research has not focused on how young children use analogies in science. This may reflect perspectives of developmental limitations on children's abilities for theoretical inquiry (e.g., Kuhn, 1993). Recent work has challenged those perspectives (Metz, 1995, 1997). We have seen almost all of these aspects of expertise in children's analogical reasoning. We present an example in the following section.

7 THIRD-GRADE STUDENTS THINK ABOUT EARTHQUAKES

Case Studies of K-8 Student Inquiry in Physical Science, funded by the National Science Foundation, is a collaboration of classroom teachers and university researchers to develop written and video case studies of students' scientific inquiry. These case studies were primarily for the purposes of professional development materials, to help inservice and preservice teachers learn to assess children's scientific thinking in the classroom.

Patricia Roy is one of the teachers in the project, and this case study concerns a conversation in her third-grade class about earthquakes. There were 26 students present for a 30-min inquiry lesson which consisted entirely of a loosely guided student discussion on a single topic. The whole class had been reading and talking about natural disasters, including volcanoes and tornadoes but not earthquakes. One of the small reading groups, reading below grade level, had read a story about earthquakes, and this led Ms. Roy to start a conversation with the full class on their ideas about how earthquakes happen. Ms. Roy's purpose in the discussion was to help the children learn to express and discuss their ideas, rather than to guide them to any particular answer; she was also hoping to draw the students from the reading group into participating.

In the first 15–20 min of the discussion, several students proposed various ideas for what might trigger earthquakes, from "scientists digging in the earth trying to find dinosaur bones" to "it's broken ground already and it just starts to crack again." Students mentioned dry land, the heat of the earth's core, crashing spaceships, and ground that is too thin or too old as possible causes. They also had ideas that the earth's rotation might cause it to shake or that the rain makes the ground "soft and crumbly."

Skander was a participant throughout, agreeing with other students' ideas about the "heat from dry land" as somehow causing earthquakes. He also put forth his own general idea that something must "crack the ground" all the way down to the earth's "lava center" for an earthquake to happen. He suggested that phenomena such as meteors, tornadoes, or a fictitious "giant drill" could start the process by cracking the ground, but did not seem to think it necessary to come up with a single explanation.

We focus our analysis on 10 min of conversation, that begins after about 20 min, when Skander has a new idea:

165. Skander: You know if the ground is closed and there's lava, like, a giant rock, er a giant rock might fall into the lava and which would cause the lava to go up because it's pressing it to go up—
166. Teacher: What's pressing it to go up, the rock?
167. Skander: Yeah.
168. Teacher: And where does that rock come from?
169. Skander: Um, part of the um ground. The ground cracks and if it goes into the lava it cause it to go up and then the ground starts shaking to um open.

This explanation is consistent with his general idea that something must "crack the earth," although in this case the earth is cracked from below. Here Skander is suggesting that a rock falls into the lava that lies underneath the earth's surface, causing the lava to rise. The lava then presses on the ground from below, causing the ground to shake and crack.

In keeping with the style of the conversation so far, the students listen to Skander, but they do not actively address his explanation. Two other students speak about two other ideas, and then Skander repeats his, this time explaining it in terms of an analogy:

176. Skander: Another thing that can, you know how if you fill your water up and you put like too many ice cubes in it, it can flood?
177. Teacher: Mm hm.
178. Skander: That's what I mean. A rock could—like, the volcano is this big [motions with hands] and you're on this side of the ground, a rock could go in, and pretend like, pretend the lava is water and the giant rock is a cube [Teacher: okay] it goes up and since it's blocked the ground has to shake which causes it to crack open so it it'll actually like go up farther.
179. Teacher: Okay, so you're . . .
180. Skander: So it's like you're actually flooding the cup of the water.
181. Teacher: And so the rock acting as the ice cube is flooding the lava so it has to come up and go out?
182. Skander: It doesn't have to, it just makes the ground come, it just needs space to go up. It's just causing it to shake and crack open.

Skander is making an analogy between how ice cubes make the water level rise and how rocks can make the lava level rise. His contribution shows several aspects of analogical reasoning seen in older students and experts. First, he generates his analogy spontaneously. His reason for generating and using it appears to be to help his classmates understand his original idea about rocks in lava, although it is also possible it helps him develop his own understanding of the situation. More specifically, he establishes familiarity with the base for his classmates by inviting them to consider a familiar situation, using phrases like "You know . . .?" and "pretend." To explain the analogy (or simply to clarify it for himself), he carefully maps elements of the base to the target, and in fact goes back and forth between the two. Also, he seems to do all this unselfconsciously, not perceptibly worrying that an analogy would be suspect or irrelevant.

When the conversation continues, other students take up Skander's idea, including two students, Hugo and Andrew, from the reading group Ms. Roy had hoped to engage.

183. Teacher: Okay. Yes, Hugo.
184. Hugo: I don't agree with Skander because . . .
185. Teacher: You said you do or you don't?
186. Hugo: I don't.
187. Teacher: You don't agree with Skander, okay. Why?
188. Hugo: Because um if the um a giant rock goes into a lava that will make it melt.
189. Teacher: You think the lava will melt the rock, and not cause it to push back up?
190. Andrew: I don't agree with Hugo because he said, he said the rock lava will melt but . . .
191. Teacher: 'Scuse me, wait a minute. [Talks to another student briefly.]
192. Andrew: He said the rock will melt but what if it's only a little bit of lava and it's a big rock, a big, big rock?
193. Teacher: Good question.
194. Ben: But it'll still melt, melt because of the lava's heat.
195. Teacher: Okay. So what do think about Skander theory then, that the . . .
196. Ben: I don't think about Skander's was right about that because a rock will automatically melt, melt right when it touch the lava.
197. Teacher: Okay.
198. Hugo: It's like acid.
199. Teacher: Okay, so but it's, if you think about his comparison to the, the ice cube into the water, the ice will melt eventually but it doesn't melt like right away. Before it melts, it pushes that water level up, right? But you don't think lava works in that way with rocks? Skander?

Apparently Skander was right to expect that using an analogy was not suspect or irrelevant. On the contrary, as soon as Skander presents his analogy, the focus of the class discussion shifts. Now students are actively considering Skander's original explanation about rocks in lava, although in different ways. Almost immediately, Hugo and Ben disagree and present a counterargument that if "a giant rock goes into the lava, that will make it melt." To elaborate on the effect of lava on a rock, Hugo spontaneously generates an analogy of his own, "It's like acid," although he uses it differently than Skander uses his—to illustrate a single point rather than an entire explanatory mechanism. It is not evident from their comments whether Hugo and Ben are criticizing Skander's explanation of what might trigger an earthquake (rocks in lava), or if they take issue with his choice of ice water as an appropriate analogy for the explanation.

When Skander next gets the floor, he defends his analogy.

200. Skander: I don't agree with Ben because the earth, the lava would actual melt but if the ground was like this . . .
201. Teacher: The lava would actually do what?
202. Skander: I kinda agree with Hugo and Ben, but I also agree with myself because if the lava's right here and the ground was right here, the rock would actually go into the lava but melt but cause *more* lava because when it melts, it's like it's like you're adding more lava and it'll cause, it still crack to make an earthquake . . .

203. Teacher: Okay, very interesting.
204. Kander: . . .because it's a solid.
205. Teacher: Because it's a solid?
206. Skander: It could melt and make more lava.
207. Teacher: Okay.

At first, Skander prefaces his response with "I don't agree with Ben," but then changes to "I kinda agree with Hugo and Ben, but I also agree with myself," an indication that he has reconciled their argument with his. He achieves this reconciliation by revising his original explanation only slightly to account for the fact that the rock does melt, but in melting it makes more lava.

Skander does not mention ice or water here. One possibility is that the analogy was still guiding his reasoning, as he thought of ice melting and becoming liquid water. If so, it is an example of applying an existing analogy to make new inferences about the target situation. Another possibility is that Skander was thinking in more general terms about conservation of matter, in which case the analogy had helped him synthesize (or call to mind) a generalization.

208. Jovan: I agree with Skander because if you um put a rock in, um, in um lava once it melts the um rock it's like, it's like the rock is um still in the lava so it still goes up.
209. Andrew: I agree with Skander too because if you put a ice cube in [inaudible] and wait, and some water and wait for a long time, it melts and makes more water.

Not only does Skander's revised explanation meet with agreement from at least two students, but they each have different creative ways to express their agreement. Jovan clarifies that when the rock melts, "it's like the rock is um still in the lava," and thus still has the effect that Skander has explained. Andrew explicitly *extends* the ice and water analogy, making the connection clear between the target and the analogy with respect to this new attribute, that the melting solid makes more liquid.

Skander reiterates Andrew's idea, saying that "if you put the um the ice in it, it would melt but also makes more water," and then Alex presents another counterargument:

223. Alex: I disagree with Skander because water and ice cube is practically the same. An ice cube is just frozen water, and rock is different than lava, 'cause lava isn't, isn't, isn't made, doesn't become a rock when it's frozen.

Alex is making an error here with respect to specific content knowledge—lava does in fact become a rock when it is frozen. Given what he thinks, however, he may be quite right to worry that rock is a different kind of thing. If the "rock" were dry ice or styrofoam, for example, it would take up much less space in its melted form. His argument thus reveals aspects of sophistication, not only in the fact that he is criticizing the analogy at all (rather than rejecting ice and water as irrelevant *prima facie*), but also in the form his criticism takes: identifying what he sees as a key difference between the target (rock in lava) and base (ice in water). He may believe that Skander's explanation is generally true (he does not say), but it is clear that he contests the claim that the melting rock "makes more lava."

In the last several minutes of conversation, Jovan introduces another line of reasoning:

226. Jovan: I agree with Skander because if you get a giant ice cube and um, with the lava [inaudible] underground, and a earthquake was happening? And if you put the ice cube in the um, if you put the ice cube in the, with the lava, it will um—
227. Teacher: The ice cube? With the lava?
228. Jovan: Uh huh.
229. Teacher: Or the ice cube with the water?
230. Jovan: The ice cube with the lava, [inaudible] little bit melt some in the lava, but the um the um lava will still um go higher.

Several other students follow suit, talking about what would happen to an *ice cube* if *it* were placed in lava, in this way conflating the ice/water analogy base with the rock/lava target. At this moment, they seem not to understand how analogies work. An alternative possibility is that they were constructing a *bridging analogy* (Clement, 1993), an intermediate situation between the base and target that can help transfer knowledge from one to the other. Thinking of ice melting into lava, Jovan could describe the liquid taking up space, whether or not the solid and liquid are the same substance. Alternatively, the case of ice in lava could simply be a *closer* analog to the target situation, and therefore easier to apply for these students, and not actually used to bridge from the ice water case.

Skander appears to accept this intermediate situation and sees it as helping his case.

236. Skander: Jovan was kinda right: if you put a giant ice cube as in a giant rock, you, the um, the ice would actually melt which would cause a flood, because if your water was like this and the cup was this big, if you put a giant ice cube in it, in a couple of minutes the ice would cause a flood, or the water will, because um, there's a giant um ice cube, which would causing it to flood.

To Skander, Jovan's argument is not in conflict with his original analogy. The class is still talking about putting ice in lava when time runs out and the lesson ends.

8 DISCUSSION

This case study illustrates young children's nascent understanding and abilities for analogical reasoning in science. Students in this class are able to use an analogy unselfconsciously in a systematic way, moving from target to base and back again, refining and clarifying each in an attempt to "bootstrap" (Kurtz et al., 2001) their way to a consistent understanding of both (even if they do not quite get there).

The case revolves around one student, Skander, for whom there is the most evidence of sophistication. He spontaneously generates an analogy not to illustrate just a single idea, but to explain an entire mechanism to his classmates (and perhaps also to refine his own understanding). He establishes familiarity with the base (ice cubes in water) and maps elements of the base to the target. He may also have applied his analogy to make new inferences about his original explanation, and his analogy may have helped him reconcile his classmates' counterarguments with apparent ease. Indeed, Else and colleagues make several recommendations for analogy use *by the teacher*, most of which we can see this student follow: use a simple analogy, explicitly introduce the analogy and explain its purpose, establish familiarity with the base, identify the target and establish grounds for comparison, map the base to the target, establish the limits of mapping, and confirm understanding of target knowledge (Else et al., to appear).

There is evidence as well of other students' understanding and abilities. First, the students tacitly accepted the analogy as a legitimate move in the conversation and in reasoning, to compare rocks melting in lava to an entirely different situation. In fact, several students focused on the idea for several minutes of conversation. Several students had criticisms, but these all concerned particular aspects of the comparison, not the fact of the comparison in general. (Teaching university introductory physics, we have learned not to take this for granted: Our students are often distrustful of analogical reasoning, preferring to talk only about "what is actually going on." See Hammer, 2004.)

Andrew successfully extended and refined Skander's analogy. Alex (and possibly Hugo and Ben as well) criticized Skander's analogy and sought to find its limitations by identifying differences between target and base. Jovan and others spontaneously generated and considered their own alternate analogy of ice cubes in lava. Andrew, Alex, and Jovan seemed to have had trouble figuring out what it means for the target when they find the analogy to be inadequate; this may require more sophisticated reasoning.

Other Cases of Children's Analogy Use in Science

The generation and use of analogies by elementary-age children doing science are not unusual. Other cases from our own project, as well as other studies from the literature, provide additional evidence that children have the ability to reason analogically in science.

In one lesson from *Case Studies of K-8 Student Inquiry in Physical Science*, a fifth-grade class discussed the results of an experiment they performed in which they measured the temperature rise of different containers of water placed under heat lamps. One student, Wasolla, explained his observation that the temperature in the "black, covered" container remained constant for a few minutes before rising by using an analogy:

> Wasolla: I think that what happens for the black covered, that it was, that it stayed um that it stayed on 24 [degrees] or a little bit off for a little while is because it's like when you get in the pool and the water's really cold you like freezing and then you get used to it so you start saying, oh this is not like . . . So it's the same thing what happened to the black covered that it stayed there for a little while and then the temperature rose up, just like your body.
> Teacher: So it took a little while to adjust?
> Wasolla: Yeah.

Wasolla is comparing the variable rate of change of the thermometer reading with that of a person's sensory reaction to getting in a swimming pool. He refers to this analogy at various points in the conversation, and some of his classmates appear to make moves to incorporate some of the ideas it brings up into their own thinking.

In another case from our project, described by Atkins (2004), a fifth-grade class considers what will happen when a tray is quickly pulled out from under an inverted cup filled with water. Miranda predicts that the water will "stay in the cup until it gets down to the floor and then it'll splash." To justify her prediction, she spontaneously generates an analogy:

> Miranda: Cause at home when I have like something in a basket and when I go like that real quick [motions that the basket is swung overhead and quickly pulled down] it stays in. So when—and when I pull it down like this [motions again] like upside down on the way down it stays in until it gets to the bottom and then it comes out.

The object she puts in her basket, she says, is "a little toy cat."

> Alyssa: Um. Um what she's also talking about it's the air—it's like pushing the cat up against the—the bottom of the basket which is holding it back from going out. . . .
> Miranda: And it'll be the same thing with the water the air will push the water up until it falls down and then it will go everywhere.

Alyssa identifies the mechanism by which she thinks the cat stays in the basket, and Miranda applies it to the target situation of cup with water. Later in the discussion, several students generate multiple spontaneous analogies from their personal experience to illustrate the same phenomenon.

Other researchers have also described science discussions in which children use analogies. Some are analogies involving objects, such as second grader Michael's claim that "the moon is like a mirror" (Shapiro, 1994, p. 61). Others involve processes, such as how babies grow inside their mother (Gallas, 1995). After one first grader asserts that the baby is "like a seed, not an egg," another responds with "It's just like caterpillars when they grow. They turn into butterflies. You know how butterflies grow? It makes more sense if the baby grows like butterflies" (Gallas, 1995, pp. 85–86). Still other analogies are epistemological in nature, as when children use them to talk about scientific inquiry itself. One sixth grader, when assigned to write an essay about the nature of learning, makes an analogy for learning in science:

> I think a good analogy for learning is a puzzle. You can have all 1000 pieces but if you don't take the time to fit them together you will never see the picture. Most school learning

is like collecting the pieces of the puzzle and keeping them in a box. Teachers reward you for collecting enough pieces, the more pieces you collect the better rewards you get. . . . I think learning in science is much different. Back to my analogy of the puzzle. In science class we spend a lot of time trying to fit the pieces of the puzzle together. Sometimes it takes all of us working together to fit one piece of the puzzle into its right place in the picture. The analogy isn't perfect because there is only one way to fit the pieces into the puzzle but in science there is much more than just one way to fit science ideas together. (Hennessey, 2003)

Older students have also been observed generating and using analogies while thinking about science. Eilam (2004) describes seventh-graders' experimentation with soap solution and water droppers. In the process of constructing written explanations for the phenomena they observe, many of the students spontaneously generate analogies to help them make sense of the phenomena and support their explanations. For example, one student compares the vacuum formed in the rubber dropper head when it is squeezed to the vacuum that forms behind a fish as it swims. He considers the "pull" effect of the vacuum in each case and claims that energy is required to overcome it (Eilam, 2004).

According to Gallas (1994), children make sense of science largely by telling stories, and analogies and metaphors are natural devices with which children tell stories in science. What is more, by using analogies in this way, they are able to "push [their] thinking to new levels of sophistication and reasoning" (Gallas, 1995, p. 46). There are also signs of children's related expert-like behavior in analogical modeling (Lehrer & Schauble, 2000, 2002; Lising, 2004).

9 CONCLUSION

As the above examples show, children's use of analogies in learning science is not unusual. Ms. Roy's class is not a specially selected class—they are ordinary children with varied performance in different subjects, and the curriculum included no formal instruction in analogies.

As we noted, we chose this instance because (1) it provides evidence of children's abilities for analogical reasoning and (2) the analogy supports an incorrect understanding: A rock melting in lava is indeed analogous to an ice cube melting in water, and the lava would rise, but this mechanism has nothing to do with earthquakes. Discussing this case with other science educators, privately and at conferences, we have found it polarizing: Some are immediately impressed with the students' reasoning, commenting about the articulateness and sophistication of the analogy; and some are appalled that the students could not only voice but develop a misconception in this way and have it go unchallenged. We believe the difference in these reactions exposes an important divide of understanding with respect to the nature and purpose of student inquiry.

There are often calls for increased emphasis on student inquiry in science education, but the calls and the attention they have engendered often conflate inquiry as an *objective* of science education and inquiry as a *method* for teaching "content," where content is construed in a traditional sense. In the latter view, the reason to promote student inquiry is that it is an approach for teaching the target, canonical concepts. There is no value to student inquiry that diverges from those concepts, except insofar as it exposes incorrect thinking that instruction should address. We consider inquiry as an essential objective in its own right; in other words, we consider it part of how science educators should conceptualize "content." In this view, it is important to be able to recognize and respond to nascent expertise, and that recognition should not require alignment with the canon.

Part of expertise in scientific inquiry involves the generation and use of analogies. This objective may be harder to measure than whether a student has "the right answer," but it is an important one nonetheless. Inasmuch as expertise at inquiry supports, in the long run, students and scientists developing conceptual understanding, young children's development of understanding and abilities for analogical reasoning will serve them better than learning the content knowledge of an expert.

If educators are to be successful in helping students develop expert-like thinking skills, it is crucial that we can identify the beginnings of those abilities as they appear in students.

We would like to thank our colleagues in the Physics Education Research Group at the University of Maryland for their help in analyzing this episode, and our colleagues from around the world for giving us their different interpretations of the value of this science lesson.

REFERENCES

Atkins, L. J. (2004). Analogies as categorization phenomena: Studies from scientific discourse. Unpublished Doctoral dissertation. University of Maryland, College Park, MD.

Baker, W. P., & Lawson, A. E. (2001). Complex instructional analogies and theoretical concept acquisition in college genetics. Science Education, 85, 665–683.

Blanchette, I., & Dunbar, K. (2001). Analogy use in naturalistic settings: The influence of audience, emotion, and goals. Memory and Cognition, 29, 730–735.

Chiu, M.-H., & Lin, J.-W. (2005). Promoting fourth graders' conceptual change of their understanding of electric current via multiple analogies. Journal of Research in Science Teaching, 42, 429–464.

Clement, J. (1988). Observed methods for generating analogies in scientific problem solving. Cognitive Science, 12, 563–586.

Clement, J. (1989). Generation of spontaneous analogies by students solving science problems. In D. Topping, D. Crowell, & V. Kobayashi (Eds.), Thinking across cultures (pp. 303–308). Hillsdale, NJ: Erlbaum.

Clement, J. (1993). Using bridging analogies and anchoring intuitions to deal with students' preconceptions in physics. Journal of Research in Science Teaching, 30, 1241–1257.

Clement, J. (1998). Expert novice similarities and instruction using analogies. International Journal of Science Education, 20, 1271–1286.

Dagher, Z. (1995a). Review of studies on the effectiveness of instructional analogies in science education. Science Education, 79, 295–312.

Dagher, Z. (1995b). Analysis of analogies used by science teachers. Journal of Research in Science Teaching, 32, 259–270.

Didierjean, A., & Cauzinille-Marmeche, E. (1998). Reasoning by analogy: Is it schema-mediated or case-based? European Journal of Pshychology of Education, 13, 385–398.

Driver, R., & B. Bell, B. (1986). Students' thinking and the learning of science: A constructivist view. School Science Review, 67, 443–456.

Duit, R. (1991). On the role of analogies and metaphors in learning science. Science Education, 75, 649–672.

Duit, R., Roth, W.-M., Komorek, M., and Wilbers, J. (2001). Fostering conceptual change by analogies—Between Scylla and Charybdis. Learning and Instruction 11, 283–303.

Dunbar, K., & Blanchette, I. (2001). The in vivo/in vitro approach to cognition: The case of analogy. Trends in Cognitive Science, 5, 334–339.

Eilam, B. (2004). Drops of water and of soap solution: Students' constraining mental models of the nature of matter. Journal of Research in Science Teaching, 41, 970–993.

Else, M. J., Clement, J., and Ramirez, M. A. (to appear). Using analogies in science teaching and curriculum design: Some guidelines. In J. Clement & M. Ramirez (Eds.), Model based learning and instruction in science. Dordrecht: Kluwer.

Gallas, K. (1994). The languages of learning: How children talk, write, dance, draw, and sing their understanding of the world. New York: Teachers College Press.

Gallas, K. (1995). Talking their way into science: Hearing children's questions and theories, responding with curricula. New York: Teachers College Press.

Gentner, D. (1983). Structure mapping: A theoretical framework for analogy. Cognitive Science, 7, 155–170.

Gick, M. L., & Holyoak, K. J. (1980). Analogical problem solving. Cognitive Science, 12, 306–355.

Gick, M. L., & Holyoak, K. J. (1983). Schema induction and analogical transfer. Cognitive Science, 15, 1–38.

Glynn, S. M., & Takahashi, T. (1998). Learning from analogy-enhanced science text. Journal of Research in Science Teaching, 10, 1129–1149.

Hammer, D. (2004). The variability of student reasoning, Lecture 2: Transitions. In E. Redish, C. Tarsitani, & M. Vicentini (Eds.), Proceedings of the Enrico Fermi Summer School, Course CLVI: Italian Physical Society.

Hennessey, M. G. (2003). Epistemological sophistication: Helping elementary students learn about learning. Paper presented at the Physics Education Research Seminar, University of Maryland, December 2003.

Hesse, M. (1966). Models and analogies in science. Notre Dame, IN: The University of Notre Dame Press.

Heywood, D., & Parker, J. (1997). Confronting the analogy: Primary teachers exploring the usefulness of analogies in the teaching and learning of electricity. International Journal of Science Education, 19, 869–885.

Hodson, D. (1988). Toward a philosophically more valid science curriculum. Science Education, 72, 19–40.

Hofstadter, D. (2003). Analogy as the central motor of discovery in physics. Paper presented at a Physics Department Colloquium, Ohio State University, May 2003.

Kaufman, D. R., Patel, V. L., and Magder, S. A. (1996). The explanatory role of spontaneously generated analogies in reasoning about physiological concepts. International Journal of Science Education, 18, 369–386.

Kuhn, D. (1993). Science as argument: Implications for teaching and learning scientific thinking. Science Education, 77(3), 319–337.

Kurtz, K., Miao, C.-H., & Gentner, D. (2001). Learning by analogical bootstrapping. Journal of the Learning Sciences, 10, 417–446.

Leatherdale, W. H. (1974). The role of analogy, model and metaphor in science. Amsterdam: North-Holland.

Lehrer, R., & Schauble, L. (2000). Developing model-based reasoning in mathematics and science. Journal of Applied Developmental Psychology, 21(1), 39–48.

Lehrer, R., & Schauble, L. (2002). Modeling in mathematics and science. In R. Glaser (Ed.), Advances in instructional psychology: Educational design and cognitive science, 2000 (Vol. 5, pp. 101–159). Mahwah, NJ: Erlbaum.

Lising, L. J. (2004). Scientific analogical modeling capabilities of third-grade students. Paper presented at the semi-annual meeting of the American Association of Physics Teachers, Miami Beach, FL.

Mason, L. (1994). Cognitive and metacognitive aspects in conceptual change by analogy. Instructional Science, 22, 157–187.

Mason, L., & Sorzio, P. (1996). Analogical reasoning in restructuring scientific knowledge. European Journal of Psychology of Education, 11, 2–23.

Mayo, J. A. (2001). Using analogies to teach conceptual applications of developmental theories. Journal of Constructivist Psychology, 14, 187–213.

Metz, K. E. (1995). Reassessment of developmental constraints on children's science instruction. Review of Educational Research, 65(2), 93–127.

Metz, K. E. (1997). On the complex relation between cognitive developmental research and children's science curricula. Review of Educational Research, 67(1), 151–163.

National Committee on Science Education Standards and Assessment, N. R. C. (1996). National Science Education Standards. Washington, DC: National Academy Press.

Nersessian, N. J. (1992). How do scientists think? Capturing the dynamics of conceptual change in science. In R. N. Giere (Ed.), Cognitive models of science (Vol. XV, pp. 3–44). Minneapolis, MN: University of Minneapolis Press.

Newby, T. J., Ertmer, P. A., & Stepich, D. A. (1995). Instructional analogies and the learning of concepts. Educational Technology Research and Development, 43, 5–18.

Pittman, K. M. (1999). Student-generated analogies: Another way of knowing? Journal of Research in Science Teaching, 36, 1–22.

Rouvray, D. H. (1994). The necessity for analogies in the development of science. Journal of Chemical Information and Computer Sciences, 34, 446–452.

Rumelhart, D. E., & Normann, D. A. (1981). Analogical processes in learning. In J. R. Anderson (Ed.), Cognitive skills and their acquisition (pp. 335–359). Hillsdale, NJ: Erlbaum.

Shapiro, B. L. (1994). What children bring to light: A constructivist perspective on children's learning in science. New York: Teachers College Press.

Stavy, R. (1991). Using analogy to overcome misconceptions about conservation of matter. Journal of Research in Science Teaching, 28, 305–313.

Swain, D. P. (2000). The water-tower analogy of the cardiovascular system. Advances in Physiology Education, 24, 43–50.

Wong, E. D. (1993a). Self-generated analogies as a tool for constructing and evaluating explanations of scientific phenomena. Journal of Research in Science Teaching, 30, 367–380.

Wong, E. D. (1993b). Understanding the generative capacity of analogies as a tool for explanation. Journal of Research in Science Teaching, 30, 1259–1272.

CRACK THE CASE
The Case of the Reading Incentive Program

Catherine teaches second grade in an economically disadvantaged elementary school. Many of her students read below grade level. Some of her students have had little exposure to reading outside of school, and most do not choose to read during their free time at school. Knowing that reading skills are important to future success in school, Catherine is justifiably concerned.

In an effort to entice her students to read more, Catherine develops a reading incentive program. She places a large chart on the classroom wall to track student progress. Each time a student completes a book, he or she tells Catherine, who then places a star next to the student's name on the chart. Each student who reads five books per month receives a small prize from the class prize box. The student who reads the most books in any given month receives a larger prize. When Catherine tells her students about the new incentive program, they are very excited.

"This is great!" says Joey. "I'm gonna get the most stars!"

"No, you won't," says Peter. "Sami will. She's always got her nose stuck in a book. She's the best reader in the class."

Sami is a very good reader. She is reading well above grade level and generally favors novels from the young adult section of the library. These books are rather lengthy and take her quite some time to finish. However, she really enjoys them. Catherine has brought her several from her own collection as well, since none of her classroom books seem to interest Sami.

The first week of the program is quite exciting. Every day students tell Catherine about the books they have read. The chart begins to fill with stars. By the end of the week, all the students have at least one star next to their name except Sami. During the last week of the month many students choose reading as a free-time activity. The students are anxious to ensure that they will earn at least one prize, and many

are devouring books in anticipation of being the month's "top reader." At the end of the month, 23 of Catherine's 25 students have 5 stars on the chart. The only exceptions are Sami, who has only 1 star, and Michael, who had chicken pox during the month. True to his word, Joey receives the most stars—15. The students excitedly choose their prizes.

The following month, the reading frenzy continues. This time Sami joins her classmates in their accumulation of stars and receives 30, making her the top reader. Joey is right behind her with 25. Every student in the class earns at least 5 stars, entitling all to a prize. Because they are all reading so much, Catherine gives them a Friday afternoon party, at which they watch an animated movie and eat popcorn.

A similar pattern is repeated over the next several months. The star chart fills quickly. Catherine believes that the students are reading enough that they will do quite well on the annual state achievement test. She is thrilled with their progress. She decides that after the test, she will drop the incentive program and just quietly keep track of how much her students read. After doing this, she notices that once again very few students are reading during their free time. Even Sami is no longer reading when she is finished with her other work. Now she draws instead.

1. What are the issues in this case?

2. Analyze the case from the perspective of extrinsic and intrinsic motivation.

3. Analyze the case from a goal orientation perspective.

4. Why do you think Sami went from receiving 1 star the first month to receiving 30 stars the next? Why does she no longer read in her free time at school?

5. What are the problems with this type of incentive program? How might an incentive program be developed that does not undermine students' motivation to read?

Caution—Praise Can be Dangerous

—By Carol S. Dweck

The Self-esteem movement, which was flourishing just a few years ago, is in a state of decline. Although many educators believed that boosting students' self-esteem would boost their academic achievement, this did not happen. But the failure of the self-esteem movement does not mean that we should stop being concerned with what students think of themselves and just concentrate on improving their achievement. Every time teachers give feedback to students, they convey messages that affect students' opinion of themselves, their motivation, and their achievement. And I believe that teachers can and should help students become high achievers who also feel good about themselves. But how, exactly, should teachers go about doing this?

In fact, the self-esteem people were on to something extremely important. Praise, the chief weapon in their armory, is a powerful tool. Used correctly it can help students become adults who delight in intellectual challenge, understand the value of effort, and are able to deal with setbacks. Praise can help students make the most of the gifts they have. But if praise is not handled properly, it can become a negative force, a kind of drug that, rather than strengthening students, makes them passive and dependent on the opinion of others. What teachers—and parents—need is a framework that enables them to use praise wisely and well.

⑩ WHERE DID THINGS GO WRONG?

I believe the self-esteem movement faltered because of the way in which educators tried to instill self-esteem. Many people held an intuitively appealing theory of self-esteem, which went something like this: Giving students many opportunities to experience success and then praising them for their successes will indicate to them that they are intelligent. If they feel good about their intelligence, they will achieve. They will love learning and be confident and successful learners.

Much research now shows that this idea is wrong. Giving students easy tasks and praising their success tells students that you think they're dumb.[1] It's not hard to see why. Imagine being lavishly praised for something you think is pretty Mickey Mouse. Wouldn't you feel that the person thought you weren't capable of more and was trying to make you feel good about your limited ability?

But what about praising students' ability when they perform well on challenging tasks? In such cases, there would be no question of students' thinking you were just trying to make them feel good. Melissa Kamins, Claudia Mueller, and I decided to put this idea to the test.

Mueller and I had already found, in a study of the relationship between parents' beliefs and their children's expectations, that 85 percent of parents thought they needed to praise their children's intelligence in order to assure them that they were smart.[2] We also knew that many educators and psychologists thought that praising children for being intelligent was of great benefit. Yet in almost 30 years of research, I had seen over and over that children who had maladaptive achievement patterns were already obsessed with their intelligence—and with proving it to others. The children worried about how smart they looked and feared that failing at some task—even a relatively unimportant one—meant they were dumb. They also worried that having to work hard in order to succeed at a task showed they were dumb. Intelligence seemed to be a label to these kids, a feather in their caps, rather than a tool that, with effort, they could become more skillful in using.

In contrast, the more adaptive students focused on the process of learning and achieving. They weren't worried about their intelligence and didn't consider every task a measure of it. Instead, these students were more likely to concern themselves with the effort and strategies they needed in order to master the task. We wondered if praising children for being intelligent, though it seemed like a positive thing to do, could hook them into becoming dependent on praise.

11) PRAISE FOR INTELLIGENCE

Claudia Mueller and I conducted six studies, with more than 400 fifth-grade students, to examine the effects of praising children for being intelligent.[3] The students were from different parts of the country (a Midwestern town and a large Eastern city) and came from varied ethnic, racial, and socioeconomic backgrounds. Each of the studies involved several tasks, and all began with the students working, one at a time, on a puzzle task that was challenging but easy enough for all of them to do quite well. After this first set, we praised one-third of the children for their *intelligence*. They were told: "Wow, you got x number correct. That's a really good score. You must be smart at this." One-third of the children were also told that they got a very good score, but they were praised for their *effort*: "You must have worked really hard." The final third were simply praised for their *performance*, with no comment on why they were successful. Then, we looked to see the effects of these different types of praise across all six studies.

We found that after the first trial (in which all of the students were successful) the three groups responded similarly to questions we asked them. They enjoyed the task equally, were equally eager to take the problems home to practice, and were equally confident about their future performance.

In several of the studies, as a followup to the first trial, we gave students a choice of different tasks to work on next. We asked whether they wanted to try a challenging task from which they could learn a lot (but at which they might not succeed) or an easier task (on which they were sure to do well and look smart).

The majority of the students who had received praise for being intelligent the first time around went for the task that would allow them to keep on looking smart. Most of the students who had received praise for their effort (in some studies, as many as 90 percent) wanted the challenging learning task. (The third group, the students who had not been praised for intelligence or effort, were right in the middle and I will not focus on them.)

These findings suggest that when we praise children for their intelligence, we are telling them that this is the name of the game: Look smart; don't risk making mistakes. On the other hand, when we praise children for the effort and hard work that leads to achievement, they want to keep engaging in that process. They are not diverted from the task of learning by a concern with how smart they might—or might not—look.

12) THE IMPACT OF DIFFICULTY

Next, we gave students a set of problems that were harder and on which they didn't do as well. Afterwards, we repeated the questions we had asked after the first task: How much had they enjoyed the task? Did they want to take the problems home to practice? And how smart did they feel? We found that the students who had been praised for being intelligent did not like this second task and were no longer interested in taking the problems home to practice. What's more, their difficulties led them to question their intelligence. In other words, the same students who had been told they were smart when they succeeded now felt dumb because they had encountered a setback. They had learned to measure themselves from what people said about their performance, and they were dependent on continuing praise in order to maintain their confidence.

In contrast, the students who had received praise for their effort on the easier task liked the more difficult task just as much even though they missed some of the problems. In fact, many of them said they liked the harder problems even more than the easier ones, and they were even more eager to take them home to practice. It was wonderful to see.

Moreover, these youngsters did not think that the difficulty of the task (and their relative lack of success) reflected on their intelligence. They thought, simply, that they had to make a greater effort in order to succeed. Their interest in taking problems home with them to practice on presumably reflected one way they planned to do this.

Thus, the students praised for effort were able to keep their intellectual self-esteem in the face of setbacks. They still thought they were smart; they still enjoyed the challenge; and they planned to work toward future success. The students who had been praised for their intelligence received an initial boost to their egos, but their view of themselves was quickly shaken when the going got rough. As a final test, we gave students a third set of problems that were equal in difficulty to the first set—the one on which all the students had been successful. The results were striking. Although all three groups had performed equally well on the first trial, the students who had received praise for their intelligence (and who had been discouraged by their poor showing on the second trial) now registered the worst performance of the three groups. Indeed, they did significantly worse than they had on the first trial. In contrast, students who were praised for working hard performed the best of the three groups and significantly better than they had originally. So the different kinds of praise apparently affected not just what students thought and felt, but also how well they were able to perform.

Given what we had already seen, we reasoned that when students see their performance as a measure of their intelligence, they are likely to feel stigmatized when they perform poorly and may even try to hide the fact. If, however, students consider a poor performance a temporary setback, which merely reflects how much effort they have put in or their current level of skill, then it will not be a stigma. To test this idea, we gave students the opportunity to tell a student at another school about the task they had just completed by writing a brief description on a prepared form. The form also asked them to report their score on the second, more difficult trial.

More than 40 percent of the students who had been praised for their intelligence lied about their score (to improve it, of course). They did this even though they were reporting their performance to an anonymous peer whom they would never meet. Very few of the students in the other groups exaggerated their performance. This suggests that when we praise students for their intelligence, failure becomes more personal and therefore more of a disgrace. As a result, students become less able to face and therefore deal with their setbacks.

13 THE MESSAGES WE SEND

Finally, we found that following their experiences with the different kinds of praise, the students believed different things about their intelligence. Students who had received praise for being intelligent told us they thought of intelligence as something innate—a capacity that you just had or didn't have. Students who had been praised for effort told us they thought of intelligence more in terms of their skills, knowledge, and motivation—things over which they had some control and might be able to enhance.

And these negative effects of praising for intelligence were just as strong (and sometimes stronger) for the high-achieving students as for their less successful peers.

Perhaps it is even easier to get these youngsters invested in looking smart to others. Maybe they are even more attuned to messages from us that tell them we value them for their intellects.

How can one sentence of praise have such powerful and pervasive effects? In my research, I have been amazed over and over again at how quickly students of all ages pick up on messages about themselves—at how sensitive they are to suggestions about their personal qualities or about the meaning of their actions and experiences. The kinds of praise (and criticism) students receive from their teachers and parents tell them how to think about what they do—and what they are.

This is why we cannot simply forget about students' feelings, their ideas about themselves and their motivation, and just teach them the "facts." No matter how objective we try to be, our feedback conveys messages about what we think is important, what we think of them, and how they should think of themselves. These messages, as we have seen, can have powerful effects on many things including performance. And it should surprise no one that this susceptibility starts very early.

Melissa Kamins and I found it in kindergarten children.[4] Praise or criticism that focused on children's personal traits (like being smart or good) created a real vulnerability when children hit setbacks. They saw setbacks as showing that they were bad or incompetent—and they were unable to respond constructively. In contrast, praise or criticism that focused on children's strategies or the efforts they made to succeed left them hardy, confident, and in control when they confronted setbacks. A setback did not mean anything bad about them or their personal qualities. It simply meant that something needed to be done, and they set about doing it. Again, a focus on process allowed these young children to maintain their self-esteem and to respond constructively when things went wrong.

14 WAYS OF PRAISING

There are many groups whose achievement is of particular interest to us: minorities, females, the gifted, the underachieving, to name a few. The findings of these studies will tell you why I am so concerned that we not try to encourage the achievement of our students by praising their intelligence. When we worry about low-achieving or vulnerable students, we may want to reassure them they're smart. When we want to motivate high-achieving students, we may want to spur them on by telling them they're gifted. Our research says: Don't do that. Don't get students so invested in these labels that they care more about keeping the label than about learning. Instead of empowering students, praise is likely to render students passive and dependent on something they believe they can't control. And it can hook them into a system in which setbacks signify incompetence and effort is recognized as a sign of weakness rather than a key to success.

This is not to say that we shouldn't praise students. We can praise as much as we please when they learn or do well, but should wax enthusiastic about their strategies, not about how their performance reveals an attribute they are likely to view as innate and beyond their control. We can rave about their effort, their concentration, the effectiveness of their study strategies, the interesting ideas they came up with, the way they followed through. We can ask them questions that show an intelligent appreciation of their work and what they put into it. We can enthusiastically discuss with them what they learned. This, of course, requires more from us than simply telling them that they are smart, but it is much more appreciative of their work, much more constructive, and it does not carry with it the dangers I've been describing.

What about the times a student really impresses us by doing something quickly, easily—and perfectly? Isn't it appropriate to show our admiration for the child's ability? My honest opinion is that we should not. We should not be giving students the impression that we place a high value on their doing perfect work on tasks that are easy for them. A better approach would be to apologize for wasting their time with something that was too easy, and move them to something that is more challenging. When students make progress in or master that more challenging work, that's when our admiration—for their efforts—should come through.

15 A CHALLENGING ACADEMIC TRANSITION

The studies I have been talking about were carried out in a research setting. Two other studies[5] tracked students with these different viewpoints in a real-life situation, as they were making the transition to junior high school and during their first two years of junior high. This is a point at which academic work generally becomes more demanding than it was in elementary school, and many students stumble. The studies compared the attitudes and achievement of students who believed that intelligence is a fixed quantity with students who believed that they could develop their intellectual potential. We were especially interested in any changes in the degree of success students experienced in junior high school and how they dealt with these changes. For the sake of simplicity, I will combine the results from the two studies, for they showed basically the same thing.

First, the students who believed that intelligence is fixed did indeed feel that poor performance meant they were dumb. Furthermore, they reported, in significantly greater numbers than their peers, that if they did badly on a test, they would seriously consider cheating the next time. This was true even for students who were highly skilled and who had a past record of high achievement.

Perhaps even worse, these students believed that having to make an effort meant they were dumb—hardly an attitude to foster good work habits. In fact, these students reported that even though school achievement was very important to them, one of their prime goals in school was to exert as little effort as possible.

In contrast to the hopelessly counterproductive attitude of the first group, the second group of students, those who believed that intellectual potential can be developed, felt that poor performance was often due to a lack of effort, and it called for more studying. They saw effort as worthwhile and important—something necessary even for geniuses if they are to realize their potential.

So once again, for those who are focused on their fixed intelligence and its adequacy, setbacks and even effort bring a loss of face and self-esteem. But challenges, setbacks, and effort are not threatening to the self-esteem of those who are concerned with developing their potential; they represent opportunities to learn. In fact, many of these students told us that they felt smartest when things were difficult; they gained self-esteem when they applied themselves to meeting challenges.

What about the academic achievement of the two groups making the transition to junior high school? In both studies, we saw that students who believed that intelligence was fixed and was manifest in their performance did more poorly than they had in elementary school. Even many who had been high achievers did much less well. Included among them were many students who entered junior high with high intellectual self-esteem. On the other hand, the students who believed that intellectual potential could be developed showed, as a group, clear gains in their class standing, and many blossomed intellectually. The demands of their new environment, instead of causing them to wilt because they doubted themselves, encouraged them to roll up their sleeves and get to work.

These patterns seem to continue with students entering college. Research with students at highly selective universities found that, although they may enter a situation with equal self-esteem, optimism, and past achievement, students respond to the challenge of college differently: Students in one group by measuring themselves and losing confidence; the others by figuring out what it takes and doing it.[6]

16 BELIEVING AND ACHIEVING

Some of the research my colleagues and I have carried out suggests that it is relatively easy to modify the views of young children in regard to intelligence and effort in a research setting. But is it possible to influence student attitudes in a real-life setting? And do students become set in their beliefs as they grow older? Some exciting new research shows that even college students' views about intelligence and effort can be modified—and that these changes will affect their level of academic achievement.[7] In their study, Aronson and Fried taught minority students at a prestigious university to view their intelligence as a potentiality that could be developed through hard work. For example, they created and showed a film that explained the neural changes that took place in the brain every time students confronted difficulty by exerting effort. The students who were instructed about the relationship between intelligence and effort went on to earn significantly higher grades than their peers who were not. This study, like our intelligence praise studies, shows that (1) students' ideas about their intelligence can be influenced by the messages they receive, and (2) when these ideas change, changes in performance can follow.

But simply getting back to basics and enforcing rigorous standards—which some students will meet and some will not—won't eliminate the pitfalls I have been describing. This approach may convey, even more forcefully, the idea that intelligence is a gift only certain students possess. And it will not, in itself, teach students to value learning and focus on the *process* of achievement or how to deal with obstacles. These students may, more than ever, fear failure because it takes the measure of their intelligence.

17 A DIFFERENT FRAMEWORK

Our research suggests another approach. Instead of trying to convince our students that they are smart or simply enforcing rigorous standards in the hopes that doing so will create high motivation and achievement, teachers should take the following steps: first, get students to focus on their potential to learn; second, teach them to value challenge and learning over looking smart; and third, teach them to concentrate on effort and learning processes in the face of obstacles.

This can be done while holding students to rigorous standards. Within the framework I have outlined, tasks are challenging and effort is highly valued, required, and rewarded. Moreover, we can (and must) give students frank evaluations of their work and their level of skill, but we must make clear that these are evaluations of their current level of performance and skill, not an assessment of their intelligence or their innate ability. In this framework, we do not arrange easy work or constant successes, thinking that we are doing students a favor. We do not lie to students who are doing poorly so they will feel smart: That would rob them of the information they need to work harder and improve. Nor do we just give students hard work that many can't do, thus making them into casualties of the system.

I am not encouraging high-effort situations in which students stay up studying until all hours every night, fearing they will displease their parents or disgrace themselves if they don't get the top test scores. Pushing students to do that is not about valuing learning or about orienting students toward developing their potential. It is about pressuring students to prove their worth through their test scores.

It is also not sufficient to give students piles of homework and say we are teaching them about the importance of effort. We are not talking about quantity here but about teaching students to seek challenging tasks and to engage in an active learning process.

However, we as educators must then be prepared to do our share. We must help students acquire the skills they need for learning, and we must be available as constant resources for learning. It is not enough to keep harping on and praising effort, for this may soon wear thin. And it will not be effective if students don't know *how* to apply their effort appropriately. It is necessary that we as educators understand and teach students how to engage in processes that foster learning, things like task analysis and study skills.[8]

When we focus students on their potential to learn and give them the message that effort is the key to learning, we give them responsibility for and control over their achievement—and over their self-esteem. We acknowledge that learning is not something that someone gives students; nor can they expect to feel good about themselves because teachers tell them they are smart. Both learning and self-esteem are things that students achieve as they tackle challenges and work to master new material.

Students who value learning and effort know how to make and sustain a commitment to valued goals. Unlike some of their peers, they are not afraid to work hard; they know that meaningful tasks involve setbacks; and they know how to bounce back from failure. These are lessons that cannot help but serve them well in life as well as in school.

These are lessons I have learned from my research on students' motivation and achievement, and they are things I wish I had known as a student. There is no reason that every student can't know them now.

Endnotes

1. Meyer, W. U. (1982). Indirect communications about perceived ability estimates. *Journal of Educational Psychology, 74,* 888–897.
2. Mueller, C. M., & Dweck, C. S. (1996). Implicit theories of intelligence: Relation of parental beliefs to children's expectations. Paper presented at the Third National Research Convention of Head Start, Washington, D.C.
3. Mueller, C. M., & Dweck, C. S. (1998). Intelligence praise can undermine motivation and performance. *Journal of Personality and Social Psychology; 75,* 33–52.
4. Kamins, M., & Dweck, C. S. (1999). Person vs. process praise and criticism: Implications for contingent self-worth and coping. *Developmental Psychology.*
5. Henderson, V., & Dweck, C. S. (1990). Achievement and motivation in adolescence: A new model and data. In S. Feldman and G. Elliott (Eds.), *At the threshold: The developing adolescent.* Cambridge, MA: Harvard University Press; *and* Dweck, C. S., & Sorich, L. (1999). Mastery-oriented thinking. In C. R. Snyder (Ed.). *Coping.* New York: Oxford University Press.
6. Robins, R. W. & Pals, J. (1998). Implicit self-theories of ability in the academic domain: A test of Dweck's model. Unpublished manuscript, University of California at Davis; *and* Zhao, W., Dweck, C. S., & Mueller, C. (1998). Implicit theories and depression-like responses to failure. Unpublished manuscript, Columbia University.
7. Aronson, J., & Fried, C. (1998). Reducing stereotype threat and boosting academic achievement of African Americans: The role of conceptions of intelligence. Unpublished manuscript, University of Texas.
8. Brown, A. L. (1997). Transforming schools into communities of thinking and learning about serious matters. *American Psychologist, 52,* 399–413.

Carol S. Dweck is a professor of psychology at Columbia University, who has carried out research on self-esteem, motivation, and academic achievement for thirty years. Her new book, Self-Theories: Their Role in Motivation, Personality, and Development, *was just published by The Psychology Press.*

Unit 2

Neural Plasticity and Human Development

——Charles A. Nelson[1]

Institute of Child Development and Department of Pediatrics, University of Minnesota, Minneapolis, Minnesota

Preview

ABSTRACT: In this article, I argue that experience-induced changes in the brain may be a useful way of viewing the course of human development. Work from the neurosciences supports the claim that most of the behavioral phenomena of interest to psychologists (e.g., cognition, perception, language, emotion) are instantiated by the process of neural plasticity. When development is viewed in this manner, the fallaciousness of the longstanding and often contentious debate over nature versus nurture becomes apparent. Moreover, by utilizing the neuroscientific tools used to examine the effects of experience on brain and behavioral development (e.g., functional neuroimaging), we may improve how we conceptualize our notions of intervention, competence, and resilience.

Keywords brain; plasticity; behavior

Neural plasticity can best be thought of as the subtle but orchestrated dance that occurs between the brain and the environment; specifically, it is the ability of the brain to be shaped by experience and, in turn, for this newly remolded brain to facilitate the embrace of new experiences, which leads to further neural changes, *ad infinitum*. As a rule, there are three mechanisms by which experience induces changes in the brain. An *anatomical* change might be the ability of existing synapses (i.e., connections between nerve cells) to modify their activity by sprouting new axons or by expanding the dendritic surface. A *neurochemical* change might be reflected in the ability of an existing synapse to modify its activity by increasing synthesis and release of chemicals that transmit nerve impulses (i.e., neurotransmitters). Finally, an example of a *metabolic* change might be the fluctuations in metabolic activity (e.g., use of glucose or oxygen) in the brain in response to experience.

All of these changes can occur at virtually any point in the life cycle, although to varying degrees of success. For example, some domains of behavior can be acquired only during a sensitive or critical period. Examples include song learning in the Zebra finch, social imprinting[2] in some mammals, and the development of binocular vision (for discussion, see Knudsen, 1999). Other behaviors, such as learning and memory, depend less on experience occurring at a particular point in development, and thus occur throughout the life span (see Nelson, in press). Regardless of whether there is or is not a critical period, experience is responsible for the changes that occur in the brain, which in turn determines the behavioral profile and development of the organism. Alas, this malleability is a two-edged sword, in that such changes can be both adaptive and maladaptive for the organism.

16 MALADAPTIVE CHANGES

Let us begin with the bad news, which is that the wrong experiences can have deleterious effects on the brain. Perhaps the clearest example concerns the effects of stress on the developing and developed brain. Rats exposed to stress pre- or postnatally show a wide range of changes in the brain's serotonin, catecholamine, and opiate systems.[3] Similarly, rats raised in social isolation make more learning errors than socially raised rats. Finally, brief maternal deprivation in the rat pup can alter the sensitivity of the hypothalamic pituitary adrenal (HPA) axis (see Black, Jones, Nelson, & Greenough, 1998, for review), thereby potentially altering the animal's ability to regulate and mount a behavioral response to threat.

Similarly, pregnant Rhesus monkeys exposed to different stressors at different points in time give birth to offspring that show seemingly permanent neurobehavioral changes. For example, at the cognitive level, the achievement of object permanence (the concept that objects out of sight continue to exist) can be delayed, and performance on tests of explicit memory[4] can be impaired. At the behavioral level, these animals display long-lasting changes in their ability to control their emotional state (see Schneider, in press).

The effects of prenatal exposure to stress are not limited to the rat or monkey. For example, Lou et al. (1994) reported that stress during pregnancy affected the head circumference of human newborns. (Head circumference is a coarse measure of brain growth.) In addition, prenatal stress was related to less than optimal outcome in the newborn period. As researchers have hypothesized for the rat and monkey, Lou et al. speculated that the effects of maternal stress on fetal brain development might be mediated by stress hormones (glucocorticoids) circulating in the bloodstream. A similar mechanism has been proposed to account for the observation that adults who have survived abuse as children show reduced volume of the hippocampus (a brain structure important for explicit memory) and, correspondingly, impairments on memory tasks. In this case, glucocorticoids act toxically on the hippocampus, which is well endowed with glucocorticoid receptors (see McEwen & Sapolsky, 1995).

Overall, there is clear evidence that early or late exposure to stress can deleteriously affect a range of brain systems, and thus a range of behaviors. In this context, one may view stress as something akin to a psychological lesion that exerts its effects to varying degrees depending on what system is targeted, the age of the organism when the stress occured, and whether there are protective or exacerbating factors that can moderate the effects.

17 ADAPTIVE CHANGES

Having begun with the bad news, let us now turn to the good news, which is that being exposed to the "right" experiences can have beneficial effects on brain and behavior. Greenough and his colleagues have demonstrated that rats raised in complex environments (e.g., those filled with lots of toys and other rats) perform better than rats reared in normal laboratory cages on a variety of cognitive tasks (see Greenough & Black, 1992, for review). Correspondingly, the brains of these rats show improved synaptic contacts, and a greater number of dendritic spines. Even more impressive changes are observed in perceptual-motor tasks. For example, Black and Greenough (see Black et al., 1998) required rats to learn complex motor coordination tasks and found the rats developed more synapses within the cerebellum, a brain structure important for performance of such tasks. Kleim, Vij, Ballard, and Greenough (1997) demonstrated that these changes can be long lasting.

Reorganization of the brain based on selective experience is not limited to the rat. For example, Mühlnickel, Elbert, Taub, and Flor (1998) have reported that adults suffering from tinnitus (ringing in the ears) show a dramatic reorganization of the region of the cortex that deals with hearing. This same group (Elbert, Pantev, Wienbruch,

Rockstroh, & Taub, 1995) has also shown that in musicians who play string instruments, the region of the somatosensory cortex (the region of the brain that subserves the sense of touch) that represents the fingers of the left hand (the hand requiring greater fine-motor learning) is larger than the area that represents the right hand (which is used to bow), and larger than the left-hand area in nonmusicians. Finally, Ramachandran, Rogers-Ramachandran, and Stewart (1992) have observed similar findings in patients who have experienced limb amputation. The region of the somatosensory cortex that sits adjacent to the region previously representing the missing limb encroaches on this area. This, in turn, may account for why patients experience sensation in the missing limb (e.g., the forearm) when this new area (e.g., that representing the cheek) is stimulated (Ramachandran et al., 1992). Collectively, this work suggests that the adult human cortex can be reorganized based on experiences that occur relatively late in life.

What of plasticity during childhood? Tallal and Merzenich (Merzenich et al., 1996; Tallal et al., 1996) have speculated that in some children, difficulty in parsing ongoing speech into sound segments leads to difficulty discriminating speech sounds. These authors have reported improvements in both speech discrimination and language comprehension when such children are given intensive training in speech processing. Although the brains of these children were not examined, presumably changes at the level of the auditory-thala-mo-cortical pathway were modified by this experience.

These are but a few examples of how the brain is modified by experience; many others, in various domains of functioning, and at various points in development, could be provided. This is not to say, however, that experience-induced changes are possible in all domains of behavior at all points in time. For example, there is evidence from studies of deprivation that children not exposed to normal caretaking environments during their first few years of life may suffer long-lasting changes in their socioemotional functioning (although some individuals show sparing or recovery of function that is quite remarkable). Similarly, we have known for many years that being able to see with only one eye in the first few years of life yields intractable deficits in binocular depth perception, and that prolonged linguistic deprivation yields similarly intractable long-term deficits in language, speech perception, or both. Even these cases, however, speak to the importance of experience, as without normative experiences normal development goes awry.

(18) IMPLICATIONS OF WORK ON NEURAL PLASTICITY FOR BEHAVIORAL DEVELOPMENT

The foregoing observations suggest that the "innate"-versus-"learned" debate is fallacious. An example from the literature on face perception illustrates this point (some aspects of language development may be another example). Some investigators have argued that face recognition is innate, by which they (presumably) mean that it develops without benefit of experience. However, we know that infants come into contact with faces as soon as they are born. Thus, it seems just as reasonable to argue that experience drives the development of the neural tissue (perhaps selected by evolutionary pressures, given the importance of face recognition in survival) that takes on this function and that this tissue becomes specialized rather quickly. (The brain structures responsible for face recognition in the adult are in the right temporal cortex and include the fusiform gyrus.) This process would allow the ability to recognize faces to appear early in development, but this is not the same thing as saying this ability is innate *qua* innate. Conversely, to argue that face recognition is "learned" does not do justice to the fact that such learning by default necessitates changes in the brain, which in turn alter which genes are expressed (i.e., activated). Even if one argues that an ability is "genetic" (although proving such a case would seem insurmountable without benefit of being able to specify the genes), gene expression is influenced by experience, and once experience occurs, the brain is altered, which in turn alters gene expression, and so on and so forth.

What are the practical implications of the approach I am advocating? Two come to mind. The first pertains to intervention. By understanding precisely how the brain is modified by experience, we can better identify the experiences needed to bring children back on a normal developmental trajectory, or prevent them from moving off this trajectory. In addition, we can target our interventions more judiciously, rather than targeting the whole child. Finally, using the tools of the neuroscientist, we may be able to examine the brain before and after an intervention, and in so doing better determine where in the nervous system change occurred. For example, if damage to the auditorythalamo-cortical pathway appears to be responsible for some language-learning disorders, might noninvasive procedures such as event-related potentials (electrical activity generated by the brain in response to discretely presented events) or functional magnetic resonance imaging be used to (a) confirm or disconfirm this hypothesis and (b) evaluate the effectiveness (or lack thereof) of a given intervention and its effects on brain structure and function (see Nelson & Bloom, 1997)?

A second implication of the perspective advocated in this essay pertains to our understanding of competence and resilience. As work by Masten and Garmezy (Masten et al., in press) has shown, not all children reared in suboptimal conditions (including those at significant risk for psychopathology) move off a normal trajectory. Similarly, not all children who suffer frank brain damage experience disastrous outcomes. And, in both cases, many of those who do fall off a normal trajectory show some recovery—even considerable recovery in some instances. Might we view those children who are otherwise at risk but do not show any deleterious effects as an example of neural sparing, and those who show some deficits followed by a return to a normal trajectory as an example of recovery of function? If so, can we identify how the brains of these children incorporated experience differently than the brains of children who show no sparing or recovery of function? And can we evaluate these changes using the latest tools from the neurosciences?

19 CONCLUSIONS

It is indisputable that some aspects of pre- and postnatal human development have their origin in the expression of genetic scripts conserved through evolution and expressed at key points in development. One example may be the prenatal expression of the genes that regulate the formation of body parts (i.e., homeotic genes); another may be the postnatal expression of genes (not yet identified) that lead to the cascade of hormonal changes that usher in puberty. Even in these cases, of course, experience may influence the outcome; for example, the presence of teratogens may corrupt the influence of the homeotic genes (e.g., thalidomide can cause limb deformities), and culture or other experiences can influence pubertal timing. These examples notwithstanding, the changes in behavior that occur over time and that are of most interest to behavioral scientists (e.g., changes in perception, cognition, social-emotional behavior) are likely mediated by experientially induced changes in the nervous system. Thus, it may serve us well to rethink how the brain develops and changes across the life span by considering the important role of experience in sculpting neural systems. In so doing, we may be able to shed some of the contentious history that has plagued our discipline for years (e.g., nature vs. nurture; innate vs. learned), and embrace new theoretical and empirical approaches to human development and brain function.

Recommended Reading

Black, J.E., Jones, T.A., Nelson, C.A., & Greenough, W.T. (1998). (See References)

Greenough, W.T., & Black, J.E. (1992). (See References)

Kolb, B., Forgie, M., Gibb, R., Gorny, G., & Rowntree, S. (1998). Age, experience, and the changing brain. *Neuroscience and Bio-behavioral Reviews, 22,* 143–159.

Nelson, C.A. (in press). The neurobiological bases of early intervention. In J.P. Shonkoff & S.J. Meisels (Eds.), *Handbook of early childhood intervention* (2nd ed.). New York: Cambridge University Press.

Nelson, C.A., & Bloom, F.E. (1997). (See References)

Acknowledgments—The writing of this essay was made possible by a grant to the author from the John D. and Catherine T. MacArthur Foundation and the J.S. McDonnell Foundation, through their support of their research network on Early Experience and Brain Development. The author wishes to thank Floyd Bloom, John Bruer, and Richard Weinberg for their helpful comments on an earlier draft of this article.

Endnotes

1. Address correspondence to Charles A. Nelson, Institute of Child Development, University of Minnesota, 51 East River Rd., Minneapolis, MN 55455; e-mail: canelson@tc.umn.edu.
2. Social imprinting is the process by which an animal forms a relationship of some kind to another animal, such as the famous case of the ducklings that followed Konrad Lorenz around.
3. Serotonin and catecholamines are neurotransmitters that play a role in social and emotional behavior. The natural opiates produced by the body can induce feelings of euphoria or wellbeing.
4. Explicit memory is a form of memory that can be stated explicitly or declared, that can be brought to mind as an image or proposition in the absence of ongoing perceptual support, or of which one is consciously aware.

References

Black, J.E., Jones, T.A., Nelson, C.A., & Greenough, W.T. (1998). Neuronal plasticity and the developing brain. In N.E. Alessi, J.T. Coyle, S.I. Harrison, & S. Eth. (Eds.), *Handbook of child and adolescent psychiatry: Vol, 6. Basic psychiatric science and treatment* (pp. 31–53). New York: John Wiley & Sons.

Elbert, T., Pantev, C., Wienbruch, C., Rockstroh, B., & Taub, E. (1995). Increased cortical representation of the fingers of the left hand in string players. *Science, 270,* 305–307.

Greenough, W.T., & Black, J.E. (1992). Induction of brain structure by experience: Substrates for cognitive development. In M.R. Gunnar & C.A. Nelson (Eds.), *Developmental behavioral neuroscience* (Minnesota Symposia on Child Psychology, Vol. 24, pp. 155–200). Hillsdale, NJ: Erlbaum.

Kleim, J.A., Vij, K., Ballard, D.H., & Greenough, W.T. (1997). Learning-dependent synaptic modifications in the cerebellar cortex of the adult rat persist for at least four weeks. *Journal of Neuroscience, 17,* 717–721.

Knudsen, E.I. (1999). Early experience and critical periods. In M.J. Zigmond, F.E. Bloom, S.C. Landis, J.L. Roberts, & L.R. Squire (Eds.)., *Fundamental neuroscience* (pp. 637–654). New York: Academic Press.

Lou, H.C., Hansen, D., Nordentoft, M., Pryds, O., Jensen, F., Nim, J., & Hemmingsen, R. (1994). Prenatal stressors of human life affect fetal brain development. *Developmental Medicine and Child Neurology, 36,* 826–832.

Masten, A.S., Hubbard, J.J., Gest, S.D., Tellegen, A., Garmezy, N., & Ramirez, M. (in press). Adaptation in the context of adversity: Pathways to resilience and maladaption from childhood to late adolescence. *Development and Psychopathology.*

McEwen, B.S., & Sapolsky, R.M. (1995). Stress and cognitive function. *Current Opinion in Neurobiology, 5,* 205–216.

Merzenich, M.M., Jenkins, W.M., Johnston, P., Schreiner, C., Miller, S.L., & Tallal, P. (1996). Temporal processing deficits of language learning impaired children ameliorated by training. *Science, 271,* 77–81.

Mühlnickel, W., Elbert, T., Taub, E., & Flor, H. (1998). Reorganization of auditory cortex in tinnitus. *Proceedings of the National Academy of Sciences, USA, 95,* 10340–10343.

Nelson, C.A. (in press). Neural plasticity and human development: The role of early experience in sculpting memory systems. *Developmental Science.*

Nelson, C.A., & Bloom, F.E. (1997). Child development and neuroscience. *Child Development, 68,* 970–987.

Ramachandran, V.S., Rogers-Ramachandran, D., & Stewart, M. (1992). Perceptual correlates of massive cortical reorganization. *Science, 258,* 1159–1160.

Schneider, M.L. (in press). Effect of prenatal stress on development: A nonhuman primate model. In C.A. Nelson (Ed.), *The effects of early adversity on neurobehavioral development* (Minnesota Symposia on Child Psychology, Vol. 31). Mahwah, NJ: Erlbaum.

Tallal, P., Miller, S.L., Bedi, G., Byma, G., Wang, X., Nagarajan, S.S., Schreiner, C., Jenkins, W.M., & Merzenich, M.M. (1996). Language comprehension in language-learning impaired children improved with acoustically modified speech. *Science, 271,* 81–84.

Memory

Twentieth-century playwright Tennessee Williams once commented that life is all memory except for that one present moment that goes by so quickly that you can hardly catch it going. But just what is memory?

22 WHAT IS MEMORY?

Memory is the retention of information over time. Educational psychologists study how information is initially placed or encoded into memory, how it is retained or stored after being encoded, and how it is found or retrieved for a certain purpose later. Memory anchors the self in continuity. Without memory you would not be able to connect what happened to you yesterday with what is going on in your life today. Today, educational psychologists emphasize that it is important not to view memory in terms of how children add something to it but, rather, to underscore how children actively construct their memory (Schacter, 2001).

The main body of our discussion of memory will focus on encoding, storage, and retrieval. Thinking about memory in terms of these processes should help you to understand it better (see Figure 2.1). For memory to work, children have to take information in, store it or represent it, and then retrieve it for some purpose later.

As you learned earlier, *encoding* is the process by which information gets into memory. *Storage* is the retention of information over time. *Retrieval* means taking information out of storage. Let's now explore each of these three important memory activities in greater detail.

Encoding
Getting information into memory

Storage
Retaining information over time

Retrieval
Taking information out of storage

FIGURE 2.1 Processing Information in Memory

As you read about the many aspects of memory in this chapter, think about the organization of memory in terms of these three main activities.

23 ENCODING

In everyday language, encoding has much in common with attention and learning. When a student is listening to a teacher, watching a movie, listening to music, or talking with a friend, he or she is encoding information into memory. In addition to attention, which we just discussed, encoding consists of a number of processes: rehearsal, deep processing, elaboration, constructing images, and organization.

Rehearsal

Rehearsal is the conscious repetition of information over time to increase the length of time information stays in memory. For example, when you make a date to meet your best friend for lunch, you are likely to repeat, or rehearse, the date and time: "OK—Wednesday at 1:30." Rehearsal works best when you need to encode and remember a list of items for a brief period of time. When you must retain information over long periods of time, as when you are studying for a test you won't take until next week, other strategies usually work better than rehearsal. Rehearsal does not work well for retaining information over the long term because it often involves just rote repetition of information without imparting any meaning to it. When you construct your memory in meaningful ways, you remember better. As we will see next, you also remember better when you process material deeply and elaborate it.

memory The retention of information over time, which involves encoding, storage, and retrieval.

rehearsal The conscious repetition of information over time to increase the length of time information stays in memory.

The Cobwebs of Memory

I think the point of having memories is to share them, especially with close friends or family. If you don't share them, they are just sitting inside your brain getting cobwebs. If you have a great memory of Christmas and no one to share it with, what's the point of memories?

Seventh-Grade Student
West Middle School
Ypsilanti, Michigan

FIGURE 2.2 Verbal Elaboration and Memory
Both second- and fifth-grade children remembered words better when they constructed a meaningful sentence for the word (verbal elaboration group) than when they merely heard the word and its definition (control group). The verbal elaboration worked better for the fifth-graders than the second-graders.

Deep Processing

Following the discovery that rehearsal is not an efficient way to encode information for long-term memory, Fergus Craik and Robert Lockhart (1972) proposed that we can process information at a variety of levels. Their theory, **levels of processing theory,** states that the processing of memory occurs on a continuum from shallow to deep, with deeper processing producing better memory. Shallow processing means analyzing a stimuli's sensory, or physical, features at a shallow level. This might involve detecting the lines, angles, and contours of a printed word's letters or a spoken word's frequency, duration, and loudness. At an intermediate level of processing, you recognize the stimulus and give it a label. For example, you identify a four-legged, barking object as a dog. Then, at the deepest level, you process information semantically, in terms of its meaning. For example, if a child sees the word *boat,* at the shallow level she might notice the shapes of the letters, at the intermediate level she might think of the characteristics of the word (for instance, that it rhymes with *coat*), and at the deepest level she might think about the last time she went fishing` with her dad on a boat and the kind of boat it was. Researchers have found that individuals remember information better when they process it at a deep level (Otten, Henson, & Rugg, 2001).

Elaboration

Cognitive psychologists soon recognized, however, that there is more to good encoding than just depth of processing. They discovered that when individuals use elaboration in their encoding of information, their memory benefits (Terry, 2006). **Elaboration** is the extensiveness of information processing involved in encoding. Thus, when you present the concept of democracy to students, they likely will remember it better if they come up with good examples of it. Thinking of examples is a good way to elaborate information. For instance, self-reference is an effective way to elaborate information. If you are trying to get students to remember the concept of fairness, the more they can generate personal examples of inequities and equities they have personally experienced, the more likely they are to remember the concept.

The use of elaboration changes developmentally (Nelson, 2006; Schneider, 2004; Schneider & Pressley, 1997). Adolescents are more likely to use elaboration spontaneously than children are. Elementary school children can be taught to use elaboration strategies on a learning task, but they are less likely than adolescents to use the strategies on other learning tasks in the future. Nonetheless, verbal elaboration can be an effective memory strategy even with young elementary school children. In one study, the experimenter told second- and fifth-grade children to construct a meaningful sentence for a keyword (such as "The postman carried a letter in his cart" for the keyword *cart*). As shown in Figure 2.2, both second- and fifth-grade children remembered the keywords better when they constructed a meaningful sentence containing the word than when the keyword and its definition were told to the child (Pressley, Levin, & McCormick, 1980).

One reason elaboration works so well in encoding is that it adds to the distinctiveness of memory code (Ellis, 1987; Hunt & Ellis, 2004). To remember a piece of information, such as a name, an experience, or a fact about geography, students need to search for the code that contains this information among the mass of codes in their long-term memory. The search process is easier if the memory code is unique (Hunt & Kelly, 1996). The situation is not unlike searching for a friend at a crowded airport—if your friend is 6 feet 3 inches tall and has flaming red hair, it will be easier to find him in the crowd than if he has more common features. Also, as a person elaborates information, more information is stored. And as more information is stored, it becomes easier to differentiate the memory from others. For example, if a student witnesses another student being hit by a car that speeds away, the student's memory of the car will be far better if she deliberately encodes her observations that the car is a red 1995 Pontiac with tinted windows and spinners on the wheels than if she observes only that it is a red car.

Constructing Images

When we construct an image of something, we are elaborating the information. For example, how many windows are there in the apartment or house where your family has lived for a substantial part of your life? Few of us ever memorize this information, but you probably can come up with a good answer, especially if you reconstruct a mental image of each room.

Allan Paivio (1971, 1986) argues that memories are stored in one of two ways: as verbal codes or as image codes. For example, you can remember a picture by a label (*The Last Supper*, a verbal code) or by a mental image. Paivio says that the more detailed and distinctive the image code, the better your memory of the information will be.

Researchers have found that encouraging children to use imagery to remember verbal information works better for older children than for younger children (Schneider, 2004). In one study, experimenters presented twenty sentences to first-through sixth-grade children to remember (such as "The angry bird shouted at the white dog" and "The policeman painted the circus tent on a windy day") (Pressley & others, 1987). Children were randomly assigned to an imagery condition (make a picture in your head for each sentence) and a control condition (children were told just to try hard). Figure 2.3 shows that the imagery instructions improved memory more for the older children (grades 4 through 6) than for the younger children (grades 1 through 3). Researchers have found that young elementary school children can use imagery to remember pictures better than they can verbal materials, such as sentences (Schneider & Pressley, 1997).

Organization

If students organize information when they are encoding it, their memory benefits. To understand the importance of organization in encoding, complete the following exercise: Recall the 12 months of the year as quickly as you can. How long did it take you? What was the order of your recall? Your answers are probably a few seconds and in natural order (January, February, March, and so on). Now try to remember the months in alphabetical order. Did you make any errors? How long did it take you? There is a clear distinction between recalling the months in natural order and recalling alphabetically. This exercise is a good one to use with your students to help them understand the importance of organizing their memories in meaningful ways.

The more you present information in an organized way, the easier your students will remember it. This is especially true if you organize information hierarchically or outline it. Also, if you simply encourage students to organize information, they often will remember it better than if you give them no instructions about organizing (Mandler, 1980).

levels of processing theory The theory that processing of memory occurs on a continuum from shallow to deep, with deeper processing producing better memory.

elaboration The extensiveness of information processing involved in encoding.

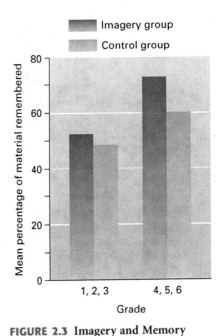

FIGURE 2.3 Imagery and Memory of Verbal Information
Imagery improved older elementary school children's memory for sentences more than younger elementary school children's memory for sentences.

Frank and Ernest

FRANK & ERNEST © Thaves/Dist. by Newspaper Enterprise Association, Inc.

"Can we hurry up and get to the test? My short-term memory is better than my long-term memory."
© 2006; reprinted courtesy of Bunny Hoest and *Parade.*

chunking Grouping, or "packing," information into "higher-order" units that can be remembered as single units.

sensory memory Memory that holds information from the world in its original form for only an instant.

short-term memory A limited-capacity memory system in which information is retained for as long as 30 seconds, unless the information is rehearsed, in which case it can be retained longer.

memory span The number of digits an individual can report back without error in a single presentation.

working memory A kind of "mental workbench" that lets individuals manipulate, assemble, and construct information when they make decisions, solve problems, and comprehend written and spoken language.

Chunking is a beneficial organizational memory strategy that involves grouping, or "packing," information into "higher-order" units that can be remembered as single units. Chunking works by making large amounts of information more manageable and more meaningful. For example, consider this simple list of words: *hot, city, book, forget, tomorrow, smile.* Try to hold these in memory for a moment; then write them down. If you recalled all six words, you succeeded in holding 30 letters in your memory. But it would have been much more difficult to try to remember those 30 letters. Chunking them into words made them meaningful.

24 STORAGE

After children encode information, they need to retain, or store, the information. Memory storage involves three types of memory with different time frames: sensory memory, working (or short-term) memory, and long-term memory.

Memory's Time Frames

Children remember some information for less than a second, some for about half a minute, and other information for minutes, hours, years, even a lifetime. The three types of memory, which correspond to these different time frames, are *sensory memory* (which lasts a fraction of a second to several seconds); *short-term memory* (also called *working memory;* lasts about 30 seconds), and *long-term memory* (which lasts up to a lifetime).

Sensory Memory **Sensory memory** holds information from the world in its original sensory form for only an instant, not much longer than the brief time a student is exposed to the visual, auditory, and other sensations.

Students have a sensory memory for sounds for up to several seconds, sort of like a brief echo. However, their sensory memory for visual images lasts only for about one-fourth of a second. Because sensory information lasts for only a fleeting moment, an important task for the student is to attend to the sensory information that is important for learning quickly, before it fades.

Short-Term Memory **Short-term memory** is a limited-capacity memory system in which information is retained for as long as 30 seconds, unless the information is rehearsed or otherwise processed further, in which case it can be retained longer. Compared with sensory memory, short-term memory is limited in capacity but relatively longer in duration. Its limited capacity intrigued George Miller (1956), who described this in a paper with a catchy title: "The Magical Number Seven, Plus or Minus Two." Miller pointed out that on many tasks, students are limited in how much information they can keep track of without external aids. Usually the limit is in the range of 7 ± 2 items.

The most widely cited example of the 7 ± 2 phenomenon involves **memory span,** the number of digits an individual can report back without error from a single presentation. How many digits individuals can report back depends on how old they are. In one study, memory span increased from two digits in 2-year-olds, to five digits in 7-year-olds, to six to seven digits in 12-year-olds (Dempster, 1981) (see Figure 2.4). Many college students can handle lists of eight or nine digits. Keep in mind that these are averages and that individuals differ. For example, many 7-year-olds have a memory span of fewer than six or seven digits; others have a memory span of eight or more digits.

Related to short-term memory, British psychologist Alan Baddeley (1993, 1998, 2000, 2001) proposed that **working memory** is a three-part system that temporarily holds information as people perform tasks. Working memory is a kind of mental "workbench" where information is manipulated and assembled to help us make decisions, solve problems, and comprehend written and spoken language. Notice that working memory is not like a passive storehouse with shelves to store information until it moves to long-term memory. Rather, it is a very active memory system (Hitch, 2006; Kane & others, 2004; Schraw, 2006).

Figure 2.5 shows Baddeley's view of working memory and its three components: phonological loop, visuospatial memory, and central executive. Think of them as an executive (central executive) with two assistants (phonological loop and visuospatial working memory) to help do your work.

- The *phonological loop* is specialized to briefly store speech-based information about the sounds of language. The phonological loop contains two separate components: an acoustic code, which decays in a few seconds, and rehearsal, which allows individuals to repeat the words in the phonological store.
- *Visuospatial working memory* stores visual and spatial information, including visual imagery. Like the phonological loop, visuospatial working memory has a limited capacity. The phonological loop and visuospatial working memory function independently. You could rehearse numbers in the phonological loop while making spatial arrangements of letters in visuospatial working memory.
- The *central executive* integrates information not only from the phonological loop and visuospatial working memory but also from long-term memory. In Baddeley's view, the central executive plays important roles in attention, planning, and organizing behavior. The central executive acts much like a supervisor who monitors which information and issues deserve attention and which should be ignored. It also selects which strategies to use to process information and solve problems. As with the other two components of working memory—the phonological loop and visuospatial working memory—the central executive has a limited capacity.

Let's examine an aspect of life in which working memory is involved. In one study, verbal working memory was impaired by negative emotion (Gray, 2001). In other words, when people are feeling bad about something, their working memory may become less efficient. In another study, college students who wrote about a negative emotional event showed sizeable improvement in working memory, compared with students who wrote about a positive emotional event and those in a control group who wrote about their daily schedule (Klein & Boals, 2001). The writing effect on working memory was associated with higher grade-point averages. This study demonstrated that working memory is malleable and can be affected by an experience such as writing about one's emotional experiences (Miyake, 2001). For example, students with math anxiety often experience deficiencies in working memory when doing math problems because of intrusive thoughts and worries about math (Ashcraft & Kirk, 2001). Such students might benefit from writing about their math anxiety.

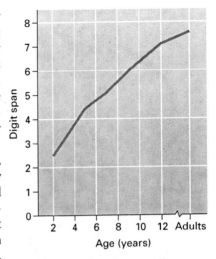

FIGURE 2.4 Developmental Changes in Memory Span
In one study, memory span increased about 3 digits from 2 years of age to 5 digits at 7 years of age (Dempster, 1981). By 12 years of age, memory span had increased on average another 1½ digits.

Working Memory

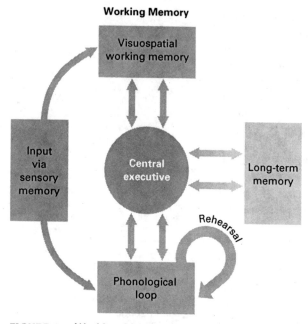

FIGURE 2.5 Working Memory

In Baddeley's working memory model, working memory is like a mental workbench where a great deal of information processing is carried out. Working memory consists of three main components: The phonological loop and visuospatial working memory serve as assistants, helping the central executive do its work. Input from sensory memory goes to the phonological loop, where information about speech is stored and rehearsal takes place, and visuospatial working memory, where visual and spatial information, including imagery, are stored. Working memory is a limited-capacity system, and information is stored there for only a brief time. Working memory interacts with long-term memory, using information from long-term memory in its work and transmitting information to long-term memory for longer storage.

Is the working memory of adolescents better than the working memory of children? One study found that it was (Swanson, 1999). Investigators examined the performances of children and adolescents on both verbal and visuospatial working memory tasks. The two verbal tasks were auditory digit sequence (the ability to remember numerical information embedded in a short sentence, such as "Now suppose somebody wanted to go to the supermarket at 8651 Elm Street") and semantic association (the ability to organize words into abstract categories) (Swanson, 1999, p. 988). In the semantic association task, the participant was presented with a series of words (such as *shirt, saw, pants, hammer, shoes,* and *nails*) and then asked to remember how they go together. The two visuospatial tasks involved mapping/directions and a visual matrix. In the mapping/directions task, the participant was shown a street map indicating the route a bicycle would take. After briefly looking at the map, participants were asked to redraw the route on a blank map. In the visual matrix task, participants were asked to study a matrix showing a series of dots. After looking at the matrix for five seconds, they were asked to answer questions about the location of the dots. As shown in Figure 2.6, working memory increased substantially from 8 through 24 years of age no matter what the task. Thus, the adolescent years are likely to be an important developmental period for improvement in working memory.

Long-Term Memory **Long-term memory** is a type of memory that holds enormous amounts of information for a long period of time in a relatively permanent fashion. A typical human's long-term memory capacity is staggering and the efficiency with which individuals can retrieve information is impressive. It often takes only a moment to search through this vast storehouse to find the information we want. Think about your own long-term memory. Who wrote the Gettysburg Address? Who was your first-grade teacher? You can answer thousands of such questions instantly. Of course, not all information is retrieved so easily from long-term memory.

A Model of the Three Memory Stores This three-stage concept of memory we have been describing was developed by Richard Atkinson and Richard Shiffrin (1968). According to the **Atkinson-Shiffrin model,** memory involves a sequence of sensory memory, short-term memory, and long-term memory stages (see Figure 2.7). As we have seen, much information makes it no further than the sensory memories of sounds and sights. This information is retained only for a brief instant. However, some information, especially that to which we pay attention, is transferred to short-term memory, where it can be retained for about 30 seconds (or longer with the aid of rehearsal). Atkinson and Shiffrin claimed that the longer information is retained in short-term memory through the use of rehearsal, the greater its chance is of getting into long-term memory. Notice in Figure 2.7 that information in long-term memory also can be retrieved back into short-term memory.

Some contemporary experts on memory believe that the Atkinson-Shiffrin model is too simple (Bartlett, 2005). They argue that memory doesn't always work in a neatly packaged three-stage sequence, as Atkinson and Shiffrin proposed. For example, these contemporary experts stress that *working memory* uses long-term memory's contents in more flexible ways than simply retrieving information from it. Despite these problems, the model is useful in providing an overview of some components of memory.

Long-Term Memory's Contents Just as different types of memory can be distinguished by how long they last, memory can be differentiated on the basis of its contents (Schraw, 2006). For long-term memory, many contemporary psychologists

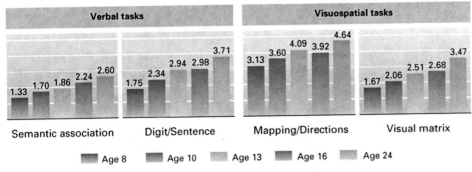

FIGURE 2.6 Developmental Changes in Working Memory

Note: The scores shown here are the means for each age group and the age also represents a mean age. Higher scores reflect superior working memory performance.

accept the hierarchy of contents described in Figure 2.8 (Bartlett, 2005; Squire, 1987). In this hierarchy, long-term memory is divided into the subtypes of declarative and procedural memory. Declarative memory is subdivided into episodic memory and semantic memory.

Declarative and Procedural Memory **Declarative memory** is the conscious recollection of information, such as specific facts or events that can be verbally communicated. Declarative memory has been called "knowing that" and more recently has been labeled "explicit memory." Demonstrations of students' declarative memory could include recounting an event they have witnessed or describing a basic principle of math. However, students do not need to be talking to be using declarative memory. If students simply sit and reflect on an experience, their declarative memory is involved.

Procedural memory is nondeclarative knowledge in the form of skills and cognitive operations. Procedural memory cannot be consciously recollected, at least not in the form of specific events or facts. This makes procedural memory difficult, if not impossible, to communicate verbally. Procedural memory is sometimes called "knowing how," and recently it also has been described as "implicit memory" (Schacter, 2000). When students apply their abilities to perform a dance, ride a bicycle, or type on a computer keyboard, their procedural memory is at work. It also is at work when they speak grammatically correct sentences without having to think about how to do it.

long-term memory A type of memory that holds enormous amounts of information for a long period of time in a relatively permanent fashion.

Atkinson–Shiffrin model A model of memory that involves a sequence of three stages: sensory memory, short-term memory, and long-term memory.

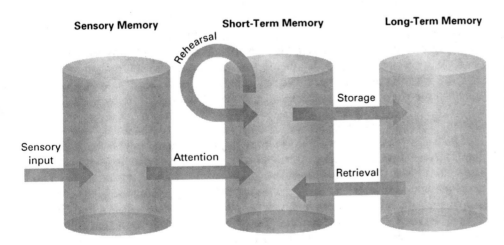

FIGURE 2.7 Atkinson and Shiffrin's Theory of Memory
In this model, sensory input goes into sensory memory. Through the process of attention, information moves into short-term memory, where it remains for 30 seconds or less, unless it is rehearsed. When the information goes into long-term memory storage, it can be retrieved over the lifetime.

declarative memory The conscious recollection of information, such as specific facts or events that can be verbally communicated.

procedural memory Knowledge in the form of skills and cognitive operations. Procedural memory cannot be consciously recollected, at least not in the form of specific events or facts.

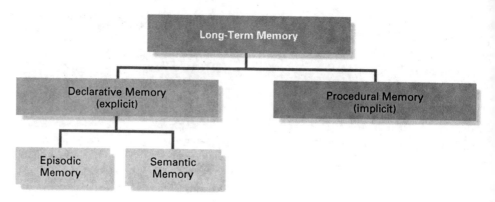

FIGURE 2.8 Classification of Long-Term Memory's Contents

Episodic and Semantic Memory   Cognitive psychologist Endel Tulving (1972, 2000) distinguishes between two subtypes of declarative memory: episodic and semantic. **Episodic memory** is the retention of information about the where and when of life's happenings. Students' memories of the first day of school, whom they had lunch with, or the guest who came to talk with their class last week are all episodic.

Semantic memory is a student's general knowledge about the world. It includes

- knowledge of the sort learned in school (such as knowledge of geometry);
- knowledge in different fields of expertise (such as knowledge of chess, for a skilled 15-year-old chess player); and
- "everyday" knowledge about meanings of words, famous people, important places, and common things (such as what the word *pertinacious* means or who Nelson Mandela is).

Semantic memory is independent of the person's identity with the past. For example, students might access a fact—such as "Lima is the capital of Peru"—and not have the foggiest idea when and where they learned it.

Representing Information in Memory

How do students represent information in their memory? Three main theories have addressed this question: network, schema, and fuzzy trace.

episodic memory The retention of information about the where and when of life's happenings.

semantic memory A student's general knowledge about the world.

network theories Theories that describe how information in memory is organized and connected; they emphasize nodes in the memory network.

schema theories Theories that when we construct information, we fit it into information that already exists in our mind.

schema Information—concepts, knowledge, information about events—that already exists in a person's mind.

Network Theories   **Network theories** describe how information in memory is organized and connected. They emphasize nodes in the memory network. The nodes stand for labels or concepts. Consider the concept "bird." One of the earliest network theories described memory representation as hierarchically arranged, with more-concrete concepts ("canary," for example) nestled under more abstract concepts (such as "bird"). However, it soon became clear that such hierarchical networks are too neat to accurately portray how memory representation really works. For example, students take longer to answer the question "Is an ostrich a bird?" than to answer the question "Is a canary a bird?" Thus, today memory researchers envision the memory network as more irregular and distorted (Schraw, 2006). A typical bird, such as a canary, is closer to the node, or center, of the category "bird" than is the atypical ostrich.

Schema Theories   Long-term memory has been compared to a library of books. The idea is that our memory stores information just as a library stores books. In this analogy, the way students retrieve information is said to be similar to the process they use to locate and check out a book. The process of retrieving information from long-term memory, however, is not as precise as the library analogy suggests. When we search through our long-term memory storehouse, we don't always find the exact "book" we want, or we might find the "book" we want but discover that only "several pages" are intact—we have to reconstruct the rest.

Schema theories state that when we reconstruct information, we fit it into information that already exists in our mind. A **schema** is information—concepts, knowledge, information about events—that already exists in a person's mind. Unlike network theories, which assume that retrieval involves specific facts, schema theory claims that long-term memory searches are not very exact. We often don't find precisely what we want, and we have to reconstruct the rest. Often when asked to retrieve information, we fill in the gaps between our fragmented memories with a variety of accuracies and inaccuracies.

We have schemas for all sorts of information. If you tell virtually any story to your class and then ask the students to write down what the story was about, you likely will get many different versions. That is, your students won't remember every detail of the story you told and will reconstruct the story with their own particular stamp on it. Suppose you tell your class a story about two men and two women who were involved in a train crash in France. One student might reconstruct the story by saying the characters died in a plane crash, another might describe three men and three women, another might say the crash was in Germany, and so on. The reconstruction and distortion of memory is nowhere more apparent than in the memories given by courtroom witnesses. In criminal court trials such as that of O. J. Simpson and Scott Peterson the variations in people's memories of what happened underscores how we reconstruct the past rather than take an exact photograph of it.

In sum, schema theory accurately predicts that people don't always coldly store and retrieve bits of data in a computer-like fashion (Chen & Mo, 2004; Schacter, 2001; Schraw, 2006). The mind can distort an event as it encodes and stores impressions of reality.

A **script** is a schema for an event. Scripts often have information about physical features, people, and typical occurrences. This kind of information is helpful when teachers and students need to figure out what is happening around them. In a script for an art activity, students likely will remember that you will instruct them on what to draw, that they are supposed to put on smocks over their clothes, that they must get the art paper and paints from the cupboard, that they are to clean the brushes when they are finished, and so on. For example, a student who comes in late to the art activity likely knows much of what to do because he has an art activity script.

Fuzzy Trace Theory   Another variation of how individuals reconstruct their memories is **fuzzy trace theory** which states that when individuals encode information it creates two types of memory representations: (1) a *verbatim memory trace*, which consists of precise details, and (2) a *fuzzy trace*, or *gist*, which is the central idea of the information (Brainerd & Reyna, 2004; Reyna, 2004; Reyna & Brainerd, 1995). For example, consider a child who is presented with information about a pet store that has 10 birds, 6 cats, 8 dogs, and 7 rabbits. Then the child is asked two different types of questions: (1) verbatim questions, such as: "How many cats are in the pet store, 6 or 8?" and (2) gist questions, such as: "Are there more cats or more dogs in the pet store?" Researchers have found that preschool children tend to remember verbatim information better than gist information, but elementary-school-aged children are more likely to remember gist information (Brainerd & Gordon, 1994). According to Brainerd and Reyna, the increased use of gist information by elementary-school-aged children accounts for their improved memory, because fuzzy traces are less likely to be forgotten than verbatim traces.

25 RETRIEVAL AND FORGETTING

After students have encoded information and then represented it in memory, they might be able to retrieve some of it but might also forget some of it. What factors influence whether students can retrieve information?

script A schema for an event.

fuzzy trace theory States that memory is best understood by considering two types of memory representations: (1) verbatim memory trace and (2) gist. In this theory, older children's better memory is attributed to the fuzzy traces created by extracting the gist of information.

serial position effect The principle that recall is better for items at the beginning and the end of a list than for items in the middle.

Retrieval

When we retrieve something from our mental "data bank," we search our store of memory to find the relevant information. Just as with encoding, this search can be automatic or it can require effort. For example, if you ask your students what month it is, the answer will immediately spring to their lips. That is, the retrieval will be automatic. But if you ask your students to name the guest speaker who came to the class 2 months earlier, the retrieval process likely will require more effort.

An item's position on a list also affects how easy or difficult it will be to remember it (Pressley & Harris, 2006). In the **serial position effect,** recall is better for items at the beginning and end of a list than for items in the middle. Suppose that when you give a student directions about where to go to get tutoring help, you say, "Left on Mockingbird, right on Central, left on Balboa, left on Sandstone, and right on Parkside." The student likely will remember "Left on Mockingbird" and "Right on Parkside" better than "Left on Balboa." The *primacy effect* is that items at the beginning of a list tend to be remembered. The *recency effect* is that items at the end of the list also tend to be remembered.

Figure 2.9 shows a typical serial position effect with a slightly stronger recency effect than primacy effect. The serial position effect applies not only to lists but also to events. If you spread out a history lesson over a week and then ask students about it the following Monday, they likely will have the best memory for what you told them on Friday of last week and the worst memory for what you told them on Wednesday of last week.

Another factor that affects retrieval is the nature of the cues people use to prompt their memory (Allan & others, 2001). Students can learn to create effective cues. For example, if a student has a "block" about remembering the name of the guest who came to class 2 months ago, she might go through the alphabet, generating names with each letter. If she manages to stumble across the right name, she likely will recognize it.

Another consideration in understanding retrieval is the **encoding specificity principle:** that associations formed at the time of encoding or learning tend to be effective retrieval cues. For example, imagine that a 13-year-old child has encoded this information about Mother Teresa: She was born in Albania, lived most of her life in India, became a Roman Catholic nun, was saddened by seeing people sick and dying in Calcutta's streets, and won a Nobel Prize for her humanitarian efforts to help the poor and suffering. Later, when the child tries to remember details about Mother Teresa, she can use words such as *Nobel Prize, Calcutta,* and *humanitarian* as retrieval cues. The concept of encoding specificity is compatible with our earlier discussion of elaboration: The more elaboration children use in encoding information, the better their memory of the information will be. Encoding specificity and elaboration reveal how interdependent encoding and retrieval are.

Yet another aspect of retrieval is the nature of the retrieval task itself. *Recall* is a memory task in which individuals must retrieve previously learned information, as students must do for fill-in-the-blank or essay questions. *Recognition* is a memory task in which individuals only have to identify ("recognize") learned information, as is often the case on multiple-choice tests. Many students prefer multiple-choice items because they provide good retrieval cues, which fill-in-the-blank and essay items don't do.

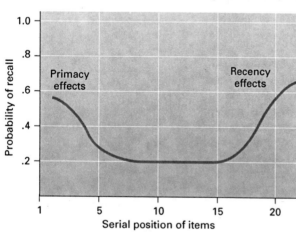

FIGURE 2.9 The Serial Position Effect
When a person is asked to memorize a list of words, the words memorized last usually are recalled best, those at the beginning next best, and those in the middle least efficiently.

Forgetting

One form of forgetting involves the cues we just discussed. **Cue-dependent forgetting** is retrieval failure caused by a lack of effective retrieval cues. The notion of cue-dependent forgetting can explain why a student might fail to retrieve a needed fact

BEST PRACTICES
Strategies for Helping Students Improve Their Memory

1. *Motivate children to remember material by understanding it rather than by memorizing it.* Children will remember information better over the long term if they understand the information rather than just rehearse and memorize it. Rehearsal works well for encoding information into short-term memory, but when children need to retrieve the information from long-term memory it is much less efficient. For most information, encourage children to understand it, give it meaning, elaborate on it, and personalize it. Give children concepts and ideas to remember and then ask them how they can relate the concepts and ideas to their own personal experiences and meanings. Give them practice on elaborating a concept so they will process the information more deeply.

2. *Assist students in organizing what they put into their memory.* Children will remember information better if they organize it hierarchically. Give them some practice arranging and reworking material that requires some structuring.

3. *Teach mnemonic strategies.* Mnemonics are memory aids for remembering information. Mnemonic strategies can involve imagery and words. Here are some different types of mnemonics:

   * *Method of loci.* In the *method of loci,* children develop images of items to be remembered and mentally store them in familiar locations. Rooms of a house and stores on a street are common locations used in this memory strategy. For example, if children need to remember a list of concepts, they can mentally place them in the rooms of their house, such as entry foyer, living room, dining room, and kitchen. Then when they need to retrieve the information, they can imagine the house, mentally go through the rooms, and retrieve the concepts. Next, teacher Rosemary Moore describes a similar idea for teaching spelling words.

THROUGH THE EYES OF TEACHERS

Seeing Words in the Mind's Eye

Many children memorize spelling words quite easily, but a few struggle with this. I wanted to help these students as much as I could, so I would write the spelling words on index cards and place them in random order and various positions (vertical, diagonal, upside down) across the front of the room. As we did spelling assignments, exercises, and games throughout the week the words were there for the students to refer to if they got "stuck." The index cards were taken down before the test on Friday, but as I called out each of the spelling words I would notice students turning their eyes to the place where that particular word had been displayed. I believe they were seeing the word in their "mind's eye." My students' spelling scores improved dramatically.

---

* *Rhymes.* Examples of mnemonic rhymes are the spelling rule "*i* before *e* except after *c,*" the month rule "Thirty days hath September, April, June, and November," the bolt-turning rule "Right is tight, left is loose," and the alphabet song.

* *Acronyms.* This strategy involves creating a word from the first letters of items to be remembered. For example, *HOMES* can be used as a cue for remembering the five original Great Lakes: *Huron, Ontario, Michigan, Erie,* and *Superior.*

* *Keyword method.* Another mnemonic strategy that involves imagery is the *keyword method,* in which vivid imagery is attached to important words. This method has been used to practical advantage in teaching students how to rapidly master new information such as foreign vocabulary words, the states and capitals of the United States, and the names of U.S. presidents. For example, in teaching children that Annapolis is the capital of Maryland, you could ask them to connect vivid images of Annapolis and Maryland, such as two apples getting married (Levin, 1980) (see Figure 2.10).

FIGURE 2.10 The Keyword Method
To help children remember the state capitals, the keyword method was used. A special component of the keyword method is the use of mental imagery, which was stimulated by presenting the children with a vivid visual image, such as two apples being married. The strategy is to help the children associate *apple* with Annapolis and *marry* with Maryland.

Some educators argue against teaching children to use mnemonics because they involve rote memorization. Clearly, as we said earlier, remembering for understanding is preferred over rote memorization. However, if children need to learn lists of concepts, mnemonic devices can do the trick. Think of mnemonic devices as a way for children to learn some specific facts that they might need to know to solve problems.

encoding specificity principle The principle that associations formed at the time of encoding or learning tend to be effective retrieval cues.

cue-dependent forgetting Retrieval failure caused by a lack of effective retrieval cues.

interference theory The theory that we forget not because we actually lose memories from storage but because other information gets in the way of what we are trying to remember.

decay theory The theory that new learning involves the creation of a neurochemical "memory trace," which will eventually disintegrate. Thus, decay theory suggests that the passage of time is responsible for forgetting.

for an exam even when he is sure he "knows" the information. For example, if you are studying for a test in this course and are asked a question about a distinction between recall and recognition in retrieval, you likely will remember the distinction better if you possess the cues "fill-in-the-blank" and "multiple-choice," respectively.

The principle of cue-dependent forgetting is consistent with **interference theory,** which states that we forget not because we actually lose memories from storage but, rather, because other information gets in the way of what we are trying to remember. For a student who studies for a biology test, then studies for a history test, and then takes the biology test, the information about history will interfere with remembering the information about biology. Thus, interference theory implies that, if you have more than one test to study for, you should study last what you are going to be tested on next. That is, the student taking the biology test would have benefited from studying history first and studying biology afterward. This strategy also fits with the recency effect we described earlier.

Another source of forgetting is memory decay. According to **decay theory,** new learning involves the creation of a neurochemical "memory trace," which will eventually disintegrate. Thus, decay theory suggests that the passage of time is responsible for forgetting. Leading memory researcher Daniel Schacter (2001) now refers to forgetting that occurs with the passage of time as *transience.*

Memories decay at different speeds. Some memories are vivid and last for long periods of time, especially when they have emotional ties. We can often remember these "flashbulb" memories with considerable accuracy and vivid imagery. For example, consider a car accident you were in or witnessed, the night of your high school graduation, an early romantic experience, and where you were when you heard about the destruction of the World Trade Center towers. Chances are, you will be able to retrieve this information many years after the event occurred.

Students Remember... What They Think About

—By Daniel T. Willingham

Daniel T. Willingham is associate professor of cognitive psychology and neuroscience at the University of Virginia and author of Cognition: The Thinking Animal. *His research focuses on the role of consciousness in learning.*

Preview

How does the mind work—and especially how does it learn? Teachers make assumptions all day long about how students best comprehend, remember, and create. These assumptions—and the teaching decisions that result—are based on a mix of theories learned in teacher education, trial and error, craft knowledge, and gut instinct. Such gut knowledge often serves us well. But is there anything sturdier to rely on?

Cognitive science is an interdisciplinary field of researchers from psychology, neuroscience, linguistics, philosophy, computer science, and anthropology who seek to understand the mind. In this regular American Educator *column, we will consider findings from this field that are strong and clear enough to merit classroom application.*

Issue: The teacher presents a strong, coherent lesson in which a set of significant facts is clearly connected to a reasonable conclusion. But, at test time, the students show no understanding of the connections. Some students parrot back the conclusion, but no facts. Others spit back memorized facts, but don't see how they fit together. Though the lesson wasn't taught in a rote way, it seems like rote knowledge is what the students took in. Why do well-integrated, coherent lessons often come back to us in a less meaningful, fragmented form? Can cognitive science help explain why this result is so common—and offer ideas about how to avoid it?

Response: Rote knowledge is devoid of all meaning (as discussed in my last column, Winter 2002). The knowledge that these students appear to be regurgitating is probably not rote knowledge. It is probably "shallow" knowledge: The students' knowledge has meaning (unlike rote knowledge), in that the students understand each isolated part, but their knowledge lacks the deeper meaning that comes from understanding the relationship among the parts. For reasons noted below, this is a common problem in the early stages of learning about a new topic. But it also has another remediable source, which is the focus of this column.

Cognitive science has shown that what ends up in a learner's memory is not simply the material presented—it is the product of what the learner thought about when he or she encountered the material. This principle illuminates one important origin of shallow knowledge and also suggests how to help students develop deep and interconnected knowledge.

Let's start with an example of shallow knowledge. Suppose that you are teaching a high school class unit on World War II and develop a lesson on the Japanese attack

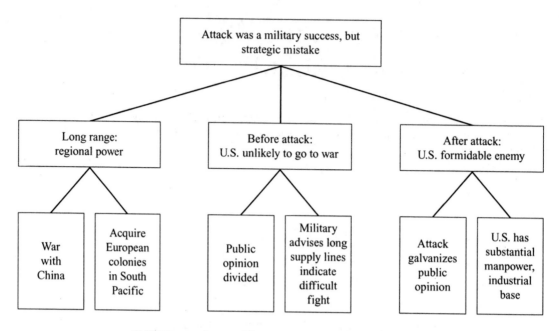

FIGURE 2.11 Lesson Diagram

on Pearl Harbor. Many facts might be included in such a lesson: (a) Japan had aspirations to be a regional power; (b) Japan was engaged in a protracted war with China; (c) because they were at war, European countries could not protect their colonies in the South Pacific; and (d) the attack on Pearl Harbor resulted in a declaration of war on Japan by the United States. The overarching point of this lesson might be to show that the attack on Pearl Harbor was a strategic mistake for the Japanese, given their war aims. (See Figure 2.11 for a diagram of the lesson.)

We can see two ways that this meaningful lesson might end up as shallow knowledge in the student's mind. The student might commit to memory some or all of these four facts. But knowing these facts without understanding how they relate to one another and can be integrated to support the conclusion leaves the facts isolated; they are not without meaning, but neither are they as rich as they might be. The student has the trees, but no view of the forest.

Alternatively, the student might commit to memory the conclusion, "The attack on Pearl Harbor, although militarily a successful battle for Japan, was ultimately detrimental to its long-range war plans." But memorizing this conclusion without understanding the reasoning behind it and knowing the supporting facts is empty. It isn't rote—the student knows Japan initiated and won a battle at the place called Pearl Harbor. But the knowledge certainly is "shallow"—it has no connections.*

We have all had students memorize phrases from class or a textbook more or less word-for-word, and although what the student says is accurate, we can't help but wonder whether he or she really understands the ideas those words represent. Let's dig deeper.

---

* My last column (Winter 2002, available at **www.aft.org/ american_educator/winter2002/CogSci.html**) discussed another common problem for students: inflexible knowledge. Like shallow knowledge, inflexible knowledge is meaningful—the catch is that it doesn't translate well to other relevant situations. To extend our World War II example, a student with inflexible knowledge may learn the conclusion and an adequate number of supporting facts, developing a real understanding of Japan's mistake. But, when the history class moved on to study another war, the student may not recognize an analogous strategic mistake. Developing flexible knowledge, such as being able to track strategic mistakes as a theme throughout military history (or to generalize, for example, to corporate history) requires much further study.

When students parrot back a teacher's or the textbook's words, they are, of course, drawing on memory. Thus, the question of why students end up with shallow knowledge is really a question about the workings of memory. Needless to say, determining what ends up in memory and in what form is a complex question, but *there is one factor that trumps most others in determining what is remembered: what you think about when you encounter the material.* The fact that the material you are dealing with has meaning does not guarantee that the meaning *will* be remembered. If you think about that meaning, the meaning will reside in memory. If you don't, it won't. For example, if I teach about Pearl Harbor, some sailing enthusiasts may start thinking about the ships of the era and pay minimal attention to the rest of the class—just a few minutes after the bell rings they won't remember much about the causes and consequences of Pearl Harbor. Memory is as thinking does.

A classic experiment illustrating this principle was conducted by Thomas Hyde and James Jenkins in 1969. It examined how one thinks about material and the effect of that thinking on memory. Subjects in their experiment listened to a list of words at a rate of one word every two seconds. Different groups of subjects were to perform different tasks upon hearing each word. Some were to rate each word as to whether it made them think of pleasant or unpleasant things, whereas others were asked to count the number of times the letter *E* appeared in the word. Rating the pleasantness forces the subject to think about the word's meaning; the word *garbage* is unpleasant because of what it means—what it is associated with in one's memory. Counting *Es*, on the other hand, forces one to think about the spelling of the word, but not its meaning. Thus, the experimenters manipulated what subjects thought about when they encountered each word. Subjects were not told that their memory for the words would later be tested; they thought they were merely to make the pleasantness or the *E*-counting judgment.

One other detail of the experiment is especially important. The word list actually consisted of 12 pairs of very highly associated words, such as *doctor–nurse*, although this fact was not pointed out to any of the subjects. The order in which the words were read was random (except that related words were not allowed to be next to one another in the list).

The results are shown in Figure 2.12. First look at the left side of the chart, which shows the mean number of words recalled. Memory was much better when subjects

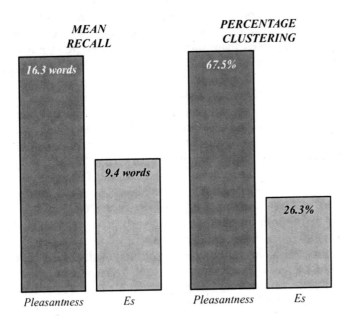

FIGURE 2.12 Thinking About Meaning Helps Memory

made the pleasantness ratings. Thinking about the meaning of material is especially helpful to memory. This finding is consistent across hundreds of other experiments.

The right side of the figure shows a measure of clustering—the extent to which subjects paired the associated words as they tried to remember them. When a subject recalled a word (e.g., *doctor*), what percentage of the time was the next word recalled the highly associated one (*nurse*)? As the figure shows, subjects who thought about the word's meaning (i.e., rated pleasantness) not only remembered more words, they tended to remember the related words together, even though the related words did not appear together in the list. The subjects who counted *Es* did not tend to remember related words together.

These results forcefully make the point that meaningful structure that is in the environment may or may not end up being stored in memory. In the Hyde and Jenkins experiment, the fact that some of the words were related in meaning was largely lost on the subjects who counted *Es* because thinking about *Es* did not encourage the subjects to process meaning. Subjects who made the pleasantness ratings tended to group the words together by meaning as they recalled them. Whatever subjects thought about when they heard the words (which, teachers will note, depends on what they were *asked* to think about) was what ended up in memory.

In the Hyde and Jenkins experiment, the "what they think about" principle is divided into thinking about meaning versus not thinking about meaning. Other experiments show that even if one thinks about meaning, the particular *aspect* of the meaning that one considers will be stored in memory, and other aspects of meaning will not. For example, in one experiment (Barclay et al., 1974), subjects were presented with words to remember in the context of a sentence. The sentence biased subjects to think of one or another feature of the to-be-remembered word: For example, some subjects read "The man lifted the *piano*," which encouraged thinking about the fact that pianos are heavy. Other subjects read "The man tuned the *piano*," which encouraged considering that pianos produce music. In the next phase of the experiment subjects were told that their memory for some of the nouns in the sentences would be tested and that for each sentence they would get a hint. For *piano*, some subjects were given the hint, "something heavy." If they had read the sentence about lifting the piano, this hint matched the feature they had thought about, but if they read the sentence about tuning the piano, the hint didn't match. (Other subjects saw a hint that matched the piano tuning sentence; that hint was "something with a nice sound.")

The results showed that subjects remembered about three times as many words when the hint for the test matched what subjects had thought about when they first read the word. Again, the point is that what is stored in memory is quite specific to what you think about when you encounter the material. It is not the case that if you think about *piano*, then *piano* and all of its features are stored in memory. You might think about its music-producing qualities, its weight, its cost, and so on. Or you might not focus on the referent at all, but rather on the physical properties of the word itself, as when Hyde and Jenkins asked subjects to count *Es*. In each case, what you think about is what you remember.

So what does this have to do with shallow knowledge? It shows where shallow knowledge might come from. Meaning that is in the environment won't end up in memory if students don't think about it. Students with shallow knowledge have apparently thought about the material in a shallow way. This conclusion reframes the question we might ask: Why would students think about the material in a shallow way, given that we didn't present it to them that way? Obviously, a student would learn only isolated facts or unsupported conclusions if that is what the teacher taught, but I find it difficult to believe that this is a common practice. The notion that education should emphasize meaning is deeply ingrained in our system and has been for a generation or more. There cannot be many teachers who ask their students to learn facts without concern for a larger picture. So how do students end up with shallow knowledge? There are several possible answers.

1. As noted at the beginning of this article, in one form, shallow knowledge is simply a step on the way to deep knowledge. Consider again the hierarchical diagram shown in Figure 1. I argued that shallow knowledge could either be memorization of the conclusion (top of the hierarchy) without knowing the facts that back it up (bottom of the hierarchy), or memorization of the facts without integrating them into a conclusion. Clearly the sort of deep knowledge we want our students to have is objectively harder to obtain than shallow knowledge, because knowledge of the facts *and* knowledge of the conclusion *and* knowledge of their interrelationships are prerequisite to it. We want students to know how the different levels of hierarchy relate to one another; it's not enough to have memorized each level in isolation of the others. That connected knowledge will inevitably be the last thing that the student acquires. Thus, some students' knowledge will be shallow simply because they are not far enough along yet.

2. Other students may effectively quit learning before they reach the deep understanding that is our goal for them. A student may learn the facts about Pearl Harbor and think "All right, I've learned a lot about this stuff." The student is correct (so far as it goes) and simply doesn't realize that there is yet more to do.

3. Students' perception of what they are supposed to learn—and what it means to learn—may contribute to shallow knowledge. A student may seek to memorize definitions and pat phrases word-for-word from the book because the student *knows* that this information is correct and cannot be contested. When I was in eighth grade, we were given a list of vocabulary terms that we were to define and then study in preparation for a weekly test. A friend defined "cherub" as "an angel of the second order." My friends and I teased him because his definition missed what we thought was the key aspect of the word—that a cherub is small, chubby, and rosy-cheeked. He was unmoved and kept repeating "that's what the dictionary said." He liked the fact that his answer was uncontestable. Students may memorize exactly what the teacher or textbook says in order to be certain that they are *correct*, and worry less about the extent to which they understand.

4. Despite what was offered to students in the teacher's lesson, the students attended to (thought about) something different—and that's what they remembered.

27) WHAT DOES THIS MEAN FOR TEACHERS?

This fundamental principle of memory—memory is as thinking does—yields a clear strategy to encourage deep, meaningful knowledge. If students think about the meaning of material, meaning will end up in memory. How can teachers be sure that students are thinking about meaning?

Obviously there is no one way to ensure that students think about the meaning of material. A compelling story may be appropriate for one lesson, whereas a carefully designed laboratory project works for a second, and a well-structured group discussion for a third. One possible common misconception is that learners can only understand meaning if they themselves construct the meaning in a physically active way. A moment's reflection should tell us that "listening" does not imply passivity or shallowness. We have all been to "active, participatory" workshops that felt like a waste of time, and we have been to lectures where we "just listened" that were gripping and informative. Constructing meaning is a matter of being *mentally* engaged; being physically engaged might help at times, but it is not necessary.

How can we ensure that students are mentally engaged? While there is still more to learn about applying this research on thinking and memory to teaching, several key principles have emerged to guide teachers in developing assignments, classroom activities, and assessments.

- **Anticipate what your lesson will lead students to think about.** The direct relationship between thought and memory is so important that it could be used as a self-check for a teacher preparing virtually any assignment: *Always try to anticipate what students will be thinking when they are doing the assignment.* Doing so may make it clear that some assignments designed with one purpose in mind will achieve another. For example, a teacher once told me that, as part of a unit on the Underground Railroad, he had his students bake biscuits so that they would appreciate what escaped slaves ate most nights. He asked what I thought of the assignment and my reply was that his students will remember baking biscuits. In other words, his students probably thought for 30 seconds about the relation of the baking to the course material, and then spent 30 minutes thinking about measuring flour, mixing dough, and so on.

  Another example comes from my recent observation of my nephew as he completed a book report. The teacher asked the students to draw a poster that depicted all of the events of the book. The purpose of the assignment was to have students think of the book as a whole, and to consider how the separate events related to one another. This purpose got lost in the execution. My nephew spent a lot more time thinking about how to draw a good castle than he did about the plot of the book.

- **Use discovery learning carefully.** The principle above—anticipate the students' thoughts—also illuminates the use and misuse of discovery learning. There is little doubt that students remember material they generate themselves better than material that is handed to them. This "generation effect," as it is called (Slamecka & Graf, 1978), is indeed powerful, and it is due, in part, to forcing the learner to think about the meaning of material (although other techniques can do that as well). Part of the effect does seem to be unique to the actual generation of the answer, over and above thinking about meaning. One might suppose, therefore, that discovery learning should be employed whenever possible. However, given that memory follows thought, one thing is clear: *Students will remember incorrect "discoveries" just as well as correct ones.*

  Considerable care must be taken to ensure that the path of students' thoughts will be a profitable one. For example, advocates of discovery learning often point out that children learn to use some computer software rapidly and effectively merely by "playing around with it." That may be true, but that learning environment is also quite structured in that profitless actions are immediately discouraged by the system not working. In effect, the system is so structured that profitless discoveries are impossible; but few classroom activities can achieve this kind of structure. How much anatomy will students learn by "playing around" with frog dissection? Can one anticipate the thoughts of students who dissect frogs with little direction? Although discovery learning may be powerful in highly structured contexts that make the correct discovery virtually inevitable, in others it is likely to prove unproductive.

Constructing Meaning is a Matter of Being Mentally Engaged

- **Design reading assignments that require students to actively process the text.** Many concrete strategies have been suggested for helping students to get more out of reading that likely have some or all of their effect by making readers think about the meaning of what they are reading. *Techniques such as writing outlines, self-examination during learning, review questions, and previews can encourage or require students to integrate the material and to thereby process (i.e., think about) the meaning.* These different techniques are more or less effective in different situations, perhaps due to the specific materials being studied (e.g., McDaniel & Einstein, 1989); general principles guiding when each technique should be used have not been forthcoming. Nevertheless, although one technique or another may be more effective for a given lesson or group of students, using any strategy that encourages the processing of meaning is almost always better than not using one.

- **Design lessons so that students can't avoid thinking about the lesson's goal.** On a more positive note, the "memory is as thinking does" principle can yield steps teachers can take to help students develop deep, interconnected knowledge: *Lessons should be directed so that students are very likely to think (or can't help but think) about the goal of the lesson.* The goal of the Underground Railroad lesson was not really about biscuits—it was to encourage students to consider the experience of escaped slaves. Therefore, a more effective starting point for that lesson would be to ask students leading questions that encourage consideration of what escaped slaves' experiences would be like, which might include questions of how they would obtain food, and what the constraints were on the food they could get (inexpensive, cooked rapidly, etc.). My nephew would have gotten more out of his book report project if it had emphasized what the teacher was really interested in (the connection among the book's events), perhaps by having the students label the events and connections among them (e.g., this event moves the character towards his goal; this event causes that event) and de-emphasizing the students' artistic contribution by having them use clip art or simply writing the events in words.

- **Design tests that lead students to think about and integrate the most important material.** The "memory is as thinking does" principle may also be applied to methods of assessing student knowledge: *Like lessons, study guides for texts should be developed that force students to think about the goals of the lessons being assessed.* For better or worse, some students expend their greatest effort to understand material as they prepare for an examination. Even if you would rather see such students motivated by a passion to learn, you can use the students' motivation to earn a good grade to ensure that they are getting the most out of your lessons. Announcing the general topics to be covered on an exam leaves the specifics of what to learn up to the student. Even if the teacher emphasizes that deep understanding will be tested, the student may misconstrue what is deep or, as noted earlier, the student may quit once some facts have been memorized, believing that he or she has already done quite a bit of studying. Suppose, however, that the teacher provides a list of integrative questions for the students to study from, such as "Describe why the attack on Pearl Harbor was a strategic mistake by Japan, given its war aims." Suppose further that the students know that the examination will consist of five questions from the 30-question list that they have been given, with an essay to be written on each of the five questions. Students will very likely restrict their studying to the 30 question list, but that might be just fine with the teacher if he or she feels that any student who can answer those 30 questions has mastered the material. This method of testing has the advantage of ensuring that while students are highly motivated, they think about the deepest meaning of the material that the teacher intended.

In summary, in the early stages of learning, students may display "shallow" learning. These students have acquired bits of knowledge that aren't well-integrated into a larger picture. Research tells us that deep, connected knowledge can be encouraged by getting students to think about the interrelation of the various pieces of knowledge that they have acquired. Cognitive science has not progressed to the point that it can issue prescriptions of exactly how that can be achieved—that job is very much in the hands of experienced teachers. But in considering how to encourage students to acquire meaningful knowledge, teachers will do well to keep the "memory is as thinking does" principle in mind.

References

Barclay, J. R., Bransford, J. D., Franks, J. J., McCarrel, N. S., & Nitsch, K. (1974). Comprehension and semantic flexibility. *Journal of Verbal Learning & Verbal Behavior, 13,* 471–481.

Hyde, T. S. & Jenkins, J. J. (1969). Differential effects of incidental tasks on the organization of recall of a list of highly associated words. *Journal of Experimental Psychology, 82,* 472–481.

McDaniel, M. A. & Einstein, G. O. (1989). Material-appropriate processing: A contextualist approach to reading and studying strategies. *Educational Psychology Review, 1,* 113–145.

Slamecka, N. J. & Graf, P. (1978). The generation effect: Delineation of a phenomenon. *Journal of Experimental Psychology: Human Learning & Memory, 4,* 592–604.

Readers can pose specific questions to "Ask the Cognitive Scientist," American Educator, *555 New Jersey Ave. N.W., Washington, DC 20001 or to **amerend@aft.org***

Development as a Dynamic System

—Linda B. Smith and Esther Thelen

Department of Psychology, Program in Cognitive Science, Indiana University, 1101 East 10th Street, Bloomington, IN 47405, USA

Preview

Development is about creating something more from something less, for example, a walking and talking toddler from a helpless infant. One current theoretical framework views the developmental process as a change within a complex dynamic system. Development is seen as the emergent product of many decentralized and local interactions that occur in real time. We examine how studying the multicausality of real-time processes could be the key to understanding change over developmental time. We specifically consider recent research and theory on perseverative reaching by infants as a case study that demonstrates this approach.

Contemporary developmental psychologists are still asking the same question that has intrigued philosophers and scientists since ancient times. How does the human mind, with all its power and imagination, emerge from the human infant, a creature so unformed and helpless? Some see the transformation as so remarkable that they endow infants with genetically programmed and pre-existing mental structures trapped in an immature body: latent capabilities for language, number, and physical and social reasoning that await revelation as infants mature. We also see the transformation as remarkable, but suggest that development is better understood as the emergent product of many decentralized and local interactions that occur in real time. That is, the developmental process is viewed as change within a complex dynamic system. There are several good introductions available to the concepts and mathematics of dynamic systems theory for cognitive scientists [1,2].

29 DEVELOPMENT AS A DYNAMIC SYSTEM

The idea of emergence—the coming into existence of new forms through ongoing processes intrinsic to the system—are not new to developmental psychology. Developmental theorists such as Kuo, Oyama and Gottlieb have long emphasized the probabilistic, epigenetic nature of ontogenetic processes. Biologists and psychologists such as Waddington, von Bertalanffy, Lewin and Gesell have envisioned behaviour and development as morphogenetic fields that unify multiple, underlying components. But only in the past decade or so have the concepts and models of non-linear dynamic systems made in-roads into traditional developmental psychology, becoming a contender for a new developmental theory [3–9] and fundamentally changing the way development is studied (see Box 1).

Developmental psychologists have used dynamic systems ideas both as a conceptual theory [3,7,9] and in various formal mathematical treatments of developmental change. These include connectionist models [10], catastrophe theories of structural change from a neo-Piagetian perspective [11] and models based on prey–predator relationships in which skills are envisioned as arising from recursive interacting 'growers' [6,12]. Moreover, dynamic views of development have

Box 1. Variability: A New Meaning

Traditionally, variability in behavioural data is a researcher's nightmare. Too much within- or between-subject variability swamps any experimental effects. Thus, researchers deliberately choose tasks to make people look alike. But real behaviour in real children is not like that. Their performance is notably fragile and context dependent. Abilities seemingly come and go. Indeed, even skilled adults might perform tasks differently each time [35]. Dynamic systems theory turns variability from a scourge into a blessing. In dynamic systems theory, the metric is not whether a child 'has' some static ability or unchanging concept. Rather, as systems are always in flux, the important dimension is the relatively stability of behaviour in its particular context over time [36]. New measures of variability allow researchers to see trajectories of change over the short timescales of problem-solving or over a longer developmental span. For example, Yan and Fischer [35] tracked adults learning a new computer programme and found that the performance of each person varied, but that the patterns of variability differed in novices and experts. Weerth and van Geert [37] collected dense longitudinal samples of basal cortisol in infants and their mothers. Cortisol levels in infants decreased with age and did not show circadian rhythms, but each infant had great variability from measurement to measurement. Mothers, conversely, were individually very stable, but more different from each other than were the infants.

Box 2. Emotional Episodes, Moods and Personality Development

How do we shift from being happy to sad when we are told of an unhappy event? How and why do moods settle in (e.g. depressions, contentment)? Why are some of us more prone to these moods than others? How do these happy and unhappy episodes and these moods create our personalities? How do our personalities create and play out in our emotional episodes, in our mood swings?

Understanding emotion requires understanding how processes at different timescales influence each other. In a recent new theory of emotion and personality development, Lewis [38] likens the relationship between emotional episodes, moods and personality to circular causality across different scales of analyses that characterize coastlines. The large-scale or macroscopic properties of a coastline—the bays, the ridges, the peninsulas—set the conditions for the small-scale or microscopic processes—waves, tidal forces, erosion. But these microscopic properties causally contribute to the long-standing macroscopic properties. This is an example of circular causality. Understanding emotion and personality development requires working out the same kind of circularly causal relationships—from the microsopic emotional states through the mid-scale of moods to the more stable personality.

Table 2.1 summarizes Lewis's three scales of emotional development, showing parallels and distinctions across scales and the current understanding of the psychological and neurobiological mechanisms.

Table 2.1. Scales of emotional development (from Lewis [38])

	Emotional episode	Mood	Personality
Timescale	Seconds, minutes	Hours, days	Years
Description	Rapid convergence of a cognitive interpretation with an emotional state	Lasting entrainment of interpretative bias with a narrow emotional range Temporary modification of state space	Lasting interpretive–emotional habits specific to classes of situations Permanent structure of state space
Dynamic system formalism	Atttractor		
Possible neurobiological mechanism	Cortical coherence mediated by orbito-entrained with limbic circuits	Orbitofrontal-corticolimbic entrainment, motor rehearsal, and preafference, sustainded neurohormone release	Selection and strengthening of some corticocortical and corticolimbic connections, pruning of others, loss of plasiticity
Higher-order form	Intention, goal	Intentional orientation	Sense of self

encompassed many different content domains, including mother–infant relationships, imitation, language, social relationships, perception and action, and atypical patterns of developmental change [13–18].

What unifies these diverse applications is their commitment to self-organization and emergence: systems can generate novelty through their own activity. We amplify these shared assumptions of dynamic approaches and show how we have applied them conceptually and formally to understand a particular task. We concentrate on two major tenets of dynamic systems theory as it applies to the self-organization of human development.

29 MULTICAUSALITY

The first assumption of the dynamic approach is that developing organisms are complex systems composed of very many individual elements embedded within, and open to, a complex environment. As in many other complex systems in nature, such systems can exhibit coherent behaviour: the parts are coordinated without an executive agent or a programme that produces the organized pattern. Rather, the coherence is generated solely in the relationships between the organic components and the constraints and opportunities of the environment. This self-organization means that no single element has causal priority.

When such complex systems self-organize, they are characterized by the relative stability or instability of their states. Development can be envisioned, then, as a series of evolving and dissolving patterns of varying dynamic stability, rather than an inevitable march towards maturity. Take infant crawling as an example. Crawling is a coherent behaviour that infants use to locomote when they have sufficient strength and coordination to assume a hands-and-knees posture, but are not balanced and strong enough to walk upright. Crawling is a stable behaviour for several months. But when infants learn to walk, the crawling pattern becomes destablilized by the patterns of standing and walking. There is no 'programme' for crawling assembled in the genes or wired in the nervous system. It self-organizes as a solution to a problem (move across the room), later to be replaced by a more efficient solution.

30 NESTED TIMESCALES

The second key assumption of the dynamics systems approach is that behavioural change occurs over different timescales. Neural excitation, for example, happens in milliseconds. Reaction times are of the order of hundreds of milliseconds. People learn skills after hours, days and months of practice. Developmental change occurs over weeks, months and years, and evolution over a much longer time period. Traditionally, psychologists have considered action, learning, development and evolution as distinct processes. But for the organism (and its descendants), time is unified and coherent, as are the collaborating elements of the system. Every neural event is the initial condition for the next slice of time. Every cell division sets the stage for the next. The coherence of time and levels of the complex system mean that the dynamics of one time-scale (e.g. neural activity) must be continuous with and nested within the dynamics of all other time-scales (e.g. growth, learning and development). Thus, in the study of development, we must be concerned with how different timescales interact (see Box 2).

31 THE A-NOT-B ERROR

We present an example of how we have used the dynamic concepts of multicausality and nested time to revisit a classic issue in developmental psychology. The question originally posed by Piaget [19] was 'when do infants acquire the concept of object permanence?' He devised a simple object-hiding task, which has been adopted by several generations of researchers. The experimenter hides a tantalizing toy under a lid at location A and the infant reaches for the toy. This A-location trial is repeated several times. Then, there is the crucial switch trial: the experimenter hides the object at new location, B. At this point, 8- to 10-month-old infants make a curious 'error'. If there is a short delay between hiding and reaching, they reach not to where they saw the object disappear, but back to A, where they found the object previously.

This 'A-not-B' error is especially interesting because it is tightly linked to a highly circumscribed developmental period: infants older than 12 months of age search correctly on the crucial B trials. Why this dramatic shift? Do 12-month-old infants know something that 10-month-old infants do not? Piaget suggested that only at 12 months of age do infants know that objects can exist independently of their own

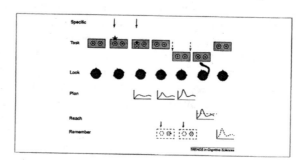

FIGURE 2.13

A task analysis of the A-not-B error, depicting a typical A-location hiding event. The box and hiding wells constitute the continually present visual input. The specific or transient input (top row) consists of the hiding of the toy in the 'A' well (on the left here). A delay is imposed between hiding and allowing the infant to search. During these events, the infant looks at the objects in view, remembers the cued location and undertakes a planning process leading to the activation of reach parameters, followed by reaching itself. Finally, the infant remembers the parameters of the current reach.

actions. Others have suggested that during that two month period, infants shift their representations of space, change the functioning of their prefrontal cortices, learn to inhibit responses, change their understanding of the task or increase the strength of their representations [20–23].

There is merit to all of these ideas, but none can explain the full pattern of experimental results [24]. This might be because these accounts seek an explanation in terms of a single cause when there is no single cause. In collaboration with Schoner and Scheier [25], we offer a formal theory, the dynamic field model [26], to explain how the A-not-B error is the emergent product of multiple causes interacting over nested timescales. The account begins with an analysis of the looking, reaching and memory events that comprise the task, as illustrated in Figure 2.13.

32 TASK DYNAMICS

The dynamic field simulates the decisions of infants to reach to location A or B by integrating, over time, the various influences on that decision. The field model is neurally inspired, of the type described and characterized analytically by Amari [27], but it is abstract and not anatomically specific. The model has a one-dimensional activation field, defining a parameter space of potential activation states (in this case the locations of targets A and B). Inputs are represented by their location and their influence on the field. Most importantly, points within the field provide input to one another, which allows the field to become self-organizing. A highly activated point will exert a strong inhibitory influence over the points around it, allowing an activation to be maintained in the absence of external input.

Figure 2.14a illustrates the evolution of activation on the very first A trial. Before the infant has seen any object hidden, there is activation in the field at both the A and B locations from the two covers. As the experimenter directs attention to the A location by hiding the toy, it produces a high, transient activation at A. Then the field evolves a decision over time. When the activation peak crosses a threshold, the infant reaches to that location.

Most crucial for this account is that once infants reach, a memory of that reach becomes another input to the next trial. Thus, at the second A trial, there is some increased activation at site A because of the previous activity there. This combines with the hiding cue to produce a second reach to A. Over many trials to A, a strong memory of previous actions builds up. Each trial embeds the history of previous trials.

Now consider the crucial B trial (Figure 2.14b). The experimenter provides a strong cue to B. But as that cue decays, the lingering memory of the actions at A begin to dominate the field, and indeed, over time, to shift the decision back to the habitual, A side. The model clearly predicts that the error is time dependent: there is a brief period immediately after the hiding event when infants should search correctly, and indeed they do [28].

Using this model as a guide, experimenters can experimentally make the error come and go, almost at will. This is achieved by changing the delay, by heightening the attention-grabbing properties of the covers or the hiding event, and by increasing and decreasing the number of prior reaches to A [24,29]. We have even made the error occur (and not occur!) even when there is no toy to be hidden [24]. Directing attention to an in-view object (A) heightens activation at the location and, in the experiment, infants reach to that continually in-view object. Subsequently, when the experimenter directs attention to a different nearby in-view object (B), infants watch, but then reach back to the original object (A).

Experimenters have also made the error vanish by making the reaches on the B trials different in some way from the A trial reaches. In the model, these differences

FIGURE 2.14 (A)

The time evolution of activation in the planning field on the first A trial. The activation rises as the object is hidden and, owing to self-organizing properties in the field, is sustained during the delay.

FIGURE 2.14 (B)

The time evolution of activation in the planning field on the first B trial. There is heightened activation at A before the hiding event, owing to memory for prior reaches. As the object is hidden at B, activation rises at B, but as this transient event ends, owing to the memory properties of the field, activation at A declines and that at B rises.

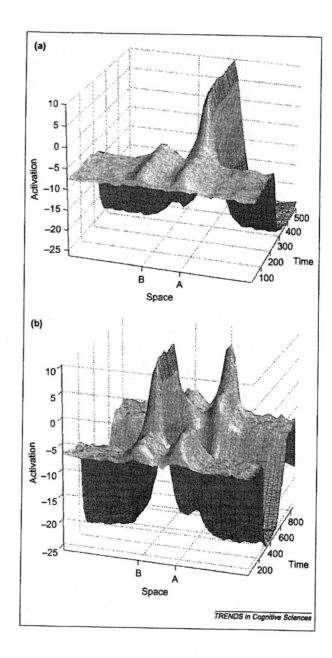

FIGURE 2.15

An infant sitting for an A trial (left) and standing for a B trial (right). This change in posture causes younger infants to search as 12-month-old infants do (see text for details).

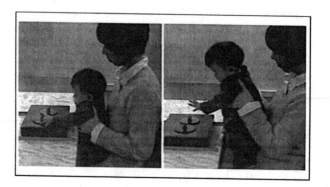

decrease the influence of the A trial memories on the activations in the field. One experiment achieved this by shifting the posture of the infant [24]. An infant who sat during the A trials would then be stood up, as shown in Figure 2.15, to watch the hiding event at B, during the delay and during the search. This posture shift causes even 8- and 10-month-old infants to search correctly, just like 12-month-olds. In another experiment, we changed the similarity of reaches on A and B trials by putting on and taking off wrist weights [25]. Infants who reached with 'heavy' arms on A trials but 'light' ones on B trials (and vice versa) did not make the error, again performing as if they were 2–3 months older. These results suggest that the relevant memories are in the language of the body and close to the sensory surface. In addition, they underscore the highly decentralized nature of error: the relevant causes include the covers on the table, the hiding event, the delay, the past activity of the infant and the feel of the body of the infant.

This multicausality demands a rethinking of what is meant by knowledge and development. Do 10-month-old infants know something different when they make the error compared with when they do not? The answer is 'yes' if we conceptualize knowledge and knowing as emergent, that is, made at a precise moment from multiple components in relation to the task and to the immediately preceding activity of the system. What do 12-month-olds know that 10-month-olds do not? There can be no single cause, no single mechanism and no one knowledge structure that distinguishes 10-month-olds from 12-month-olds because there are many causes that make the error appear and disappear. Instead, both 10-and 12-month-olds can be regarded as complex systems that self-organize in the task. However, just as trial dynamics are nested in task dynamics, so are task dynamics nested in developmental dynamics.

33 DEVELOPMENTAL DYNAMICS

The A-not-B error has been important to developmental theory because it is tightly linked to a few months in infancy. However, the neural field model suggests that the dynamics that create the error in infants are basic processes involved in goal-directed actions at all ages. Indeed, by changing the task, researchers can make perseverative errors come and go in older children and adults, just as in infants. Recently, Spencer and colleagues [30] invented an A-not-B task that was suitable for 2-year-olds by hiding toys in a sandbox. The surface of the sand presents a uniform field so there are no markers to indicate the two possible hiding locations. Experimenters gave toddlers many trials at location A, then hid the toy at location B. With a delay of 10 s, the toddlers, having watched the toy being hidden at location B, still returned to the A location to dig in the sand for the toy. Indeed there are many other situations in which both children and adults fall back on a habit despite new information [31,32]. Nonetheless, in the standard A-not-B task, infants change their behaviour over 2 months. In the field model, this is simulated this by increasing the resting activation of the field. This makes it easier for the input from the hiding cue to form a self-sustaining peak at B to compete with the A memory. Similarly, in her model of the error (also a dynamics systems model), Munakata [23] simulates development by stronger self-sustaining memories for the hiding event. If self-sustaining memories drive the successes of older children, then we must ask where they come from. What are infants doing every day that improves their location memory? One possibility is their self-locomotion. Crawling appears to improve the spatial memories of infants [33]. But there are also other possibilities. Their fine motor control improves markedly during the last part of the first year after birth. Perhaps more experience perceiving objects and manipulating them improves the flexibility of infants to notice differences in the targets or to be less tied to their previous actions. Indeed simply practising the A-not-B task repeatedly improves performance [34]. In this way, real-time activity in the task is unified with developmental time. Developmental change evolves from the real-time activities of the infant.

Box 3. Questions for Future Research

- How can we identify when behavioural patterns are stable and when they are unstable and easily changed?
- Can we design research paradigms to address multiple contributions to developmental change?
- Can we understand the interaction of real-time task dynamics and change on a longer time-scale?
- What is the nature of real experiences of infants and children in the world?
- What are the limits of developmental predictability?

---

34 IMPLICATIONS OF A DYNAMIC APPROACH

A dynamic systems theory of development helps to resolve an apparent theoretical contradiction. At a very global level, the constraints imposed by our biological heritage and by the similarities in human environments seem to result in similar developmental outcomes. All intact human infants learn to walk, to progress from making the A-not-B error to not making it, to speak their native language and to form intense social relationships. But when one looks at the details of development, the picture seems far less deterministic. Children from the same family grow up to be amazingly different from one another. Children with social and economic advantages sometimes fail in life, whereas those from impoverished backgrounds sometimes overcome them. There is considerable indeterminancy within processes that have globally similar outcomes.

Complex systems of embedded levels and timescales can have both of these properties. On the one hand, they can self-organize to produce cohesive patterns. On the other, they may be highly non-linear, sometimes called 'sensitivity to initial conditions'. This means that small changes in one or more components of the dynamic system can lead to reorganization and to large differences in behaviour. Such non-linearities might be reflected in development as stage-like shifts and might underlie the dramatic differences between 10- and 12-month-olds in the standard A-not-B task. But if development is made from real-time events, then these non-linearities might also create individual differences. Even very small differences in beginning states and in developmental histories can amplify and lead to large individual differences. If this is so, then at the microlevel, development will be messier and very much tied to the idiosyncratic real-time activities of the infant. From a dynamic perspective, then, it is important to understand the processes by which the everyday activities of children create developmental change—both the universal attainments and the individual pathways (see also Box 3. Questions for Future Research).

35 CONCLUSION

The major problem for a theory of development is to explain how to get something more from something less. At multiple levels of analysis at multiple timescales, many components open to influence from the external world interact and in so doing yield coherent higher-order behavioural forms that then feedback on the system, and change that system. In human development, every neural event, every reach, every smile and every social encounter sets the stage for the next and the real-time causal force behind change. If this is so, then we will gain a deeper understanding of development by studying multicausality, nested timescales and self-organization.

References

Acredolo, L. (1979) Laboratory versus home: the effect of the environment on the 9-month-old infant's choice of spatial reference system. *Dev. Psychol.* 15, 666–667

Amari, S. (1977) Dynamics of pattern formation in lateral inhibition type neural fields. *Biol. Cybern.* 27, 77–87

Beer, R.D. (2000) Dynamical approaches to cognitive science. *Trends Cogn. Sci.* 4, 91–99

Bertenthal, B.I. and Campos, J.J. (1990) A systems approach to the organizing effects of self-produced locomotion during infancy. In *Advances in Infancy Research* 6(Rovee-Collier, C. and Lipsitt, L.P., eds), pp. 134–156, Elsevier

Bremner, J.G. (1978) Egocentric versus allocentric spatial coding in none-month-old infants: factors influencing the choice of a code, *Dev. Psychol.* 14, 346–355

Butler, S.C *et al.* (2002) Two-year-olds' search strategies and visual tracking in a hidden displacement task. *Dev. Psychol.* 38, 581–590

Courage, M. and Howe, L. From infant to child: the dynamics of cognitive change in the second year of life. *Psychol. Bull.* 128, 250–277

De Weerth, C. and van Geert, P. (2002) A longitudinal study of basal cortisol in infants: intra-individual variability, circadian rhythm, and developmental trends. *Infant Behav. Dev.* 25, 375–398

Diamond, A. (1998) Understanding the A-not-B error: working memory vs. reinforced response, or active vs. latent trace. *Dev. Sci.* 1, 185–189

Diamond, A. (1990) The development and neural bases of memory functions as indexed by the AB and delayed response tasks in human infants and infant monkeys. In *The Development and Neural Bases of Higher Cognitive Functions* (Diamond, A., ed.), pp. 637–676, New York Academy of Sciences

Diedrich, F.J. *et al.* (2001) The role of target distinctiveness in infant perseverative reaching. *J. Exp. Child Psychol.* 78, 263–290

Elman, J. *et al.* (1996) *Rethinking Innateness: A Connectionist Perspective on Development*, MIT Press

Erlhagen, W. and Schoener, G. (2002) Dynamic field theory of movement preparation. *Psychol. Rev.* 109, 545–572

Fischer, K.W. and Bidell, T.R. (1998) Dynamic development of psychological structures in action and thought. In *Handbook of Child Psychology* In *Theoretical Models of Human Development* (Vol. 1), 5th edn, (Lerner, R.M. and Damon, W., eds), pp. 117–121, Plenum

Fogel, A. (1999) Systems, cycles, and developmental pathways, *Hum. Dev.* 42, 213–216

Fogel, A. (2000) Systems, attachment, and relationships. *Hum. Dev.* 43, 314–320

Gerhskoff-Stowe, L. (2002) Object naming, vocabulary growth, and the development of word retrieval abilities. *J. Mem, Lang.* 46, 665–687

Gogate, L. *et al.* (2001) The intersensory origins of word comprehension: an ecological–dynamic systems view. *Dev. Sci.* 4, 1–18

Hood, B. *et al.* (2000) Predicting the outcomes of physical events: two-year-olds fail to reveal knowledge of solidity and support. *Child Dev.* 71, 1540–1554

Johnson, M. *et al.* (2002) Neuroimaging of typical and atypical development: a perspective from multiple levels of analysis. *Dev. Psychopathol.* 14, 521–536

Kelso, J.A.S. (2000) Principles of dynamic pattern formation and change for a science of human behavior. In *Developmental Science and the Holistic Approach* (Bergman, L.R. and Cairns, R.B., eds), pp. 63–83, Erlbaum

Lewis, M.D. and Granic, I. (2000) *Emotion, Development, and Self-Organization: Dynamic Systems Approaches to Emotional Development*, Cambridge University Press

Lewis, M.D. (2000) Emotional self-organization at three time scales. In *Emotion, Development, and Self-Organization* (Lewis, M.D. and Granic, I., eds), pp. 37–69, Cambridge University Press

MacWhinney, B. (1999) *The Emergence of Language*, Erlbaum

Munakata, Y. (1998) Infant perseveration and implications for object permancence theories: a PDP model of the A-not-B task. *Dev. Sci.* 1, 161–184

Newell, K.M. and Molenaar, P.C.M. (1998) *Applications of Nonlinear Dynamics to Developmental Process Modeling*, Erlbaum

Piaget, J. (1963) *The Origins of Intelligence in Children*, W.W. Norton

Smith, L.B. and Thelen, E. (1993) *A dynamic Systems Approach to Development: Applications*, MIT Press

Smith, L.B. *et al.* (1999) Knowing in the context of acting: the task dynamics of the A-not-B error. *Psychol. Rev* 106, 235–260

Spencer, J.P. *et al.* (2001) Tests of a dynamic systems account of the A-not-B error: the influence of prior experience on the spatial memory abilities of two-year-olds. *Child Dev.* 72, 1327–1346

Thelen, E. and Ulrich, B.D. (1991) Hidden skills: a dynamic systems analysis of treadmill stepping during the first year. *Monogr. Soc. Res. Child Dev.* 56, 104

Thelen, E. and Smith, L.B. (1994) *A Dynamic System Approach to the Development of cognition and Action*, MIT Press

Thelen, E. *et al.* (2001) The dynamics of embodiment: a field theory of infant perseverative reaching. *Behav. Brain Sci.* 24, 1–86

van der Maas, H.L.J. and Molenaar, P.C.M. (1992) Stage-wise cognitive development: an application of catastrophe theory. *Psychol. Rev.* 99, 395–417

Van Geert, P. (2000) The dynamics of general developmental mechanisms: from Piaget and Vygotsky to dynamic systems models. *Curr. Dir. Psychol. Sci.* 9, 64–68

Van Geert, P. (2002) Developmental dynamics, intentional action, and fuzzy sets. In *Microdevelopment: Transition Processes in Development and Learning* (Granott, N. and Parziale, J., eds), Cambridge University Press

Wellman, H.M. *et al.* (1986) Infant search and object permanence: a meta-analysis of the A-not-B error. *Monogr.Soc. Res. Child Dev.* No.54

Yan, Z. and Fischer, K. (2002) Always under construction: dynamic variations in adult cognitive microdevelopment. *Hum. Dev.* 45, 141–160

Unit 3

Chapter Outline

Vygotsky's Theory

VYGOTSKY'S THEORY OF COGNITIVE DEVELOPMENT

Lev Vygotsky (1896–1934) was a major figure in Russian psychology. Vygotsky provided a theory of children's development that was greatly influenced by the historical events of his time. Following the Russian Revolution in 1917, leaders of the new Soviet society emphasized the role of each person in transforming society through labor and education. Vygotsky constructed a psychological theory of development that fit the view of this new Soviet state.

Vygotsky's theory stresses relations between the individual and society. He asserted that it is not possible to understand a child's development without some understanding of the culture in which the child is raised. Vygotsky believed that an individual's thinking patterns are not primarily due to innate factors but are products of cultural institutions and social activities. Adult society has a responsibility to share its collective knowledge with younger and less advanced members in order to promote intellectual development. Through social activities, children learn to incorporate cultural tools such as language, counting systems, writing, art, and other social inventions into their thinking. Cognitive development occurs as children internalize the products of their social interactions. According to Vygotsky's theory, both the history of the child's culture and the history of the child's own experiences are important for understanding cognitive development. This tenet in Vygotsky's theory represents a cultural-historical or sociocultural view of children's development. Vygotsky stressed that development could only be understood by looking at the *mutual* influences of individual, interpersonal, and cultural-historical factors on one another (e.g., Rogoff, 2003; Scrimsher & Tudge, 2003).

Vygotsky's career as a psychologist was brief, due to his premature death at age 38 from tuberculosis. During his 10-year career, however, Vygotsky wrote more than 100 books and articles. His most influential book, *Thought and Language,* was not published until the year of his death. From 1936 to 1956, Vygotsky's work was banned in the Soviet Union, because it contained references to Western psychologists. Consequently, Vygotsky's work did not become widely available to researchers until the 1960s, almost 30 years after his death.

In the last two decades, Vygotsky's influence on developmental psychology has steadily grown. His views regarding the social context of learning also have a major impact on educational practices today. See the Focus on Research box, "Learning Arithmetic in Context" on page 101. In the next sections, we consider the major contributions of Vygotsky's theory for understanding children's cognitive development and learning in the classroom.

Key Concepts in Vygotsky's Theory

Social Origins of Thought   Vygotsky is considered one of the earliest critics of Piaget's theory of cognitive development. In Vygotsky's view, knowledge is not individually constructed, as Piaget proposed, but socially *co-constructed* between people as they interact. Social interactions with more knowledgeable peers and adults provide the main vehicles for intellectual development. For Vygotsky, knowledge is not located in the environment nor in the child. Rather, it is situated in a particular social or cultural context. In other words, Vygotsky believed that individual mental processes, such as remembering, problem solving, or planning, have a social origin (Wertsch & Tulviste, 1992).

Focus On Research   Learning Arithmetic in Context

A group of British and Brazilian researchers studied the computational skills of 9- to 15-year-old street vendors in Brazil. In many Brazilian towns, it is common for younger sons and daughters of street vendors to help their parents at the market. Adolescents may develop their own businesses to sell roasted peanuts, popcorn, coconut milk, or corn on the cob. These researchers found that children and adolescents develop sophisticated arithmetic skills in the context of buying and selling, but they are unable to perform the same mathematical operations when they are presented out of context. For example, a typical interview with a 12-year-old street vendor in the market might go like this (Carraher, Carraher, & Schliemann, 1985):

Customer:	How much is one coconut?
Child:	35 cruzerios.
Customer:	I would like ten. How much is that?
Child:	(pause) Three will be 105, with three more, that will be 210. (pause) I need four more. That is . . . (pause) 315. I think it is 350.

After the interviewers posed a number of such questions, the children were given a paper and pencil and asked to solve identical problems. For example, they were asked: 35 × 10 = _____? The math operation that was performed on the street was also represented in a word problem: Each banana costs 12 cruzerios. Mary bought 10 bananas. How much did she pay altogether?

The results of this interesting study showed that when mathematical problems were embedded in real-life contexts (e.g., buying and selling), they were solved at a much higher rate than the same problems presented out of context. Children correctly answered the context-specific question 98 percent of the time. When the same operation was embedded in a word problem, children correctly solved the problem 73 percent of the time. In contrast, children correctly solved the mathematical operation with no context 37 percent of the time.

The results of this study show that context can have an important influence on whether or not children are able to use their existing mathematical knowledge. The children in this study were unable to use the computational strategies they used while selling on the streets for solving problems in school-type situations. This study raises questions about teaching mathematics as a set of conventions and routines that are divorced from children's daily problem-solving activities.

According to Vygotsky, children are born with elementary mental abilities such as perception, attention, and memory. As they interact with more knowledgeable peers and adults, these "innate" abilities are transformed into higher mental functions. More specifically, Vygotsky believed that cognitive development involves the internalization of functions that first occur on what he called a *social plane*. **Internalization** refers to the process of constructing an internal representation of external physical actions or mental operations. James Wertsch (1985) described Vygotsky's ideas about the social origins of cognition in this way:

> An important point to note about Vygotsky's ideas on the social origins of cognition is that it is at this point that he uses the notion of *internalization*. He is not simply claiming that social interaction leads to the development of the child's abilities in problem solving, memory, etc.; rather, he is saying that the *very means* (especially speech) used in social interactions are taken over by the individual child and internalized. Thus, Vygotsky is making a very strong statement here about internalization and the social foundations of cognition. (p. 146; italics added)

A good example of this internalization process may be observed when an adult reads to a young child. For instance, a parent may point to objects on a page and count off "one," "two," "three," and so forth. The next time this parent and child read the book together, the child may point to the pictures and try to count the objects on his or her own. A very young child will have difficulty remembering the order of number tags, so the parent is likely to say the number words too. In the Vygotskian sense, the child is internalizing a way of using numbers to give meaning to a set of objects. When children begin to count off objects in the absence of a parent's prompts or assistance, then they have truly made this external operation their own. The counting operation has become a part of the children's own internal organization, and it is carried out without the support of others.

internalization Vygotsky's term for the process of constructing a mental representation of external physical actions or cognitive operations that first occur through social interaction.

Tools for Thought Similar to Piaget's way of thinking, Vygotsky defined cognitive development in terms of qualitative changes in children's thinking processes. However, he described these developmental changes in terms of the technical and psychological tools children use to make sense of their world. Technical tools are generally used to change objects or to gain mastery over the environment, whereas psychological tools are used to organize or control thought and behavior.

In the example described previously, the child is learning to use a counting system as a way of ordering objects. Numbers, words, and other symbol systems are different examples of psychological tools. Other examples include systems of logic, social norms and conventions, theoretical concepts, maps, plans, literary forms, or drawings. Some examples of technical tools include pencil and paper, protractors, machines, scales, hammers, and so on. According to Vygotsky, every culture has its own set of technical and psychological tools that are passed on to children through social interactions. For example, Gauvain (2001) studied how mothers assist their children with using plans or directions that accompany toys and games. These cultural tools in turn shape the mind.

What are some other ways children's thinking is molded by society? In the early 1900s, for instance, mothers taught their daughters to churn butter and to weave cloth by the time they reached puberty. Few young women today learn these skills. Before the availability of inexpensive calculators, students of all ages were required to memorize arithmetic facts, including square roots of numbers. Most schools today allow students to use calculators in mathematics and science classes. Currently, another technological tool, the computer, is becoming more and more common in classroom and home environments. It is interesting to consider how computers are influencing the way children and adolescents think.

Language and Development For Vygotsky, language is the most important psychological tool influencing children's cognitive development. In Vygotsky's (1962) words, "The child's intellectual development is contingent on mastering the social means of thought, that is, language" (p. 24). He identified three different stages in children's use of language: social, egocentric, and inner speech.

In the first stage, **social speech,** language is used primarily for communicative functions. Thought and language have separate functions. Children enter the next stage of development, **egocentric speech,** when they begin to use speech to regulate their behavior and thinking. For example, many 5- and 6-year-old children talk aloud to themselves as they work on various tasks. Because children are not trying to communicate with others, these self-verbalizations are viewed as private rather than social speech. At this point in development, speech begins to serve an intellectual as well as communicative function. Berk and Garvin (1984) observed the following examples of *private speech* in an Appalachian mission school for low-income children aged 5 to 10 years old.

> [Student] O. Sits down at the art table and says to himself, "I want to draw something. Let's see. I need a big piece of paper. I want to draw my cat."
>
> [Student] C., working in her arithmetic workbook says out loud to no one in particular, "Six." Then counting on her fingers she continues, "Seven, eight, nine, ten. It's ten, it's ten. The answer's ten." (p. 277)

In Vygotsky's last stage of speech development, **inner speech,** children internalize egocentric speech. They use language internally to guide their thinking and behavior. At this stage, children can think about problem solutions and action sequences by manipulating language "in their heads."

Zone of Proximal Development One of the most important contributions of Vygotsky's theory to psychology and education is the *zone of proximal development.* Vygotsky (1978) was interested in children's *potential* for intellectual growth rather than

social speech One of three stages of children's use of language identified by Vygotsky that is used primarily for communicative purposes in which thought and language have separate functions; contrast with *egocentric speech* and *inner speech.*

egocentric speech One of three stages of children's use of language identified by Vygotsky, during which children begin to use speech to regulate their behavior and thinking through spoken-aloud self-verbalizations; contrast with *social speech* and *inner speech.*

inner speech One of three stages of children's use of language identified by Vygotsky, during which children internalize their self-verbalizations and are able to manipulate language in their heads to think about problem solutions and action sequences. A self-regulatory process by which children guide their own thinking and behavior; also called *private speech*; contrast with *social speech* and *egocentric speech.*

their *actual* level of development. The **zone of proximal development** includes those functions that are in the process of developing but not yet fully developed.

> The zone of proximal development defines those functions that have not yet matured but are in the process of maturation, functions that will mature tomorrow but are currently in an embryonic state. These functions could be termed the "buds" or "flowers" of development rather than the "fruits" of development. The actual development level characterizes mental development retrospectively, while the zone of proximal development characterizes mental development prospectively. (pp. 86–87)

In practice, the zone of proximal development represents the gap between what children can do on their own and what they can do with the assistance of others, as illustrated in Figure 3.1. For example, a 6-year-old might have difficulty assembling a model airplane alone, but with the assistance and guidance of an older, more experienced sibling, the child can successfully complete the task.

In the example presented at the beginning of the chapter about boiling tap water, the students are acquiring a more sophisticated understanding of their science experiment with the teacher's guidance. Note that the teacher is not telling students what they should learn from the experiment. He is guiding their thinking through the use of questions ("What happens when the water is boiled?") and prompts ("Think about density."). At the end of the discussion, the students can use what they learned from the experiment to make hypotheses about other liquids. As a result, the students are thinking about the experiment at a level that was not evident when they were carrying out the experiment on their own. The kindergarten teacher is also interacting with children to stimulate ideas about learning languages ("How are you learning all these English words now?").

Vygotsky assumed that interactions with adults and peers in the zone of proximal development help children to move to a higher level of functioning. We will examine how adults can help learn from and "build scaffolds" for children when we consider the educational implications of Vygotsky's theory.

Contrasts Between Piaget's and Vygotsky's Theories

There are several important differences in the basic assumptions of Vygotsky's and Piaget's theories. Both theorists agree that knowledge must be mentally constructed by the child, but Vygotsky placed a much stronger emphasis on the role of social interactions in this construction process. To Vygotsky, the construction of knowledge is not an individual process. In James Wertsch's (1999) words, cognition does not only go on "within the skin" (p. 311). Rather, it is primarily a social process in which higher mental functions are products of socially mediated activity. Collaborative learning and problem solving are the main vehicles of cognitive change.

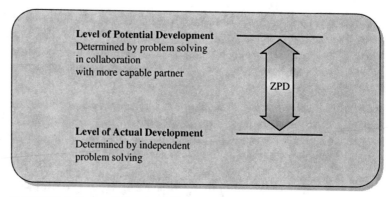

FIGURE 3.1 Zone of Proximal Development
Source: After Hamilton & Ghatala (1994).

Compared with Piaget, Vygotsky also placed a stronger emphasis on culture in shaping children's cognitive development. As children develop, they learn to use tools for thought that are valued by their culture. There are no universal patterns of development because cultures emphasize different kinds of tools, intellectual skills, and social conventions. The intellectual skills needed for survival in a highly technical society differ from those needed for survival in a largely agrarian society.

Another important difference between Piaget's and Vygotsky's views concerns the importance placed on learning. As we know, Piaget believed that cognitive development limits what children are capable of learning from social experiences. It is not possible to accelerate development through learning experiences. Although Vygotsky (1978) agreed that learning is not the same as development, he argued that "learning is a necessary and universal aspect of the process of developing culturally organized, specifically human, psychological functions" (p. 90). Vygotsky believed instruction (both formal and informal) by more knowledgeable peers or adults is at the heart of cognitive development. Vygotsky believed that learning precedes development.

In addition, Vygotsky's zone of proximal development offers a very different view of readiness than the one provided by Piaget's theory. According to Piaget, children's readiness for learning is defined by their existing level of competence and knowledge. If a teacher attempts to teach a concept or operation before a child is mentally ready, it can result in what Piaget called "empty learning." In contrast, Vygotsky (1978) argued that instruction should be directed toward children's potential level of development, the level of competence they can demonstrate with the assistance and guidance of others. In his words, "The only 'good learning' is that which is in advance of the child's development" (p. 89).

Finally, Vygotsky and Piaget had very different opinions about the role of language in development. In Piaget's view, the egocentric speech of young children reflects the child's inability to take the perspective of others. It plays no useful role in their development. Thinking processes develop from children's actions on objects, not from talking. Vygotsky, on the other hand, thought that egocentric speech is an extremely important developmental phenomenon. He believed that egocentric speech helps children organize and regulate their thinking. When children talk to themselves, they are trying to solve problems and think on their own. According to Vygotsky, egocentric speech, or private speech, is the means by which children move from being regulated by others (other-regulated) to being regulated by their own thinking processes (self-regulated). Egocentric speech has both an intellectual and a self-regulatory function for young children.

Observational Learning

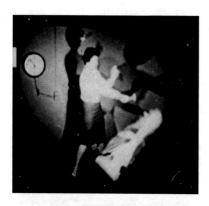

FIGURE 3.2 Bandura's Classic Bobo Doll Study: The Effects of Observational Learning on Children's Aggression
In the top frame, an adult model aggressively attacks the Bobo doll. In the bottom frame, a kindergarten-age girl who has observed the model's aggressive actions follows suit. In Bandura's experiment, under what conditions did the children reproduce the model's aggressive actions?

observational learning Learning that involves acquiring skills, strategies, and beliefs by observing others.

Observational learning is learning that involves acquiring skills, strategies, and beliefs by observing others. Observational learning involves imitation but is not limited to it. What is learned typically is not an exact copy of what is modeled but rather a general form or strategy that observers often apply in creative ways. The capacity to learn behavior patterns by observation eliminates tedious trial-and-error learning. In many instances, observational learning takes less time than operant conditioning.

The Classic Bobo Doll Study   A classic experiment by Bandura (1965) illustrates how observational learning can occur even when a student watches a model who is not reinforced or punished. The experiment also illustrates a distinction between learning and performance.

Equal numbers of kindergarten children were randomly assigned to watch one of three films in which a person (the model) beat up an adult-size plastic toy called a Bobo doll (see figure 3.2). In the first film, the aggressor was rewarded with candy, soft drinks, and praise for aggressive behavior. In the second film, the aggressor was criticized and spanked for the aggressive behavior. And in the third film, there were no consequences for the aggressor's behavior.

Subsequently, each child was left alone in a room filled with toys, including a Bobo doll. The child's behavior was observed through a one-way mirror. Children who watched the films in which the aggressor's behavior either was reinforced or went unpunished imitated the aggressor's behavior more than did the children who saw the aggressor get punished. As you might expect, boys were more aggressive than girls. An important point in this study, however, is that observational learning occurred just as extensively when modeled aggressive behavior was *not* reinforced as when it was reinforced.

A second important point in this study focuses on the distinction between learning and performance. Just because students don't perform a response doesn't mean they didn't learn it. In Bandura's study, when children were given an incentive (stickers or fruit juice) to imitate the model, differences in the children's imitative behavior in the three conditions were eliminated. Bandura believes that when a child observes behavior but makes no observable response, the child may still have acquired the modeled response in cognitive form.

Bandura's Contemporary Model of Observational Learning   Since his early experiments, Bandura (1986) has focused on exploring specific processes that are involved in observational learning. These include attention, retention, production, and motivation (see figure 3.3):

- *Attention.* Before students can imitate a model's actions, they must attend to what the model is doing or saying. Attention to the model is influenced by a host of characteristics. For example, warm, powerful, atypical people command more attention than do cold, weak, typical people. Students are more likely to be attentive to high-status models than to low-status models. In most cases, teachers are high-status models for students.

- *Retention.* To reproduce a model's actions, students must code the information and keep it in memory so that they retrieve it. A simple verbal description or a vivid image of what the model did assists students' retention. For example, the teacher might say, "I'm showing the correct way to do this. You have to do this step first, this step second, and this step third," as she models how to solve a math problem. A video with a colorful character demonstrating the importance of considering other students' feelings might be remembered better than if the teacher just tells the students to do this. Such colorful characters are at the heart of the popularity of *Sesame Street* with children. Students' retention will be improved when teachers give vivid, logical, and clear demonstrations.

- *Production.* Children might attend to a model and code in memory what they have seen—but, because of limitations in their motor ability, not be able to reproduce the model's behavior. A 13-year-old might watch basketball player Lebron James and golfer Michelle Wie execute their athletic skills to perfection, or observe a famous pianist or artist, but not be able to reproduce their motor actions. Teaching, coaching, and practice can help children improve their motor performances.

- *Motivation.* Often children attend to what a model says or does, retain the information in memory, and possess the motor skills to perform the action but are not motivated to perform the modeled behavior. This was demonstrated in Bandura's classic Bobo doll study when children who saw the model being punished did not reproduce the punished model's aggressive actions. However, when they subsequently were given a reinforcement or incentive (stickers or fruit juice), they did imitate the model's behavior.

FIGURE 3.3 Bandura's Model of Observational Learning
In Bandura's model of observational learning, four processes need to be considered: attention, retention, production, and motivation. *How might these processes be involved in this classroom situation in which a teacher is demonstrating how to tell time?*

Bandura argues that reinforcement is not always necessary for observational learning to take place. But if the child does not reproduce the desired behaviors, four types of reinforcement can help do the trick: (1) reward the model; (2) reward the child; (3) instruct the child to make self-reinforcing statements such as "Good, I did it!" or "Okay, I've done a good job of getting most of this right; now if I keep trying I will get the rest"; or (4) show how the behavior leads to reinforcing outcomes.

As you can see, you will be an important model in students' lives, and you have many options for providing students with an array of competent models. To evaluate the roles that models and mentors have played in your own life and can play in your students' lives. To explore the lack of male and minority role models and mentors in children's education, read the Diversity and Education interlude.

Case Study
—Marsha Warren

Preview

An experienced third-grade teacher is overwhelmed by the problems created by her heterogeneous class, which includes eight students who have unique home and personal situations that are affecting their schooling.

José glared at Tyrone. "Quit looking at me, you jerk!"

"I wasn't lookin' at nothin', creepy," replied Tyrone vehemently.

Marsha Warren looked up sharply at the two boys and made a cutting gesture through the air. "That's enough from both of you. You should both be looking at your books, not each other."

"I *was* lookin' at my book!" protested Tyrone.

"Just stop!" repeated Marsha. "Please continue reading, Angela."

Angela rolled her eyes at no one in particular and resumed reading aloud in a bored, expressionless tone. Her progress was slow and halting.

Marsha Warren was a third-grade teacher at the Roosevelt Elementary School in Littleton. She was trying to conduct a reading group with the eight slowest readers in her class of twenty-two while the other children worked in workbooks at their seats. But each time an argument erupted among the children in the reading group, most of the children at their desks snapped to attention to watch the sparks fly.

"You can stop there, Angela," interrupted Marsha as Angela came to the end of a paragraph. "Bettie Ann, will you read next?" As she spoke, Marsha also put a hand out to touch another child, Katie, on the shoulder in an attempt to stop her from bouncing in her chair.

Bettie Ann didn't respond. She was gazing out the window at the leafless November landscape, sucking her thumb and twirling her hair with her other hand. "Bettie Ann, I'm talking to you," repeated Marsha.

"Your turn," yelled José as he poked Bettie Ann's shoulder.

"Shut up, José," interjected Sarah. Sarah often tried to mediate between the members of the group, but her argumentative streak pulled her into the fray as often as not.

"Quiet!" insisted Marsha in a hushed, but emphatic, tone. As she spoke, she turned her head to glance over her shoulder at the rest of the class. The hum of conversation was growing in the room. Tension crept into her voice as she addressed the reading group. "We're distracting the other children. Do we need to discuss rule 3 again? Everyone pull out the class rules from your notebook, now."

The chemistry in the reading group—and in the class in general—had been so explosive since September that Marsha had gone beyond her normal first-of-the-year review of rules and procedures. All the children in the class had copied the four class rules into their notebooks, and she had led long discussions of what they meant. Rule 3 was "Be considerate of other people."

Loud groans from the reading group greeted Marsha's mention of rules. Simultaneously, a loud BANG sounded in the back of the room. Marsha turned and saw a student reaching to the floor for a book as his neighbor snickered. She also noticed three girls in the far-left row leaning into a conversation over a drawing, and she saw most of the students quickly turn back to their work, as if they were not enjoying the entertainment of the reading group once again.

"That's it!" Marsha exclaimed. She slammed her hand down on the reading-circle table and stood to face the entire class. "Put your heads on your desks, and don't say another word—everyone!" By the time she finished the sentence, Marsha realized she had been shouting, but she didn't care. Her class gazed at her in stunned disbelief. Mrs. Warren had always been so gentle! "Now!"

Marsha quickly turned and walked from the room, not bothering to look back to see if her command had been obeyed. She closed the door to her classroom, managing not to slam it, and tried to control her temper and collect her thoughts. "What in God's name am I going to do with this class?" she asked herself. "I've got to calm down. Here I am in the hallway with twenty-two kids inside who have driven me out—they've absolutely won." Marsha suddenly felt paralyzed.

Marsha tried to remember if there was ever a time in her eleven years of teaching when discipline and control were such a challenge. "It's not as though I were a rookie. I ought to know what to do!" she agonized. But Marsha had tried everything she had ever learned or done before to interest and control this group, and the class as a whole, yet there she was, standing in the hall.

Marsha's third-grade class was indeed a difficult group of children. There were a few students who liked school and really tried to learn, but overall it was a class full of children who were just not focused on learning. It was impossible to relax with them. If Marsha let down her guard and tried to engage them on a more friendly or casual level, the class would disintegrate. Marsha's natural inclination in teaching was to maintain a friendly, relaxed manner; she usually enjoyed her students and her enjoyment showed. But with this class she constantly had to be firm and vigilant ("witchlike," she thought) in order to keep the students under control.

Academically the class was fairly average, but Marsha did have two instructional challenges: There were three really bright students, whom Marsha tried to encourage with extra instruction and higher expectations, and there were three students (besides the Hispanic children in her slow-reading group) who spoke little or no English. The most remarkable characteristic of the students, though, was their overall immaturity. Each child seemed to feed off the antics of the others, and every issue was taken to its extreme. For example, whenever one child laughed, the entire class would begin to giggle uncontrollably. The students' behavior was simply inappropriate for their age and grade.

The core of Marsha's problem was the lowest-level reading group. This group provided the spark that set off fireworks in the entire class, day after day. The slow readers were rude and disruptive as a group, and they were instigators on their own.

When Marsha thought of each child in the lowest reading group individually, she was usually able to summon some sympathy and understanding. Each of the eight had an emotional or academic problem that probably accounted, at least in part, for his or her behavior.

José, for instance, topped her list of troublemakers. He was a loud, egocentric child. His mother, Marsha thought, probably had surrendered long ago, and his father did not live with them. José had little respect for or recognition of authority; he was boisterous and argumentative; and he was unable to take turns under any condition. When something didn't go his way, he would explode. This low flash point, Marsha felt, was just one of many signs of his immaturity, even though José was repeating the third grade and was actually older than his classmates.

José had a slight learning disability in the area of organizational skills, but Marsha didn't think this justified his behavior. His mother spoke only Spanish, and—although José was fluent in both Spanish and English—when Marsha sent notes home, she would first have to find someone to translate for her. Conferring with José's mother on the telephone was out of the question.

Angela was also repeating the third grade, and Marsha thought the child's anger over this contributed to her terrible attitude in class. The child just refused to learn. She could be a low-average achiever if she would apply herself, but it was clear that Angela's agenda was not school. She was concerned with her hair, her looks, her clothes—preoccupations that Marsha found inappropriate for a third-grader. Angela came from a middle-class black family, and her parents were also angry that she had been held back; consultations with them were not usually fruitful. Angela seemed truly upset if Marsha asked her to do any work, and Marsha was sure her frustration with the child was occasionally apparent.

Tyrone, on the other hand, was a very low average learner, but he, at least, worked to his capabilities. He even tried to mediate arguments among the members of the group. But Tyrone had a very stubborn streak, which was typical, Marsha thought, of slow learners. If he was on the wrong track, he just would not get off of it. She frequently asked him to redo work and helped him with his errors, but when he presented it to her the next day as though it were different, it would contain the same mistakes.

Sarah, too, knew right from wrong and generally wanted to do her work, but she was easily pulled into the fray. Sarah had appointed herself protector of Bettie Ann, an overweight, emotionally insecure child who had difficulty focusing on the topic at hand. Bettie Ann was the baby of her family, with several near-adult siblings at home. Marsha wondered if Bettie Ann's position in the family was the reason she assumed no responsibility for her own actions and no control over her own fate. Bettie Ann seemed hungry for Marsha's attention, but she exhibited no independence or initiative at all.

Katie was one of the brighter students in the reading group, but her hyperactivity caused her to be easily distracted and argumentative. She could neither sit still physically nor pay attention mentally. Katie had a rich home background, full of books and middle-class aspirations, but Marsha thought she also encountered pressure at home to perform, perhaps to levels beyond her capability.

Rhea, another child with at least average intelligence, was one of the more heartrending cases. Her mother was an alcoholic who neglected her, and Rhea had to do the housework and care for her older brother, who was in a special education class. She had no time for homework, and there were no books or even conversations at home. Rhea had been held back in the second grade, and while she tried to do her work, the language deficit at home was so severe that she kept falling further behind.

Finally, there was Maria, a petite, immature native of El Salvador. She had average intelligence and a cooperative spirit, but Spanish was spoken in her home and her limited English vocabulary severely limited her progress.

Marsha tried to analyze what it was among these children that fostered such animosity. Not a day passed that they didn't argue, fight, or insult one another. The reading group was not the only arena for these combatants; they fought in the playground, in line, on the bus, and in the cafeteria. They were troublemakers in previous grades, and some of the teachers at Roosevelt called them the "Infidels."

They tended to be at their worst as a group, and so Marsha had tried separating them, but with little improvement. Three weeks before, in early October, she rearranged and reorganized all three reading groups, distributing the students in the lowest section among three new groups. But she found that the inappropriate behavior did not stop; it only spread. Now all three of her reading groups, rather than one, were disrupted, and mixing her slow and her average readers dramatically reduced the pace of both groups. Finding this arrangement unfair to her other students, she reorganized back to her original group assignments last week.

Marsha also tried other remedies. She introduced popular reading material for the reading groups and tried innovations such as having the children act out the stories they read. She wrote a contingency contract with the groups when she reconstituted them last week, promising that they could use the school's audiovisual equipment to make filmstrips illustrating their current book if they behaved, but so far that wasn't working either.

Marsha did not think she was generally too lax. She had procedures for incomplete work (the students had to come to her room during lunch hour or after school to finish); she had rules for appropriate behavior in school; and she never hesitated to involve parents. She praised the children for completing work, and she sent positive notes home when they did so. She also sent home disciplinary cards (much more frequently, unfortunately), which parents were supposed to sign, and she telephoned parents when she thought it would help.

Marsha also tried punishment. She sent individual troublemakers to the office, and she held detention during lunch. She isolated children for misbehavior by separating their desks from the rest of the class, and she used denial of privileges (the children really liked using the class computer, so she withdrew that privilege frequently). Marsha even tried talking honestly with the children, giving them pep talks about the value of education and their need to read and write and think in order to participate in life. But nothing was fundamentally altering the course of the class's behavior.

Besides having the desire to teach the "Infidels," Marsha knew that the progress of the rest of the class was being slowed because of the time she was forced to spend on policing. Her patience, her ideas, and her fortitude were fast evaporating, and she knew she had to solve the problem even though she felt like giving up.

Marsha stood on tiptoe to look through the window of the classroom door. The children were sitting in their places looking at each other uneasily and at the door, clearly wondering what would happen next. With a sigh, Marsha turned the knob.

The Child as a Moral Philosopher

—by Lawrence Kohlberg

Preview

You're a good man Charlie Brown! You have humility, nobility and a sense of honor that is very rare indeed. You are kind to all the animals and every little bird. With a heart of gold, you believe what you're told, every single solitary word. You bravely face adversity; you're cheerful through the day; you're thoughtful, brave and courteous. You're a good man Charlie Brown! You're a prince, and a prince could be a king. With a heart such as yours you could open any door—if only you weren't so wishy-washy.

How can one study morality? Current trends in the fields of ethics, linguistics, anthropology and cognitive psychology have suggested a new approach which seems to avoid the morass of semantical confusions, value-bias and cultural relativity in which the psychoanalytic and semantic approaches to morality have foundered. New scholarship in all these fields is now focusing upon structures, forms and relationships that seem to be common to all societies and all languages rather than upon the features that make particular languages or cultures different.

For 12 years, my colleagues and I studied the same group of 75 boys, following their development at three-year intervals from early adolescence through young manhood. At the start of the study, the boys were aged 10 to 16. We have now followed them through to ages 22 to 28. In addition, I have explored moral development in other cultures—Great Britain, Canada, Taiwan, Mexico and Turkey.

Inspired by Jean Piaget's pioneering effort to apply a structural approach to moral development, I have gradually elaborated over the years of my study a typological scheme describing general structures and forms of moral thought which can be defined independently of the specific content of particular moral decisions or actions.

The typology contains three distinct levels of moral thinking, and within each of these levels distinguishes two related stages. These levels and stages may be considered separate moral philosophies, distinct views of the socio-moral world.

We can speak of the child as having his own morality or series of moralities. Adults seldom listen to children's moralizing. If a child throws back a few adult cliches and behaves himself, most parents—and many anthropologists and psychologists as well—think that the child has adopted or internalized the appropriate parental standards.

Actually, as soon as we talk with children about morality, we find that they have many ways of making judgments which are not "internalized" from the outside, and which do not come in any direct and obvious way from parents, teachers or even peers.

37 MORAL LEVELS

The *preconventional* level is the first of three levels of moral thinking; the second level is *conventional,* and the third *post conventional* or autonomous. While the preconventional child is often "well-behaved" and is responsive to cultural labels of good and bad, be interprets these labels in terms of their physical consequences (punishment, reward, exchange of favors) or in terms of the physical power of those who enunciate the rules and labels of good and bad.

This level is usually occupied by children aged four to 10, a fact long known to sensitive observers of children. The capacity of "properly behaved" children of this age to engage in cruel behavior when there are holes in the power structure is sometimes noted as tragic *(Lord of the Flies, High Wind in Jamaica),* sometimes as comic (Lucy in *Peanuts).*

The second or *conventional* level also can be described as conformist, but that is perhaps too smug a term. Maintaining the expectations and rules of the individual's family, group or nation is perceived as valuable in its own right. There is a concern not only with *conforming* to the individual's social order but in *maintaining,* supporting and justifying this order.

The *postconventional* level is characterized by a major thrust toward autonomous moral principles which have validity and application apart from authority of the groups or persons who bold them and apart from the individual's identification with those persons or groups.

38 MORAL STAGES

Within each of these three levels there are two discernable stages. At the preconventional level we have:

Stage 1: Orientation toward punishment and unquestioning deference to superior power. The physical consequences of action regardless of their human meaning or value determine its goodness or badness.

Stage 2: Right action consists of that which instrumentally satisfies one's own needs and occasionally the needs of others. Human relations are viewed in terms like those of the marketplace. Elements of fairness, of reciprocity and equal sharing are present, but they are always interpreted in a physical, pragmatic way. Reciprocity is a matter of "you scratch my back and I'll scratch yours" not of loyalty, gratitude or justice.

And at the conventional level we have:

Stage 3: Good-boy-good-girl orientation. Good behavior is that which pleases or helps others and is approved by them. There is much conformity to stereotypical images of what is majority or "natural" behavior. Behavior is often judged by intention—"he means well" becomes important for the first time, and is overused, as by Charlie Brown in *Peanuts.* One seeks approval by being "nice."

Stage 4: Orientation toward authority, fixed rules and the maintenance of the social order. Right behavior consists of doing one's duty, showing respect for authority and maintaining the given social order for its own sake. One earns respect by performing dutifully.

At the postconventional level, we have:

Stage 5: A social-contract orientation, generally with legalistic and utilitarian overtones. Right action tends to be defined in terms of general rights and in terms of standards which have been critically examined and agreed upon by the whole society. There is a clear awareness of the relativism of personal values and opinions and a corresponding emphasis upon procedural rules for reaching consensus.

Aside from what is constitutionally and democratically agreed upon, right or wrong is a matter of personal "values" and "opinion." The result is an emphasis upon the "legal point of view," but with an emphasis upon the possibility of *changing law* in terms of rational considerations of social utility, rather than freezing it in, the terms of Stage 4 "law and order". Outside the legal realm, free agreement and contract are the binding elements of obligation. This is the "official" morality of American government, and finds its ground in the thought of the writers of the Constitution.

Stage 6: Orientation toward the decisions of conscience and toward chosen *ethical principles* appealing to logical comprehensiveness, universality and consistency. These principles are abstract and ethical (the Golden Rule, the categorical imperative); they are not concrete moral rules like the Ten Commandments. Instead they are universal Principles of *justice*, of the *reciprocity* and *equality* of human rights, and of respect for the dignity of human beings as *individual persons*.

39 UP TO NOW

In the past, when psychologists tried to answer the question asked of Socrates by Meno "Is virtue something that can be taught (by rational discussion), or does it come by practice, or is it a natural inborn attitude?" their answers usually have been dictated, not by research findings on children's moral character, but by their general theoretical convictions.

Behavior theorists have said that virtue is behavior acquired according to their favorite general principles of learning. Freudians have claimed that virtue is superego-identification with parents generated by a proper balance of love and authority in family relations.

The American psychologists who have actually studied children's morality have tried to start with a set of labels—the "virtues" and "vices," the "traits" of good and bad character found in ordinary language. The earliest major psychological study of moral character, that of Hugh Hartshorne and Mark May in 1928–1930, focused on a bag of virtues including honesty, service (altruism or generosity), and self-control. To their dismay, they found that there were *no* character trains, psychological dispostions or entities which correspond to words like honest, service, or self-control.

Regarding honesty, for instance, they found that almost everyone cheats some of the time, and that if a person cheats in one situation, it doesn't mean that he *will* or *won't* in another. In other words, it is not an identifiable character trait, *dis*honesty, that makes a child cheat in a given situation. These early researchers also found that people who cheat express as much or even more moral disapproval of cheating as those who do not cheat.

What Hartshorne and May found out about their bag of virtues is equally upsetting to the somewhat more psychological-sounding names introduced by psychoanalytic psychology: "superego-strength," "resistance to temptation," "strength of conscience," and the like. When recent researchers attempt to measure such traits in individuals, they have been forced to use Hartshorne and May's old tests of honesty and self-control and they get exactly the same results—"superego strength" in one situation predicts little to "superego strength" in another. That is, virtue-words like honesty (or superego-strength) point to certain behaviors with approval, but give us no guide to understanding them.

So far as one can extract some generalized personality factor from children's performance on tests of honesty or resistance to temptation, it is a factor of ego-strength or ego-control, which always involves non-moral capacities like the capacity to maintain attention, intelligent-task performance, and the ability to delay response. "'Ego-strength" (called "will" in earlier days) has something to do with moral action, but it does not take us to the core of morality or to the definition of virtue. Obviously enough, many of the greatest evil-doers in history have been men of strong wills, men strongly pursuing immoral goals.

40 MORAL REASONS

In our research, we have found definite and universal levels of development in moral thought. In our study of 75 American boys from early adolescence on, these youths were presented with hypothetical moral dilemmas, all deliberately philosophical, some of them found in medieval works of casuistry.

On the basis of their reasoning about these dilernmas at a given age, each boy's stage of thought could be determined for each of 25 basic moral concepts or aspects. One such aspect, for instance, is "Motive Given for Rule Obedience or Moral Action." In this instance, the six stages look like this:

1. Obey rules to avoid punishment.
2. Conform to obtain rewards, have favors returned, and so on.
3. Conform to avoid disapproval, dislike by others.
4. Conform to avoid censure by legitimate authorities and resultant guilt.
5. Conform to maintain the respect ofthe impartial spectator judging in terms of community welfare.
6. Conform to avoid self-condemnation.

In another of these 25 moral aspects, the value of human life, the six stages can be defined thus:

1. The value of a human life is confused with the value of physical objects and is based on the social status or physical attributes of its possessor.
2. The value of a human life is seen as instrumental to the satisfaction of the needs of its possessor or of other persons.
3. The value of a human life is based on the empathy and affection of family members and others toward its possessor.
4. Life is conceived as sacred in terms of its place in a categorical moral or religious order of rights and duties.
5. Life is valued both in terms of its relation to community welfare and in terms of life being a universal human right.
6. Belief in the sacredness of human life as representing a universal human value of respect for the individual.

I have called this scheme a typology. This is because about 50 per cent of most people's thinking will be at a single stage, regardless of the moral dilemma involved. We call our types stages because they seem to represent an *invariant developmental sequence.* "True" stages come one at a time and always in the same order.

All movement is forward in sequence, and does not skip steps. Children may move through these stages at varying speeds, of course, and may be found half in and half out of a particular stage. An individual may stop at any given stage and at any age, but if he continues to move, he must move in accord with these steps. Moral reasoning of the conventional or Stage 3–4 kind never occurs before the preconventional Stage-1 and Stage-2 thought has taken place. No adult in Stage 4 has gone through Stage-6, but all Stage-6 adults have gone at least through 4.

While the evidence is not complete, my study strongly suggests that moral change fits the stage pattern just described. (The major uncertainty is whether all Stage-6s go through Stage 5 or whether these are two alternate mature orientations.)

41 HOW VALUES CHANGE

As a single example of our findings of stage-sequence, take the progress of two boys on the aspect "The Value of Human Life." The first boy Tommy, is asked "Is it better to save the life of one important person or a lot of unimportant people?". At age 10, he answers "all the people that aren't important because one man just has one house, maybe a lot of furniture, but a whole bunch of people have an awful lot of furniture and some of these poor people might have a lot of money and it doesn't look it."

Clearly Tommy is Stage 1: he confuses the value of a human being with the value of the property he possesses. Three years later (age 13) Tommy's conceptions of life's value are most clearly elicited by the question, "Should the doctor mercy kill a fatally ill woman requesting death because of her pain?". He answers, "Maybe it would be good, to put her out of her pain, she'd be better off that way. But the husband wouldn't want it, it's not like an animal. If a pet dies you can get along without it–it isn't something you really need. Well, you can get a new wife, but it's not really the same."

Here his answer is Stage 2: the value the woman's life is partly contingent on its hedonistic value to the wife herself but even more contingent on its instrumental value to her husband, who can't replace her as easily as he can a pet.

Three years later still (age 16) Tommy's conception of life's value is elicited by the same question, to which he replies: "It might be best for her, but her husband—it's a human life—not like an animal; it just doesn't have the same relationship that a human being does to a family. You can become attached to a dog, but nothing like a human you know."

Now Tommy has moved from a Stage 2 instrumental view of the woman's value to a Stage-3 view based on the husband's distinctively human empathy and love for someone in his family. Equally clearly, it lacks any basis for a universal human value of the woman's life, which would hold if she had no husband or if her husband didn't love her. Tommy, then, has moved step by step through three stages during the age 10–16. Tommy, though bright (I.Q. 120), is a slow developer in moral judgment. Let us take another boy, Richard, to show us sequential movement through the remaining three steps.

At age 13, Richard said about the mercy-killing, "If she requests it, it's really up to her. She is in such terrible pain, just the same as people are always putting animals out of their pain," and in general showed a mixture of Stage-2 and Stage-3 responses concerning the value of life. At 16, he said, "I dont know. In one way, it's murder, it's not a right or privilege of man to decide who shall live and who should die. God put life into everybody on earth and you're taking away something from that person that came directly from God, and you're destroying something that is very sacred, it's in a way part of God and it's almost destroying a part of God when you kill a person. There's something of God in everyone."

Here Richard clearly displays a Stage-4 concept of life as sacred in terms of its place in a categorical moral or religious order. The value of human life is universal, it is true for all humans. It is still, however, dependent on something else, upon respect for God and God's authority; it is not an autonomous human value. Presumably if God told Richard to murder, as God commanded Abraham to murder Isaac, he would do so.

At age 20, Richard said to the same question: "There are more and more people in the medical profession who think it is a hardship on everyone, the person, the family, when you know they are going to die. When a person is kept alive by an artificial lung or kidney it's more like being a vegetable than being a human. If it's her own choice, I think there are certain rights and privileges that go along with being a human being. I am a human being and have certain desires for life and I think everybody else does too. You have a world of which you are the center, and everybody else does too and in that sense we're all equal."

Richard's response is clearly Stage 5, in that the value of life is defined in terms of equal and universal human rights in a context of relativity ("You have a world of which you are the center and in that sense we're all equal"), and of concern for utility or welfare consequences.

42 THE FINAL STEP

At 24, Richard says: "A human life takes precedence over any other moral or legal value, whoever it is. A human life has inherent value whether or not it is valued by a particular individual. The worth of the individual human being is central where the principles of justice and love are normative for all human relationships."

This young man is at Stage 6 in seeing the value of human life as absolute in representing a universal and equal respect for the human as an individual. He has moved step by step through a sequence culminating in a deflnition of human life as centrally valuable rather than derived from or dependent on social or divine authority.

In a genuine and culturally universal sense, these steps lead toward an increased morality of value judgment, where morality is considered as a form of judging, as it has been in a philosophic tradition running from the analyses of Kant to those of the modern analytic or "ordinary language" philosophers. The person at Stage 6 has disentangled his judgments of—or language about—human life from status and property values (Stage 1), from its uses to others (Stage 2), from interpersonal affection (Stage 3), and so on; he has a means of moral judgment that is universal and impersonal. The Stage-6 person's answers use moral words like "duty" or "morally right," and he uses them in a way implying universality, ideals, impersonality: He thinks and speaks in phrases like "regardless of who it was," or ". . . I would do it in spite of punishment."

43 ACROSS CULTURES

When I first decided to explore moral development in other cultures, I was told by anthropologist friends that I would have to throw away my culturebound moral concepts and stories and start from scratch learning a whole new set of values for each new culture. My first try consisted of a brace of villages, one Atayal (Malaysian aboriginal) and the other Taiwanese.

My guide was a young Chinese ethnographer who had written an account of the moral and religious patterns of the Atayal and Taiwanese villages. Taiwanese boys in the 10–13 age group were asked about a story involving theft of food. A man's wife is starving to death but the store owner won't give the man any food unless he can pay, which be can't. Should he break in and steal some food? Why? Many of the boys said, "He should steal the food for his wife because if she dies he'll have to pay for her funeral and that costs a lot."

My guide was amused by these responses, but I was relieved: they were of course "classic" Stage-2 responses. In the Atayal village, funerals weren I t such a big thing, so the Stage 2-boys would say, "He should steal the food because he needs his wife to cook for him."

This means that we need to consult our anthropologists to know what content a Stage-2 child will include in his instrumental exchange calculations, or what a Stage-4 adult will identify as the proper social order. But one certainly doesn't have to start from scratch. What made my guide laugh was the difference in form between the children's Stage-2 thought and his own, a difference definable independently of particular cultures.

Illustrations number 1 and number 2 indicate the cultural universality of the sequence of stages which we have found. Illustration number 1 presents the age trends for middle-class urban boys in the U.S., Taiwan and Mexico. At age 10 in each country, the order of use of each stage is the same as the order of its difficulty or maturity.

In the United States, by age 16 the order is the reverse, from the highest to the lowest, except that Stage 6 is still little-used. At age 13, the good-boy, middle stage (Stage 3), is not used.

The results in Mexico and Taiwan are the same, except that development is a little slower. The most conspicuous feature is that at the age of 16, Stage-5 thinking is much more salient in the United States than in Mexico or Taiwan. Nevertheless, it is present in the other countries, so we know that this is not purely an American democratic construct.

Illustration 2 shows strikingly similar results from two isolated villages, one in Yucatan, one in Turkey. While conventional moral thought increases steadily from ages 10 to 16 it still has not achieved a clear ascendency over preconventional thought.

Trends for lower-class urban groups are intermediate in the rate of development between those for the middle-class and for the village boys. In the three divergent cultures that I studied, middle-class children were found to be more advanced in moral judgment than matched lower-class children. This was not due to the fact that the middle-class children heavily favored some one type of thought which could be seen as corresponding to the prevailing middle-class pattern. Instead, middle-class and working-class children move through the same sequences, but the middle-class children move faster and farther.

This sequence is not dependent upon a particular religion, or any religion at all in the usual sense. I found no important differences in the development of moral thinking among Catholics, Protestants, Jews, Buddhists, Moslems and atheists. Religious values seem to go through the same stages as all other values.

44 TRADING UP

In summary, the nature of our sequence is not significantly affected by widely varying social, cultural or religious conditions. The only thing that is affected is the rate at which individuals progress through this sequence.

Why should there be such a universal invariant sequence of development? In answering this question, we need first to analyze these developing social concepts in terms of their internal logical structure. At each stage, the same basic moral concept or aspect is defined, but at each higher stage this definition is more differentiated, more integrated and more general or universal. When one's concept of human life moves from Stage 1 to Stage 2 the value of life becomes more differentiated from the value of property, more integrated (the value of life enters an organizational hierarchy where it is "higher" than property so that one steals property in order to save life) and more universalized (the life of any sentient being is valuable regardless of status or property). The same advance is true at each stage in the hierarchy. Each step of development then is a better cognitive organization than the one before it, one which takes account of everything present in the previous stage, but making new distinctions and organizing them into a more comprehensive or more equilibrated structure. The fact that this is the case has been demonstrated by a series of studies indicating that children and adolescents comprehend all stages up to their own, but not more than one stage beyond their own. And importantly, *they prefer this next stage.*

We have conducted experimental moral discussion classes which show that the child at an earlier stage of development tends to move forward when confronted by the views of a child one stage further along. In an argument between a Stage-3 and Stage-4 child, the child in the third stage tends to move toward or into Stage 4, while the Stage-4 child understands but does not accept the arguments of the Stage-3 child.

Moral thought, then, seems to behave like all other kinds of thought. Progress through the moral levels and stages is characterized by increasing differentiation and increasing integration, and hence is the same kind of progress that scientific theory represents. Like acceptable scientific theory—or like *any* theory or structure of knowledge—moral thought may be considered partially to generate its own data as it goes along, or at least to expand so as to contain in a balanced, self-consistent way a wider and experiential field. The raw data in the case of our ethical philosophies may be considered as conflicts between roles, or values, or as the social order in which men live.

45 THE ROLE OF SOCIETY

The social worlds of all men seem to contain the same basic structures. All the societies we have studied have the same basic institutions—family, economy, law, government. In addition, however, all societies are alike because they are societies—systems of defined complementary roles. In order to *play* a social role in the family, school or society, the child must implicitly take the role of others toward himself and toward others in the group. These role-taking tendencies form the basis of social institutions. They represent various patternings of shared or complementary expectations.

In the preconventional and conventional levels (Stages 1–4), moral content or value is largely accidental or culture-bound. Anything from "honesty" to "courage in battle" can be the central value. But in the higher postconventional levels, Socrates, Lincoln, Thoreau and Martin Luther King tend to speak without confusion of tongues, as it were. This is because the ideal principles of any social structure are basically alike, if only because there simply aren't that many principles which are articulate, comprehensive and integrated enough to be satisfying to the human intellect. And most of these principles have gone by the name of justice.

Behavioristic psychology and psychoanalysis have always upheld the Philistine view that fine moral words are one thing and moral deeds another. Morally mature reasoning is quite a different matter, and does not really depend on "fine words." The man who understands justice is more likely to practice it.

In our studies, we have found that youths who understand justice act more justly, and the man who understands justice helps create a moral climate which goes far beyond his immediate and personal acts. The universal society is the beneficiary.

Unit 4

Attention

What Is Attention?

Attention is the focusing of mental resources. Attention improves cognitive processing for many tasks, from grabbing a toy to hitting a baseball or adding numbers. At any one time, though, children, like adults, can pay attention to only a limited amount of information. They allocate their attention in different ways. Psychologists have labeled these types of allocation as sustained attention, selective attention, and divided attention.

What are some developmental changes in attention?

- **Sustained attention** is the ability to maintain attention to a selected stimulus for a prolonged period of time. Sustained attention is also called *vigilance.* One recent study difficulties in sustaining attention were the most common type of attentional problem characterizing children with ADHD (Tsal, Shavel, & Mevorach, 2005).
- **Selective attention** is focusing on a specific aspect of experience that is relevant while ignoring others that are irrelevant. Focusing on one voice among many in a crowded room or a noisy restaurant is an example of selective attention.
- **Divided attention** involves concentrating on more than one activity at the same time. If you are listening to music while you are reading this, you are engaging in divided attention.

Developmental Changes

Some important changes in attention occur during childhood. Much of the research on attention has focused on selective attention. One recent study of 5- to 7-year-old children found that the older children and more socially advantaged children in a sample resisted the interference of competing demands and focused their attention better than the younger children and more socially disadvantaged children (Mezzacappa, 2004).

The length of time children can pay attention increases as they get older. The toddler wanders around, shifts attention from one activity to another, and seems to spend little time focused on any one object or event. In contrast, the preschool child might watch television for half an hour at a time (Giavecchio, 2001). One study that observed 99 families in their homes for 4,672 hours found that visual attention to television dramatically increased in the preschool years (Anderson & others, 1985).

Researchers have found that preschool children's attention is related to their achievement-related and social skills (Ruff & Rothbart, 1996). In regard to achievement-related skills, one recent study of more than 1,000 children found that their sustained attention at 54 months of age was linked to their school readiness (which included achievement and language skills) (NICHD Early Child Care Research Network, 2003). In regard to social skills, young children who have difficulty regulating their attention are more likely than other children to experience peer rejection and engage in aggressive behavior (Eisenberg & others, 2000).

Control over attention shows important changes during childhood (Ruff & Capozzoli, 2003). External stimuli are likely to determine the target of the preschooler's attention; what is *salient,* or obvious, grabs the preschooler's attention. For example, suppose a flashy, attractive clown presents the directions for solving

attention Concentrating and focusing mental resources.

sustained attention The ability to maintain attention to a selected stimulus for a prolonged period of time; also called vigilance.

selective attention Focusing on a specific aspect of experience that is relevant while ignoring others that are irrelevant.

divided attention Concentrating on more than one activity at a time.

BEST PRACTICES
Strategies for Helping Students Pay Attention

1. *Encourage students to pay close attention and minimize distraction.* Talk with children about how important it is to pay attention when they need to remember something. Give them exercises with opportunities to give their undivided attention to something.

2. *Use cues or gestures to signal that something is important.* This might involve raising your voice, repeating something with emphasis, and writing the concept on the board or on a transparency.

3. *Help students generate their own cue or catch phrase for when they need to pay attention.* Possibly vary this from month to month. Give them a menu of options to select from, such as "Alert," "Focus," or "Zero in." Teach them to say their word or pet phrase quietly but firmly to themselves when they catch their minds wandering.

4. *Make learning interesting.* Boredom can set in quickly for students, and when it does their attention wanes. Relating ideas to students' interests increases their attention. So does infusing the classroom with novel, unusual, or surprising exercises. Just starting off a biology exercise on heredity and aging with a question such as "Can you live to be 100?" or "Might someone be able to live to be even 400 some day?" is sure to capture students' attention. Think of dramatic questions such as these to introduce various topics.

5. *Use media and technology effectively as part of your effort to vary the pace of the classroom.* Video and television programs have built-in attention-getting formats, such as zooming in on an image; flashing a vivid, colorful image on the screen; and switching from one setting to another. Look for relevant videos and television programs that can help you vary the classroom's pace and increase students' attention. Unfortunately, too many teachers show videos only to keep students quiet, which does not promote learning. Also, if the curriculum is dull, it doesn't matter what kinds of "tricks" or "splashes" the teacher uses—students will not learn effectively. Make sure that the media and technology you use captures students' attention in meaningful ways that promote effective learning (Goldman, 1998).

6. *Focus on active learning to make learning enjoyable.* A different exercise, a guest, a field trip, and many other activities can be used to make learning more enjoyable, reduce student boredom, and increase attention. Next, middle school English and drama teacher Lynn Ayres describes how games can add interest at all grade levels.

THROUGH THE EYES OF TEACHERS
Turning Boring Exercises into Active Learning Games

I have found that the most boring exercises (such as the kind you find on worksheets and textbooks) can be turned into an active learning game. One favorite game in my seventh-grade English class was "sit-set, rise-raise." I'd put two students in chairs next to tables and place a book on each table. If I said "rise" they were to stand. If I said "raise" they were to raise the book. They were to seat themselves if I said "sit" and they were to place the book on the table if I said "set." If I said "rise" and one of them stood up and the other student lifted the book, the student with the book held up was out and was replaced by a teammate. Or if they both stood up, the one who stood up first stayed, and the other student was replaced by a teammate. The students loved that game, and they really learned the difference between those two commonly confused pairs of verbs in the process.

That game taught me the effectiveness of getting students physically involved. I developed dozens of other games involving bells and timers and teams that had students running around the room, ringing bells, trying to beat a member of the opposing team in telling me if a word was a noun or an adjective. Almost any workbook or textbook exercise can be turned into a physical activity game if you put some thought into it, and middle school students learn so much more from doing an exercise that is both physical and mental.

7. *Don't overload students with too much information.* We live in an information society where sometimes the tendency is to feel like you have to get students to learn everything. But students who are given too much information too fast might not attend to anything.

8. *Be aware of individual differences in students' attentional skills.* Some students have severe problems in paying attention. You will need to take this into account when presenting material. Before you begin an exercise, look around the room for potential distractions, such as an open window to a playground where students are being noisy. Close the window and draw the shade to eliminate the distraction.

a problem. Preschool children are likely to pay attention to the clown and ignore the directions, because they are influenced strongly by the salient features of the environment. After the age of 6 or 7, children pay more attention to features relevant to performing a task or solving a problem, such as the directions. This change reflects a shift to *cognitive control* of attention, so that children act less impulsively and reflect more. Instead of being controlled by the most striking stimuli in their environment, older children can direct their attention to more important stimuli.

Attention to relevant information increases steadily through the elementary and secondary school years (Davidson, 1996). Processing of irrelevant information decreases in adolescence.

As children grow up, their abilities both to direct selective attention and to divided attention also improve. Older children and adolescents are better than younger children at tasks that require shifts of attention. For example, writing a good story requires shifting attention among many competing tasks—spelling the words, composing

What are some good strategies teachers can use to get students' attention?

Review, Reflect, and Practice

(1) Characterize attention and summarize how it changes during development.

REVIEW

- What is attention? What are three ways attention can be allocated?
- How does attention develop in childhood and adolescence?

REFLECT

- Imagine that you are an elementary school teacher and a child is having difficulty sustaining attention on a learning task. What strategies would you try to use to help the child sustain attention?

PRAXIS™ PRACTICE

1. Ms. Samson teaches first grade. Often while she is working with one group of children, she must monitor the behavior of the rest of the class, occasionally intervening in some manner. Sometimes she has three or four students at her desk, each needing something different from her. This does not seem to faze her in the least. She can talk to one student while tying another's shoes and monitoring the behavior of the rest with no problem. What skill has Ms. Samson mastered?
   a. divided attention
   b. selective attention
   c. sustained attention
   d. personal attention

2. Mark shifts his attention very quickly from one thing to another. The more colorful and noisy the thing, the more likely it is to draw his attention. He rarely attends to any one thing for more than a few minutes. From this description, Mark is most likely to be a
   a. toddler.
   b. preschooler.
   c. elementary-school-age child.
   d. adolescent.

grammar, structuring paragraphs, and conveying the story as a whole. Children also improve in their ability to do two things at once. For example, in one investigation, 12-year-olds were markedly better than 8-year-olds and slightly worse than 20-year-olds at allocating their attention in a situation involving two tasks (divided attention) (Manis, Keating, & Morrison, 1980). These improvements in divided attention might be due to an increase in cognitive resources (through increased processing speed or capacity), automaticity, or increased skill at directing resources.

Expertise and Metacognition

In the last section we considered various aspects of memory. Our ability to remember new information about a subject depends considerably on what we already know about it (Carver & Klahr, 2001; Ericsson & others, 2006; Keil, 2006). For example, a student's ability to recount what she saw when she was at the library is largely governed by what she already knows about libraries, such as where books on certain topics are likely to be and how to check books out. If she knew little about libraries, the student would have a much harder time recounting what was there.

The contribution of prior content knowledge to our ability to remember new material is especially evident when we compare the memories of experts and novices in a particular knowledge domain (Donovan & Bransford, 2005). An expert is the opposite of a novice (someone who is just beginning to learn a content area). Experts demonstrate especially impressive memory in their areas of expertise. One reason that children remember less than adults is that they are far less expert in most areas.

46 EXPERTISE AND LEARNING

Studying the behavior and mental processes of experts can give us insights into how to guide students in becoming more effective learners. What is it, exactly, that experts do? According to the National Research Council (1999), they are better than novices at

1. detecting features and meaningful patterns of information;
2. accumulating more content knowledge and organizing it in a manner that shows an understanding of the topic;
3. retrieving important aspects of knowledge with little effort;
4. adapting an approach to new situations; and
5. using effective strategies.

In this section we will consider various ways that you can help your students learn and remember these skills that experts use so effortlessly.

Detecting Features and Meaningful Patterns of Organization

Experts are better at noticing important features of problems and contexts that novices may ignore (Bransford & others, 2006). Thus, the attentional advantage of experts starts them off at a more advantageous level than novices in a learning context. Experts also have superior recall of information in their area of expertise. The process of chunking, which we discussed earlier, is one way they accomplish this superior recall. For example, "Chess masters perceive chunks of meaningful information, which affects their memory of what they see. . . . Lacking a hierarchical, highly organized structure for the domain, novices cannot use this chunking strategy" (National Research Council, 1999, p. 21).

In areas where children are experts, their memory is often extremely good. In fact, it often exceeds that of adults who are novices in that content area. This was documented in a study of 10-year-old chess experts (Chi, 1978). These children were excellent chess players but not especially brilliant in other ways. As with most 10-year-olds, their memory spans for digits were shorter than an adult's. However, they remembered the configurations of chess pieces on chessboards far better than did the adults who were novices at chess (see Figure 4.1).

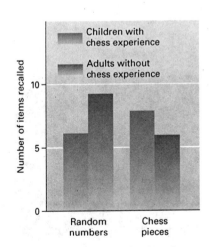

FIGURE 4.1 Memory for Numbers and Chess Pieces

Expert teachers recognize features and patterns that are not noticed by novice teachers (National Research Council, 1999, pp. 21, 25). For example, in one study, expert and novice teachers had a very different understanding of the events in a videotaped classroom lesson, in which three screens showed simultaneous events taking place throughout the classroom (left, center, and right areas) (Sabers, Cushing, & Berliner, 1991). One expert teacher said, "On the left monitor, the students' note taking indicates that they have seen sheets like this before; it's fairly efficient at this point because they're used to the format they are using." One novice teacher sparsely responded, "It's a lot to watch."

Organization and Depth of Knowledge

Experts' knowledge is organized around important ideas or concepts more than novices' knowledge is (National Research Council, 1999). This provides experts with a much deeper understanding of knowledge than novices have (Bransford & others, 2006; Simon, 2001; Voss & others, 1984).

Experts in a particular area usually have far more elaborate networks of information about that area than novices do (see Figure 4.2). The information they represent in memory has more nodes, more interconnections, and better hierarchical organization.

The implications for teaching are that too often a curriculum is designed in a way that makes it difficult for students to organize knowledge in meaningful ways. This especially occurs when there is only superficial coverage of facts before moving on to the next topic. In this context, students have little time to explore the topic in depth and get a sense of what the important, organizing ideas are. This type of shallow presentation can occur in any subject area but is common in history and science texts that emphasize facts (National Research Council, 1999).

Fluent Retrieval

Retrieval of relevant information can range from taking a lot of effort to being fluent and almost effortless (National Research Council, 1999). Experts retrieve information in an almost effortless, automatic manner, while novices expend a great deal of effort in retrieving information.

Effortless retrieval places fewer demands on conscious attention. Since the amount of information a student can attend to at one time is limited, ease of processing information in some aspects of a task frees up capacity to attend to other aspects of a task.

Consider expert and novice readers. Expert readers can quickly scan the words of a sentence and paragraph, which allows them to devote attention to understanding what they are reading. However, novice readers' ability to decode words is not yet fluent, so they have to allocate considerable attention and time to this task, which restricts the time they can give to understanding a passage. An important aspect of teaching is to help students develop the fluency they need to competently perform cognitive tasks (Beck & others, 1991).

Adaptive Expertise

An important aspect of expertise "is whether some ways of organizing knowledge are better" than others for helping people to be "flexible and adaptive to new situations than others" (National Research Council, 1999, p. 33). Adaptive experts are able to approach new situations flexibly rather than always responding in a rigid, fixed routine (Bransford & others, 2006; Hatano, 1990; Hatano & Oura, 2003). An important theme in a recent book, *Preparing Teachers for a Changing World* (Darling-Hammond & Bransford, 2005, p. 3), was to "help teachers become 'adaptive experts' who are prepared for effective lifelong learning that allows them to continually add

What are some characteristics of teachers who are adaptive experts?

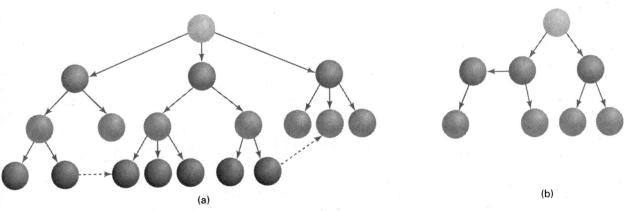

FIGURE 4.2 An Example of How Information Is Organized in the Mind of an Expert and a Novice
(a) An expert's knowledge is based on years of experience in which small bits of information have been linked with many other small pieces, which together are placed in a more general category. This category is in turn placed in an even more general category of knowledge. The dotted lines are used as pointers, associations between specific elements of knowledge that connect the lower branches and provide mental shortcuts in the expert's mind. (b) The novice's knowledge shows far fewer connections, shortcuts, and levels than an expert's knowledge.

to their knowledge and skills." Thus, teachers characterized by adaptive expertise are flexible and open to rethinking important ideas and practices to improve their students' learning (Hammerness & others, 2005).

Indeed, innovation *and* efficiency are the two main dimensions of one model of adaptive expertise (Bransford & others, 2006; Schwartz, Bransford, & Sears, 2006, in press). Experts characterized by *efficiency* can quickly retrieve and apply information in skillful ways to explain something or solve a problem. Experts characterized by *innovation* involves moving away from efficiency, at least on a short-term basis, and unlearning previous routines. Innovation occurs when individuals "let go" and rethink their routine way of doing something.

In this model, adaptive experts possess a balance of efficiency and innovation (Bransford & others, 2006; Schwartz, Bransford, & Sears, 2006). For example, efficiency is at work when a teacher teaches students to speedily complete math computations, but this efficiency may limit the students' competence when they face new math problems. When this efficiency-oriented teacher adapts and adds teaching for understanding and application, innovation is taking place. The new skills she teaches are likely to increase the students' competence when they encounter new math problems.

Adaptive experts are motivated to learn from others (Hammerness & others, 2005). This may not be that difficult when the learning involves making a teacher's existing routines and practices more efficient. However, as we just indicated, adaptive expertise also includes innovation that requires sometimes replacing or transforming prior routines and practices, which is often not easy to do. Your teaching likely will benefit if you seek feedback from other competent teachers, even if their approaches are different than yours. This might occur when you watch a videotape of your teaching with other teachers who provide feedback about your teaching or invite a colleague to come to your classroom to observe your teaching.

Strategies

Experts use effective strategies in understanding the information in their area of expertise and in advancing it (Ornstein, Haden, & Elischberger, 2006; Pressley & Hilden, 2006). Earlier in the chapter we described a number of strategies that students can use to remember information. Let's now explore some effective strategies that students can develop to become experts at learning and studying.

Patricia Alexander (2003) uses the label *acclimation* to describe the initial stage of expertise in a particular domain (such as English, biology, or mathematics). At this stage, students have limited and fragmented knowledge that restricts their ability to detect the difference between accurate and inaccurate and relevant and tangential information. To help students move beyond the acclimation stage, teachers need to guide students in determining what content is central and what is peripheral, as well as what is accurate and well supported and what is inaccurate and unsupported. In Alexander's (2003) view, students don't come to the classroom equipped with the strategies they need to move beyond the acclimation stage. Teachers must help students learn effective strategies and practice them in relevant situations before students can experience their value. Students also need to be encouraged to change and combine strategies to solve the problem at hand.

Spreading Out and Consolidating Learning Students' learning benefits when teachers talk with them about the importance of regularly reviewing what they learn. Children who have to prepare for a test will benefit from distributing their learning over a longer period rather than cramming for the test at the last minute. Cramming tends to produce short-term memory that is processed in a shallow rather than deep manner. A final, concentrated tune-up before the test is better than trying to learn everything at the last minute.

Asking Themselves Questions When children ask themselves questions about what they have read or about an activity, they expand the number of associations with the information they need to retrieve. At least as early as the middle of elementary school, the self-questioning strategy can help children to remember. For example, as children read, they can be encouraged to stop periodically and ask themselves questions such as "What is the meaning of what I just read?" "Why is this important?" and "What is an example of the concept I just read?" Students can use the same self-questioning strategy when they listen to you conduct a lesson, hear a guest give a talk, or watch a video. If you periodically remind children to generate questions about their experiences, they are more likely to remember the experiences.

Taking Good Notes Taking good notes from either a lecture or a text benefits learning. When children are left to take notes without being given any strategies, they tend to take notes that are brief and disorganized. When they do write something down, it often is a verbatim record of what they have just heard. Give children some practice in taking notes and then evaluate their note taking. Encourage children not to write down everything they hear when they take notes. It is impossible to do this, anyway, and it can prevent them from getting the big picture of what the speaker is saying. Here are some good note-taking strategies:

- *Summarizing.* Have the children listen for a few minutes and then write down the main idea that a speaker is trying to get across in that time frame. Then have the child listen for several more minutes and write down another idea, and so on.
- *Outlining.* Show the children how to outline what a speaker is saying, using first-level heads as the main topics, second-level heads as subtopics under the first-level heads, and third-level heads under the second-level heads.
- *Concept maps.* Help the children practice drawing concept maps, which are similar to outlines but visually portray information in a more spiderlike format.

All three note-taking strategies described so far—summarizing, outlining, and concept maps—help children evaluate which ideas are the most important to remember. Outlining and concept maps also help children arrange the material hier-

What are some good study strategies?

archically, which underscores an important theme of learning: It works best when it is organized.

Using a Study System   Various systems have been developed to help people to remember information that they are studying from a book. One of the earliest systems was called *SQ3R*, which stands for *Survey, Question, Read, Recite,* and *Review*. A more recently developed system is called *PQ4R,* which stands for *Preview, Question, Read, Reflect, Recite,* and *Review*. Thus, the PQ4R system adds an additional step, "Reflect," to the SQ3R system. From the later elementary school years on, students will benefit from practicing the PQ4R system (Adams, Carnine, & Gersten, 1982). The system benefits students by getting them to meaningfully organize information, ask questions about it, reflect on it, and review it. Here are more details about the steps in the PQ4R system:

- *Preview.* Tell your students to briefly survey the material to get a sense of the overall organization of ideas—to look at the headings to see the main topics and subtopics that will be covered.
- *Question.* Encourage the children to ask themselves questions about the material as they read it.
- *Read.* Now tell the children to read the material. Encourage your students to be active readers—to immerse themselves in what they are reading and strive to understand what the author is saying. This helps students to avoid being empty readers whose eyes just track the lines of text but whose minds fail to register anything important.
- *Reflect.* By occasionally stopping and reflecting on the material, students increase its meaningfulness. Encourage the children to be analytic at this point in studying. After they have read something, challenge them to break open the ideas and scratch beneath their surface. This is a good time for them to think out applications and interpretations of the information, as well as connecting it with other information already in their long-term memory.
- *Recite.* This involves children self-testing themselves to see if they can remember the material and reconstruct it. At this point, encourage the children to make up a series of questions about the material and then try to answer them.
- *Review.* Tell your students to go over the material and evaluate what they know and don't know. At this point they should reread and study the material they don't remember or understand well.

We will further explore strategies later in the chapter in our discussion of metacognition. To evaluate the extent to which you use good memory and study strategies, complete Self-Assessment 4.1.

 ACQUIRING EXPERTISE

What determines whether or not someone becomes an expert? Can motivation and practice get someone to expert status? Or does expertise also require a great deal of talent (Sternberg & Ben-Zeev, 2001)?

Practice and Motivation

One perspective is that a particular kind of practice—*deliberate practice*—is required to become an expert (Hatano & Oura, 2003; Schraw, 2006). Deliberate practice involves practice that is at an appropriate level of difficulty for the individual, provides corrective feedback, and allows opportunities for repetition (Ericsson, 1996, 2006).

SELF-ASSESSMENT 4.1

How Effective Are My Memory and Study Strategies?

Teachers who themselves practice using good memory and study strategies are more likely to model and communicate these to their students than teachers who don't use such strategies. Candidly respond to these items about your own memory and study strategies. Rate yourself on this scale: 1 = never, 2 = some, 3 = moderate, 4 = almost always, or 5 = always. Then total your points.

	1	2	3	4	5
1. I'm a good time manager and planner.					
2. I'm good at focusing my attention and minimizing distractions.					
3. I try to understand material rather than rotely memorizing it.					
4. I ask myself questions about what I have read or about class activities.					
5. I take good notes in class and from textbooks.					
6. I regularly review my notes.					
7. I use mnemonic strategies.					
8. I'm very organized in the way I encode information.					
9. I spread out my studying to consolidate my learning.					
10. I use good retrieval cues.					
11. I use the PQ4R method or a similar study method.					
Total					

Scoring and Interpretation

If you scored 50–55 total points, you likely use good memory and study strategies. If you scored 45–49 points, you likely have some reasonably good memory and study strategies. If you scored below 45, spend some time working on improving your memory and study strategies.

If you would like to learn more about effective memory and study strategies, one resource is a book called *Your Guide to College Success* (Santrock & Halonen, 2002). Also, to gain more experience in developing good memory and study strategies, contact the study skills center at your college or university; specialists there likely will be able to help you.

In one study of violinists at a music academy, the extent to which children engaged in deliberate practice distinguished novices and experts (Ericsson, Krampe, & Tesch-Romer, 1993). The top violinists averaged 7,500 hours of deliberate practice by age 18, the good violinists only 5,300 hours. Many individuals give up on becoming an expert because they won't put forth the effort it takes to engage in extensive deliberate practice over a number of years.

Such extensive practice requires considerable motivation. Students who are not motivated to practice long hours are unlikely to become experts in a particular area. Thus, a student who complains about all of the work, doesn't persevere, and doesn't extensively practice solving math problems over a number years is not going to become an expert in math.

TECHNOLOGY AND EDUCATION

Experts and Technology

As described by the National Research Council (1999), experts in many fields are using new technologies to represent information in new ways. For example, three-dimensional models of the surface of Venus or of a molecular structure can be electronically created and viewed from any angle.

One of the characteristics of expertise we have discussed involves organizing knowledge meaningfully around important ideas. The Belvedere computer technology system is designed to help students who lack a deep understanding of many areas of science, have difficulty zeroing in on the key issues in a scientific debate, and have trouble recognizing connections of ideas in scientific theories (Suthers & others, 1995). Belvedere uses graphics with specialized boxes to represent connections of ideas in an effort to support students' reasoning about scientific issues. An online advisor gives students hints to help them improve their understanding and reasoning.

The Belvedere system can also help students in nonscientific studies such as analyzing social policies. This system helps students by (1) giving arguments a concrete, diagram-like form and providing tools for focusing on particular problems encountered in the construction and evaluation of complex arguments; (2) providing access to online information resources; and (3) supporting students working in small groups to construct documents to be shared with others.

Talent

A number of psychologists who study expertise believe that it requires not only deliberate practice and motivation but also talent (Bloom, 1985; Hunt, 2006; Schraw 2006; Shiffrin, 1996; Sternberg & Ben-Zeev, 2001).

A number of abilities—music and athletic, for example—seem to have a heritable component (Plomin, 1997). For example, is it likely that Mozart could have become such an outstanding musical composer just because he practiced long hours? Is it likely that Tiger Woods became such a fantastic golfer just because he was motivated to do so? Many talented individuals have attempted to become as great as Mozart or Woods but have given up trying after only mediocre performances. Clearly, heredity matters. Nonetheless, Mozart and Woods would not have developed expertise in their fields without being highly motivated and engaging in extensive deliberate practice. Talent alone does not make an expert (Hunt, 2006; Winner, 2006).

(48) EXPERTISE AND TEACHING

Being an expert in a particular domain—such as physics, history, or math—does not mean that the expert is good at helping others learn it (Bransford & others, 2005, 2006). Indeed, "expertise can sometimes hurt teaching because many experts forget what is easy and what is difficult for students" (National Research Council, 1999, p. 32).

Some educators have distinguished between the content knowledge required for expertise and the pedagogical content knowledge necessary to effectively teach it (Shulman, 1987). *Pedagogical content knowledge* includes ideas about common difficulties that students have as they try to learn a content area; typical paths students must take to understand the area; and strategies for helping students overcome the difficulties they experience.

Expert teachers are good at monitoring students' learning and assessing students' progress. They also know what types of difficulties students are likely to encounter, are

An expert teacher monitoring a student's learning. What are some characteristics of expert teachers?

Review, Reflect, and Practice

(1) Draw some lessons about learning from the way experts think.

REVIEW

- What do experts do that novices often don't do in the process of learning?
- What does it take to become an expert?
- Is subject experience enough to make a good teacher? What else is needed?

REFLECT

- Choose an area in which you feel at least somewhat of an expert. Compare your ability to learn in that field with the ability of a novice.

PRAXIS™ PRACTICE

1. The case studies in this text are designed to help educational psychology students learn the material and begin to develop expertise. The first question of each case study asks students to identify the issues in the case. The author most likely included this question for each case because he understood that
   a. it is important for students to consolidate their learning.
   b. it is important for students to learn to determine what content is central and what is peripheral.
   c. in learning, it is important to strike a balance between efficiency and innovation.
   d. students need a great deal of help in developing fluid retrieval skills.

2. Ryan is the best player on his soccer team. His coach thinks of him as a coach's dream player because he works so hard. It is rare for Ryan to perform a skill better than his teammates when it is initially introduced, but by the time the next practice comes, he will have mastered the skill. At one point, Ryan decided that he wanted to be able to score from a corner kick. He gathered up all the soccer balls he could find and kicked them one after another from the corner, trying to curl them into the goal. When he had finished, he gathered the balls and did it again. He continued this for an entire afternoon, and thereafter for at least an hour after school each day. His coach was very happily surprised when, in the next game, Ryan scored a goal from a corner kick. Why has Ryan developed expertise in soccer?
   a. He engages in extensive deliberative practice.
   b. He is relying on an inborn talent.
   c. He has an excellent teacher in his coach.
   d. He uses the PQ4R method 3.

3. Mr. Williams is a former college history professor who is now teaching high school American history. He discusses his research and writing with his students and tries to make history come alive by telling them about how historians find out about the past. After a month of teaching, he finds that his students seem confused during class discussions and perform poorly on tests of factual knowledge. The most likely explanation is that Mr. Williams lacks
   a. content expertise.
   b. pedagogical content knowledge.
   c. metacognition.
   d. cue-dependent knowledge.

aware of students' existing knowledge, and use this awareness to teach at the right level and to make new information meaningful. Some educational psychologists argue that in the absence of expert pedagogical awareness of their own students, inexpert teachers simply rely on textbook publishers' materials, which, of course, contain no information about the particular pedagogical needs of students in the teacher's classroom (Brophy, 2004). To read further about expertise, see the Technology and Education box.

(49) METACOGNITION

So far in this chapter, we have examined a number of ways that you help students improve their ability to process information as they learn, including how to improve their attention and memory, as well as strategies that can increase the likelihood that they will make the transition from being a novice to being an expert. Another way that you can help children process information more effectively is by encouraging them to examine what they know about how their mind processes information. As you read at the beginning of this chapter, this involves metacognition, which involves cognition about cognition, or "knowing about knowing" (Flavell, 1999, 2004; Flavell, Miller, & Miller, 2002). A distinction can be made between metacognitive knowledge and metacognitive activity. *Metacognitive knowledge* involves monitoring and reflecting on one's current or recent thoughts. This includes both factual knowledge, such as knowledge about the task, one's goals, or oneself, and strategic knowledge, such as how and when to use specific procedures to solve problems. *Metacognitive activity* occurs when students consciously adapt and manage their thinking strategies during problem solving and purposeful thinking (Ferrari & Sternberg, 1998; Kuhn & others, 1995).

Metacognitive skills have been taught to students to help them solve math problems (Cardelle-Elawar, 1992). In each of thirty daily lessons involving math story problems, a teacher guided low-achieving students in learning to recognize when they did not know the meaning of a word, did not have all of the information necessary to solve a problem, did not know how to subdivide the problem into specific steps, or did not know how to carry out a computation. After the thirty daily lessons, the students who were given this metacognitive training had better math achievement and better attitudes toward math.

One expert on children's thinking, Deanna Kuhn (1999; Kuhn & Franklin, 2006), argues that metacognition should be a stronger focus of efforts to help children become better critical thinkers, especially at the middle school and high school levels. She distinguishes between first-order cognitive skills, which enable children to know about the world (and have been the main focus of critical thinking programs), and second-order cognitive skills—meta-knowing skills—which involve knowing about one's own (and others') knowing.

Developmental Changes

How does metacognition change in childhood? Are there further changes in metacognition during adolescence?

Childhood Many studies have focused on children's metamemory, or knowledge of how memory works. In the last several decades, there has been extensive interest in children's theories about how the human mind works.

Metamemory By 5 or 6 years of age, children usually know that familiar items are easier to learn than unfamiliar ones, that short lists are easier than long ones, that recognition is easier than recall, and that forgetting becomes more likely over time (Lyon & Flavell, 1993). In other ways, however, young children's metamemory is limited. They don't understand that related items are easier to remember than unrelated ones or that remembering the gist of a story is easier than remembering information verbatim (Kreutzer & Flavell, 1975). By fifth grade, students understand that gist recall is easier than verbatim recall.

Preschool children also have an inflated opinion of their memory abilities. For example, in one study, a majority of preschool children predicted that they would be

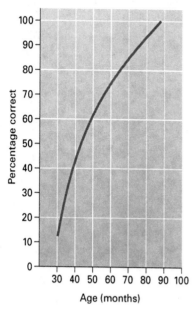

FIGURE 4.3 Developmental Changes in False-Belief Performance

False-belief performance dramatically increases from 2½ years of age through the middle of the elementary school years. In a summary of the results of many studies, 2½-year-olds gave incorrect responses about 80 percent of the time (Wellman, Cross, & Watson, 2001). At 3 years, 8 months, they were correct about 50 percent of the time, and after that, gave increasingly correct responses.

able to recall all ten items of a list of ten items. When tested, none of the young children managed this feat (Flavell, Friedrichs, & Hoyt, 1970). As they move through the elementary school years, children give more realistic evaluations of their memory skills (Schneider & Pressley, 1997).

Preschool children also have little appreciation for the importance of memory cues, such as "It helps when you can think of an example of it." By 7 or 8 years of age, children better appreciate the importance of cueing for memory. In general, children's understanding of their memory abilities and their skill in evaluating their performance on memory tasks is relatively poor at the beginning of the elementary school years but improves considerably by age 11 or 12 (Bjorklund & Rosenblum, 2000).

Theory of Mind **Theory of mind** refers to awareness of one's own mental processes and the mental processes of others. Even young children are curious about the nature of the human mind (Flavell, 1999, 2004; Wellman, 1997, 2000, 2004). Their theory of mind changes as they go through the childhood years (Flavell, Miller, & Miller, 2002; Harris, 2006; Wellman, 2004):

- *Two to Three Years of Age.* Children begin to understand three mental states: (1) *perceptions*—children realize that other people see what is in front of their eyes and not necessarily in front of the children's eyes; (2) *desires*—children understand that if someone wants something, he or she will try to get it; and (3) *emotions*—children can distinguish between positive (for example, "happy") and negative (for example, "sad") emotions. Despite these advances, children who are 2 to 3 years of age have only a minimal understanding of how mental life can be linked to behavior. They think that people are at the mercy of their desires and don't understand how beliefs influence behavior.

- *Four to Five Years of Age.* Children begin to understand that the mind can represent objects and events accurately or inaccurately. Most children realize that people have *false beliefs*—beliefs that are not true—by the time they are 5 years old (Wellman, Cross, & Watson, 2001) (see Figure 4.3). For example, in one study children were shown a Band-Aid box and asked what was inside (Jenkins & Astington, 1996). To the children's surprise, the box contained pencils. When asked what a child who had never seen the box would think was inside, 3-year-olds typically responded "pencils." The 4- and 5-year-olds, grinning in anticipation of other children's false beliefs, were more likely to say "Band-Aids."

- *Middle and Late Childhood.* It is only beyond the early childhood years that children have a deepening appreciation of the mind itself rather than just an understanding of mental states (Wellman, 2004). Not until middle and late childhood do children see the mind as an active constructor of knowledge or processing center (Flavell, Green, & Flavell, 1998). In middle and late childhood, children move from understanding that beliefs can be false to an understanding of beliefs and mind as "interpretive," exemplified in an awareness that the same event can be open to multiple interpretations (Carpendale & Chandler, 1996).

Adolescence In addition to the metacognition changes in memory and theory of mind that occur in childhood, important changes in metacognition take place during adolescence (Kuhn & Franklin, 2006). Compared with children, adolescents have an increased capacity to monitor and manage cognitive resources to effectively meet the demands of a learning task. This increased metacognitive ability results in more effective cognitive functioning and learning.

An important aspect of cognitive functioning and learning is determining how much attention will be allocated to available resources. Evidence is accumulating that adolescents have a better understanding of how to effectively deploy their attention to different aspects of a task than children have (Kuhn & Franklin, 2006). In one investigation, 12-year-olds were markedly better than 8-year-olds, and slightly worse than 20-year-olds, at allocating their attention between two tasks (Manis,

theory of mind Awareness of one's own mental processes and the mental processes of others.

Keating, & Morrison, 1980). Adolescents may have more resources available to them than children (through increased processing speed, capacity, and automaticity), or they may be more skilled at directing the resources. Further, adolescents have a better meta-level understanding of strategies—that is, knowing the best strategy to use and when to use it in performing a learning task.

Keep in mind, though, that there is considerable individual variation in adolescents' metacognition. Indeed, some experts argue that individual variation in metacognition become much more pronounced in adolescence than in childhood (Kuhn & Franklin, 2006). Thus, some adolescents are quite good at using metacognition to improve their learning, others far less effective.

The Good Information-Processing Model

Michael Pressley and his colleagues (Pressley, Borkowski, & Schneider, 1989; Pressley & Harris, 2006; Schneider & Pressley, 1997) have developed a metacognitive model called the Good Information-Processing model. It emphasizes that competent cognition results from a number of interacting factors. These include strategies, content knowledge, motivation, and metacognition. They believe that children become good at cognition in three main steps:

1. *Children are taught by parents or teachers to use a particular strategy.* With practice, they learn about its characteristics and advantages for learning *specific knowledge.* The more intellectually stimulating children's homes and schools are, the more specific strategies they will encounter and learn to use.

2. *Teachers may demonstrate similarities and differences in multiple strategies in a particular domain, such as math, which motivates students to see shared features of different strategies.* This leads to better *relational knowledge.*

3. *At this point, students recognize the general benefits of using strategies, which produces general strategy knowledge.* They learn to attribute successful learning outcomes to the efforts they make in evaluating, selecting, and monitoring strategy use *(metacognitive knowledge and activity).*

What are some changes in metacognition during adolescence?

Strategies and Metacognitive Regulation

In Pressley's (McCormick & Pressley, 1997; Pressley, 1983; Pressley & Harris, 2006; Pressley & Hilden, 2006) view, the key to education is helping students learn a rich repertoire of strategies that results in solutions of problems. Good thinkers routinely use strategies and effective planning to solve problems. Good thinkers also know when and where to use strategies (metacognitive knowledge about strategies). Understanding when and where to use strategies often results from the learner's monitoring of the learning situation.

Pressley argues that when students are given instruction about effective strategies, they often can apply strategies that they previously have not used on their own. He emphasizes that students benefit when the teacher models the appropriate strategy and overtly verbalizes its steps. Then, students subsequently practice the strategy, guided and supported by the teacher's feedback until the students can use it autonomously. When instructing students about employing a strategy, it also is a good idea to explain to them how using the strategy will benefit them. However, there are some developmental limitations to this approach. For instance, young children often cannot use mental imagery competently.

Just having students practice the new strategy is usually not enough for them to continue to use the strategy and transfer it to new situations. For effective maintenance and transfer, encourage students to monitor the effectiveness of the new strategy relative to their use of old strategies by comparing their performance on tests and other assessments (Graham, 2006). Pressley says that it is not enough to say, "Try it, you will like it"; you need to say, "Try it and compare."

BEST PRACTICES
Strategies for Helping Students Use Strategies

The following strategies are based on the recommendations of Michael Pressley and his colleagues (Pressley & Hilden, 2006; Pressley & McCormick, 1995):

1. *Recognize that strategies are a key aspect of solving problems.* Monitor students' knowledge and awareness of strategies for effective learning outcomes. Many students do not use good strategies and are unaware that strategies can help them learn.

2. *Model effective strategies for students.*

3. *Give students many opportunities to practice the strategies.* As students practice the strategies, provide guidance and support to the students. Give them feedback until they can use the strategies independently. As part of your feedback, inform them about where and when the strategies are most useful.

4. *Encourage students to monitor the effectiveness of their new strategy in comparison to the effectiveness of old strategies.*

5. *Remember that it takes students a considerable amount of time to learn how to use an effective strategy.* Be patient and give students continued support during this tedious learning experience. Keep encouraging students to use the strategy over and over again until they can use it automatically.

6. *Understand that students need to be motivated to use the strategies.* Students are not always going to be motivated to use the strategies. Especially important to students' motivation is their expectations that the strategies will lead to successful learning outcomes. It can also help if students set goals for learning effective strategies. And when students attribute their learning outcomes to the effort they put forth, their learning benefits.

7. *Encourage children to use multiple strategies.* Most children benefit from experimenting with multiple strategies, finding out what works well, when, and where.

8. *Read more about strategy instruction.* A good place to start is the recent chapter by Michael Pressley and Katherine Hilden (2006), which includes extensive ideas about how to improve children's use of strategies.

9. *Ask questions that help to guide students' thinking in various content areas.* These might include, "How can proofreading help me in writing a paper?" "Why is it important periodically to stop when I'm reading and try to understand what is being said so far?" and "What is the purpose of learning this formula?"

An important aspect of metacognition is monitoring how well one is performing on a task (Pressley & Harris, 2006; Pressley & Hilden, 2006). This might involve becoming aware that one has not studied enough for a test or needs to reread a particular section of a chapter to understand it better. Mismonitoring is common. For example, elementary school students often think they are better prepared for a test than they actually are and think they understand text material better than they do. One strategy is to encourage students who mismonitor to create practice tests and questions to assess how complete their understanding is.

Learning how to use strategies effectively often takes time. Initially, it takes time to learn to execute the strategies, and it requires guidance and support from the teacher. With practice, students learn to execute strategies faster and more competently. *Practice* means that students use the effective strategy over and over again until they perform it automatically. To execute the strategies effectively, they need to have the strategies in long-term memory, and extensive practice makes this possible. Learners also need to be motivated to use the strategies. Thus, an important implication for helping students develop strategies such as organization is that once a strategy is learned, students usually need more time before they can use them efficiently (Schneider, 2004). Further, it is important for teachers to be aware that students may drop an effective strategy or continue to use a strategy that does not help them (Miller, 2000).

Do children use one strategy or multiple strategies in memory and problem solving? They often use more than one strategy (Schneider & Bjorklund, 1998; Siegler & Alibali, 2005). Most children benefit from generating a variety of alternative strategies and experimenting with different approaches to a problem and discovering what works well, when, and where (Schneider & Bjorklund, 1998). This is especially true for children from the middle elementary school grades on, although some cognitive psychologists believe that even young children should be encouraged to practice varying strategies (Siegler & Alibali, 2005).

Pressley and his colleagues (Pressley & Hilden, 2006; Pressley & others, 2001, 2003, 2004) have spent considerable time in recent years observing the use of strategy instruction by teachers and strategy use by students in elementary and secondary school classrooms. They conclude that teachers use of strategy instruction is far less complete and intense than what is needed for students to learn how to use strategies effectively. They argue that education needs to be restructured so that students are provided with more opportunities to become competent strategic learners.

A final point about strategies is that many strategies depend on prior knowledge (Pressley & Harris, 2006; Pressley & Hilden, 2006). For example, students can't apply organizational strategies to a list of items unless they know the correct categories into which the items fall. The point about the importance of prior knowledge in strategy use coincides with the emphasis in our discussion earlier in the chapter of how experts use more effective strategies than novices.

Review, Reflect, and Practice

(2) Explain the concept of metacognition and identify some ways to improve children's metacognition.

REVIEW

- How do young children compare with older children in their metacognitive abilities?
- According to Pressley and colleagues' Good Information-Processing model, competent cognition results from what interacting factors?
- How can children be helped to learn metacognitive strategies and self-regulation?

REFLECT

- How might the three steps in the Good Information-Processing model be part of teaching a topic to children? Select a topic that you might teach one day and try working through it as an example.

PRAXIS™ PRACTICE

1. Sharmala's uncle has just played a trick on her. He presented her with a can that looked like a can of peanuts. However, when she opened the can, a cloth snake sprang out at her. Sharmala thought the trick was very funny and can hardly wait to play it on her brother. When her uncle asked her what she thought her brother would expect to be in the can, she giggled and responded, "Peanuts, but won't he be surprised." This is an example of Sharmala's development of
   a. the ability to allocate attention to different aspects of a problem.
   b. problem-solving expertise.
   c. metamemory skills.
   d. theory of mind.
2. Marvel has learned to use strategies to solve math problems but does not use them to study for history exams or spelling quizzes. According to the Good Information-Processing model, the next step for Marvel's metacognitive development would most likely be to
   a. ask his teacher for specific strategies for studying history.

continued on page 114

   b. ask his parents about the benefits of using strategies for math.

   c. understand shared features of many different strategies.

   d. learn to attribute successful learning to use of strategies.

3. Mr. Quinton has taught his students the PQ4R strategy for reading textbooks, in hopes that it will help them on their next history test. The majority of his class improves their scores. Mr. Quinton is disappointed when in spite of improved performance, many of his students don't continue using the PQ4R strategy. What is the most plausible explanation for the students' behavior?

   a. They did not compare the results of using the PQ4R with their prior strategies.

   b. They don't have the requisite background knowledge to use the PQ4R strategy effectively.

   c. They have not had enough practice to use the strategy effectively.

   d. They have not yet developed expertise in using the strategy.

CRACK THE CASE
The Case of the Test

George has a test next week in his eighth-grade history class. He is having considerable difficulty remembering terms, names, and facts. On his last test, he identified General Sherman as a Vietnam War hero and Saigon as the capital of Japan. Historical dates are so confusing to him that he does not even try to remember them. In addition, George has difficulty spelling.

The test will consist of fifty objective test items (multiple-choice, true/false, and fill-in-the-blank) and two essay items. In general, George does better on essay items. He purposely leaves out any names about which he is uncertain and always omits dates. Sometimes he mixes up his facts, though, and often loses points for misspelled words. On objective items he has real problems. Usually, more than one answer will appear to be correct to him. Often he is "sure" he is correct, only to discover later that he was mistaken.

Before the last test, George tried to design some mnemonic devices to help him understand. He used acronyms, such as *HOMES* (for *H*uron, *O*ntario, *M*ichigan, *E*rie, and *S*uperior). While he remembered his acronyms quite well, he could not recall what each letter stood for. The result was a test paper filled with acronyms. Another time a classmate suggested that George try using concept maps. This classmate lent George the concept maps she had designed for her own use. George looked at them and found them to be very busy and confusing—he couldn't figure out what they even meant. They were not at all useful to him.

George has decided he is in need of some serious help if he is to pass this class. He has sought you out for his help.

1. What are the issues in this case?

2. With what type of learning is George having difficulty?

3. What type of learning is easier for George?

4. Design a study-skills program for George drawing on principles of the cognitive information-processing approach.

Metacognition: A Bridge Between Cognitive Psychology and Educational Practice

—Deanna Kuhn, & David Dean Jr.

*Deanna Kuhn is a professor and **David Dean Jr.** is a graduate research fellow, both at Teachers College, Columbia University.*

Preview

Although they have their differences, educational practitioners and academic researchers largely agree on a broad goal: to develop in students the kinds of thinking skills that will prepare them to contribute to a democratic society. But the two groups largely speak different languages. While educators frequently talk about critical thinking as an objective, researchers have largely avoided the term, preferring constructs that can be more precisely defined and measured. How do we connect critical thinking to modern research on cognition and learning? The authors propose the construct of metacognition as having the potential to bridge the concerns of educators and researchers whose work is addressed to the development of skilled thinking. Given its growing importance in studies of cognition and learning, teachers would benefit from an understanding of the mechanisms involved in metacognition and how best to foster it.

They have their differences to be sure, but today's educational practitioners and the academic theorists and researchers who concern themselves with education would likely agree on a broad goal: to develop in students the conceptual skills that will prepare them to contribute to a democratic society. Academics are inclined to decry the growing emphasis on "objective" standardized tests and to endorse "education for understanding" (Gardner, 1999) and development of the learning and thinking skills that will equip students to thrive in tomorrow's society (Bereiter, 2002; Kuhn, in press). Practitioners have long appeared to be of the same mind. The mission statement of the school district in which one of us was recently a teacher reads, "... our students will graduate with the knowledge, skills, and values necessary to be successful contributors to our democratic society." These educational goals can be traced back at least as far as Thomas Jefferson, who proclaimed (in a personal communication to W. Jarvis in 1820),

> I know no safe depository of the ultimate powers of the society but the people themselves; and if we think them not enlightened enough to exercise their control with a wholesome discretion, the remedy is not to take it from them, but to inform their discretion by education.

The challenge comes, of course, in trying to implement these lofty goals, and here we find academics and practitioners navigating largely unconnected paths. Academics pursue their agendas isolated from the demands of the classroom, while practitioners are pressed to find methods that work, and quickly. Even if they had the time and energy to seek them out, research findings are not disseminated in a way that facilitates practitioners' consumption of them. And practitioners are unlikely to do so, having acquired the attitude, conveyed from their preservice training onward, that research studies are not going to be of any direct help—findings are inconsistent and far removed from classroom realities. Scant attention in the preservice curriculum to educational research, and to the tools needed to evaluate it, is perhaps the strongest meta-level message to practitioners as to its value.

Bereiter (2002) argues that this state of affairs needs to change dramatically. Teachers must become collaborators in the research enterprise, in close contact with knowledge building in their field, seeing themselves and being accepted as part of the endeavor. Educational reformers, Bereiter says, "are likely to fail in even their immediate objectives if they do not become more deeply engaged with the unsolved problems of pedagogy" (p. 421).

A major "unsolved problem of pedagogy," we would add, is exactly what are the higher order thinking skills that will equip students to participate in modern democratic society? Practitioners traditionally have ignored the question. "We all know good thinking when we see it," their attitude has been, "so let's focus on finding effective techniques to foster it." Increasingly, it is becoming clear that this stance will not suffice. We cannot effectively teach cognitive skills in the absence of very clear and precise understandings of what those skills are (Kuhn, 1999, in press). Given the prevalence of the "we'll know good thinking when we see it" stance, educators today are more likely to agree on promising educational activities and settings for fostering thinking than on what the thinking skills are that they seek to induce in these settings.

Educators must collaborate with researchers in achieving these understandings, creating the need for a different kind of collaborative role for the academic researcher. In the past, when educators have turned to academics for assistance, the role the academic has been asked to play is that of technician: Here is what we want students to know; can you advise us of the most efficient means for them to acquire it? Instead, both practitioners and academics need to collaborate not just with respect to devising means but also in better defining ends—the nature of the intellectual skills that need to develop.

The kinds of cognitive skills that educators think about as coming under the heading of critical thinking are amenable to empirical investigation. It is possible to learn something about their nature and about how they develop. In our research we have examined two major families of skills—inquiry and argument (Kuhn, in press). The case we make is the same with respect to both. Teachers need a roadmap of what is developing and what needs to develop. In contrast to elementary skills such as classification or number that emerge in all normal children during the early years, skills of inquiry and argument do not necessarily develop, or at least do not develop to the degree we would like. Here the efforts of educators and researchers studying cognitive development truly intersect. Researchers need to be examining forms of development that are unlikely to occur in the absence of appropriate educational environments. At the same time, educators need the developmental knowledge that will inform their efforts.

What, then, needs to develop? A cornerstone of inquiry is the idea of a thesis, or question, and potential evidence that bears on it. There must be something to find out. Entertaining a thesis that is understood as capable of being disconfirmed by evidence reflects rudimentary skill in coordinating theory and evidence. Without this understanding and intention, there can be little point to inquiry. At worst, in the student's eyes inquiry becomes nothing more than demonstration of what one already accepts as true. Skills of argument have received much less attention than those of inquiry, but they are just as important. Children are not natural-born arguers. There are skills that need to develop. Our argument research indicates that young adolescents do not have great difficulty learning how to provide support for a claim. In debating someone who holds an opposing view, however, they find it much harder than do adults to attend to and address their opponent's claim and supporting argument (Felton & Kuhn, 2001). In analyses of their argumentive discourse with a peer, we found they engaged in exposition regarding their own argument almost four times as frequently as they sought clarification of the opponent's argument and four times as frequently as they undertook to critique the opponent's argument. Adults' utterances, in contrast, more often addressed the partner's argument, usually through counterargument. Adolescents appear to interpret the goal of argumentive discourse as prevailing over an opponent by superior presentation of one's own position. This objective, if successfully met, undermines the opponent's position but without addressing the opponent's argument. Deep-level processing of the opponent's argument, in addition to exposition of one's own argument and negotiating the mechanics of discourse, may represent cognitive overload for the novice arguer.

51 METACOGNITION AND CRITICAL THINKING

Definitions of critical thinking are numerous and wide-ranging. However, one non-controversial claim we can make about critical thinking is that it entails awareness of one's own thinking and reflection on the thinking of self and others as an object of cognition. Metacognition, a construct that is assuming an increasingly central place in cognitive development research, is defined in similar terms as awareness and management of one's own thought, or "thinking about thinking." Metacognition originates early in life, when children first become aware of their own and others' minds. But like many other intellectual skills, metacognitive skills typically do not develop to the level we would like.

In cognitive psychology, metacognitive functions are most often examined under the heading of "executive control." Whatever its exact label, the management of one's own cognition is crucial, as both researchers and practitioners are likely to have observed. It is usually not difficult to teach a child to perform a particular procedure in a particular context. But it is the meta-level of operations that determines whether the child will continue to exercise this skill in other settings once instruction is withdrawn and the child resumes meta-level control of his or her own behavior.

One way of supporting metacognitive development is to encourage students to reflect on and evaluate their activities. Doing so should heighten interest in the purpose of these activities. Why are we doing this? What was gained from having done it? Questions such as these are less likely to arise when activity is imposed by authority figures without negotiation, uating students' standing relative to one another—a function that so often steals attention away from any other objective.

Another source of metacognitive development is the interiorization that both Vygotksy and Piaget talked about, which occurs when forms that are originally social become covert within the individual. If students participate in discourse where they are frequently asked, "How do you know?" or "What makes you say that?" they become more likely to pose such questions to themselves. Eventually, we hope, they will interiorize the structure of argument as a framework for much of their own individual thinking. They will think in terms of issues or claims, with facts summoned in their service, rather than the reverse—storing up facts with the idea that some conclusion may emerge from them.

Metacognitive functions can be procedural or declarative. The former invokes awareness and management of one's own thinking. The latter involves one's broader understanding of thinking and knowing in general. It has been studied under the heading of epistemological understanding. Like thinking itself, the understanding of thinking undergoes development. The study of students' developing epistemological understanding has blossomed in the last decade. As a result, we now have a fairly convergent picture of a series of steps that mark development toward more mature epistemological understanding in the years from early childhood to adulthood.

52 EPISTEMOLOGICAL UNDERSTANDING AS A METACOGNITIVE DEVELOPMENT

Preschool age children are realists. They regard what one knows as an immediate reading of what's out there. Beliefs are faithful copies of reality. They are received directly from the external world, rather than constructed by the knower. Hence, there are no inaccurate renderings of events, nor any possibility of conflicting beliefs, since everyone is perceiving the same external reality. Minds provide everyone the very same pictures of reality.

Not until about age 4 does a knower begin to emerge in children's conceptions of knowing. Children become aware that mental representations, as products of the human mind, do not necessarily duplicate external reality. Before children achieve a concept of false belief, they are unwilling to attribute to another person a belief that they themselves know to be false. Once they attain this understanding, the knower, and knowledge as mental representations produced by knowers, come to life. The products of knowing, however, are still more firmly attached to the known object than to the knower. Hence, while inadequate or incorrect information can produce false beliefs, these are easily correctable by reference to an external reality—the known object. If you and I disagree, one of us is right and one is wrong and resolving the matter is simply a matter of finding out which is which. At this absolutist level of epistemological understanding, knowledge is an accumulating body of certain facts.

Further progress in epistemological understanding can be characterized as an extended task of coordinating the subjective with the objective elements of knowing. At the realist and absolutist levels, the objective dominates. By adolescence typically comes the likelihood of a radical change in epistemological understanding. In a word, everyone now becomes right. The discovery that reasonable people—even experts—disagree is the most likely source of recognizing the uncertain, subjective aspect of knowing. This recognition initially assumes such proportions, however, that it eclipses recognition of any objective standard that could serve as a basis for evaluating conflicting claims. Adolescents typically fall into what Chandler has called "a poisoned well of doubt," and they fall hard and deep. At this multiplist (sometimes called relativist) level of epistemological understanding, knowledge consists not of facts but of opinions, freely chosen by their holders as personal possessions and accordingly not open to challenge. Knowledge is now clearly seen as emanating from knowers, rather than the known, but at the significant cost of any discriminability among competing knowledge claims. Indeed, this lack of discriminability is equated with tolerance: Because everyone has a right to their opinion, all opinions are equally right. That ubiquitous slogan of adolescence—"whatever"—holds sway.

Evidence suggests that hoisting oneself out of the "whatever" well of multiplicity and indiscriminability is achieved at much greater effort than the quick and easy fall into its depths. Many adults remain absolutists or multiplists for life. Yet, by adulthood, many adolescents will have reintegrated the objective dimension of knowing to achieve the understanding that while everyone has a right to their opinion, some opinions are in fact more right than others, to the extent they are better supported by argument and evidence. Justification for a belief becomes more than personal preference. "Whatever" is no longer the automatic response to any assertion—there are now legitimate discriminations and choices to be made. Rather than facts or opinions, knowledge at this evaluativist level of epistemological understanding consists of judgments, which require support in a framework of alternatives, evidence, and argument. An evaluativist epistemology provides the intellectual basis for judging one idea as better than another, a basis more powerful than mere personal preference.

53 INTELLECTUAL VALUES

The evolution just described is a necessary condition for the development of intellectual values. Adolescents who never progress beyond the absolutist belief in certain knowledge, or the multiplist's equation of knowledge with personal preference, lack a reason to engage in sustained intellectual inquiry. If facts can be ascertained with certainty and are readily available to anyone who seeks them, as the absolutist understands, or if any claim is as valid as any other, as the multiplist understands, there is little point to expending the mental effort that the evaluation of claims entails. Only at the evaluativist level are thinking and reason recognized as essential support for beliefs and actions. Thinking is the process that enables us to make informed choices between conflicting claims. Understanding this leads one to value thinking and to be willing to expend the effort that it entails (Table 4.1).

Table 4.1 Levels of Epistemological Understanding

Level	Assertions	Knowledge	Critical Thinking
Realist	Assertions are COPIES of an external reality.	Knowledge comes from an external source and is certain.	Critical thinking is unnecessary.
Absolutist	Assertions are FACTS that are correct or incorrect in their representation of reality.	Knowledge comes from an external source and is certain but not directly accessible, producing false beliefs.	Critical thinking is a vehicle for comparing assertions to reality and determining their truth or falsehood.
Multiplist	Assertions are OPINIONS freely chosen by and accountable only to their owners.	Knowledge is generated by human minds and therefore uncertain.	Critical thinking is irrelevant.
Evaluativist	Assertions are JUDGMENTS that can be evaluated and compared according to criteria of argument and evidence.	Knowledge is generated by human minds and is uncertain but susceptible to evaluation.	Critical thinking is valued as a vehicle that promotes sound assertions and enhances understanding.

Our research has found striking differences across cultural groups and subcultural groups within the United States in the responses of parents and children to several questions like this one:

> Many social issues, like the death penalty, gun control, or medical care, are pretty much matters of personal opinion, and there is no basis for saying that one person's opinion is any better than another's. So there's not much point in people having discussions about these kinds of issues. Do you strongly agree, sort of agree, or disagree?

Reasons respondents offer for disagreement are similar and refer to values of discussion in enhancing individual and/or collective understanding, solving problems, and resolving conflicts. Reasons offered for agreement, however, tend to be of two distinct types. Some participants respond along these lines, suggestive of the multiplist level of epistemological understanding: "It's not worth it to discuss it because you're not going to get anywhere; everyone has a right to think what they want to." Others take this position, suggestive of the absolutist's equation of knowledge with right answers: "It's not worth it to discuss it because it's not something you can get a definite answer to."

Parents and children within the cultures and subcultures we have studied respond similarly to one another. Middle school and high school students in American ethnic subcultures, however, show some movement away from their parents' response patterns in the direction of those of their American peers. These results suggest that parents do matter in transmitting intellectual values to their children. At the same time, children to a significant degree construct these values anew in a context of their peer culture, especially when the values of the culture outside the home deviate from those within the home.

The transitions from realist to absolutist to multiplist epistemological understanding don't seem to require a great deal of tending by those wishing to scaffold children's development. Unless the child's experience is unusually restricted, children become aware that people's beliefs vary and they must figure out a way of understanding this state of affairs. The vast majority take at least a brief dip, and more often a prolonged one, into the well of multiplicity. The last major transition, however, from multiplist to evaluativist, is another story. It is helping young people climb out of the multiplist well that requires the concerned attention of parents and educators, especially if it is this progression that provides the necessary foundation for intellectual values.

The goal will not be achieved by exhortation—by telling students that a particular activity is valuable, or even how or why it's valuable. A more promising adult role involves introducing young people to activities that have a value that becomes self-evident in the course of engaging them and developing the skills the activities entail. By serving as a guide, or coach, as students engage in such activities, the adult models his or her own commitment to the activity and belief in its worth. As students' skill and commitment and self-direction increase, the coach's role diminishes.

Much of what we ask students to do in school simply does not have these characteristics. We have been experimenting with involving middle school students in activities that we believe have this crucial characteristic of revealing their intrinsic value as they are engaged in them. These activities fall under the broad headings of inquiry and argument and entail the skills that have been described previously. We are able to follow students' progress microgenetically as they develop these two families of skills. Through their involvement in such activities, we hope students will discover for themselves that there is something to find out and a point to arguing, sufficient to make the effort worthwhile. It is only their own experiences that will lead them to the conviction that inquiry and reasoned argument offer the most promising path to deciding between competing claims, resolving conflicts, solving problems, and achieving goals.

CONCLUSION

The growing reliance on standardized testing of basic skills, with higher and higher stakes, poses a grave danger to the quality of education. We need better definitions of what it means to be an educated person (Bereiter, 2002; Kuhn, in press). The skills of inquiry and argument, we believe, should be central to such definitions. If so, it is essential to understand more about these skills. But these skills need to be understood not just as performance tools; it is essential that the broader meta-level structure develop that reflects understanding of how, when, and why to use them. This is the critical thinking ability that educators and researchers want to see students acquire.

We suggest that cognitive development researchers and educators can and must collaborate in constructing these more adequate definitions of the ends toward which the educational enterprise is directed. Fewer and fewer cognitive development researchers remain content to preoccupy themselves with narrow agendas while ignoring the larger, more difficult questions that the education of children poses. At the same time, educators for the most part are discouraged by the professional challenges facing them, would like to be part of the knowledge-seeking process, and appreciate the importance of evidence as a basis for policy (Feuer, Towne, & Shavelson, 2002). Without being naïve about the obstacles involved, we would conclude that both groups seem poised for meaningful collaboration.

References

Bereiter, C. (2002). *Education and mind in the knowledge age.* Mahwah, NJ: Erlbaum.

Feuer, M.J., Towne, L., & Shavelson, R.J. (2002). Scientific culture and educational research. *Educational Researcher, 31*, 4–14.

Felton, M., & Kuhn, D. (2001). The development of argumentive discourse skills. *Discourse Processes, 32*, 135–153.

Gardner, H. (1999). *The disciplined mind: What all students should understand.* New York: Simon and Schuster.

Kuhn, D. (1999). A developmental model of critical thinking. *Educational Researcher, 28*, 16–25, 46.

Kuhn, D. (in press). *Education for thinking.* Cambridge MA: Harvard University Press.

Unit 5

Piagetian Stages

Even though young children make distinctive progress in this substage, their pre-operational thought still has two important limitations: egocentrism and animism. *Egocentrism* is the inability to distinguish between one's own perspective and someone else's perspective. The following telephone interaction between 4-year-old Mary, who is at home, and her father, who is at work, typifies egocentric thought:

Father: Mary, is Mommy there?
Mary: (Silently nods)
Father: Mary, can I speak to Mommy?
Mary: (Nods again silently)

Mary's response is egocentric in that she fails to consider her father's perspective; she does not realize that he cannot see her nod.

Piaget and Barbel Inhelder (1969) initially studied young children's egocentrism by devising the three mountains task (see Figure 5.2). The child walks around the model of the mountains and becomes familiar with what the mountains look like from different perspectives. The child also can see that there are different objects on the mountains. The child then is seated on one side of the table on which the mountains are placed. The experimenter moves a doll to different locations around the table. At each location the child is asked to select from a series of photos the one that most accurately reflects the view the doll is seeing. Children in the preoperational stage often pick the view that reflects where they are sitting rather than the doll's view.

Animism also characterizes preoperational thought. It is the belief that inanimate objects have "lifelike" qualities and are capable of action. A young child might show animism by saying, "That tree pushed the leaf off and it fell down" or "The sidewalk made me mad. It made me fall down."

What further cognitive changes take place in the preoperational stage? The **intuitive thought substage** is the second substage of preoperational thought, starting at about 4 years of age and lasting until about 7 years of age. At this substage, children begin to use primitive reasoning and want to know the answers to all sorts of questions. Piaget called this substage "intuitive" because the children seem so sure about their knowledge and understanding yet are unaware of how they know what they know. That is, they say they know something but know it without the use of rational thinking.

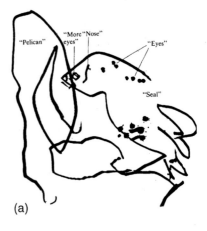

(a)

(b)

FIGURE 5.1 Developmental Changes in Children's Drawings
(a) A 3½-year-old's symbolic drawing. Halfway into this drawing, the 3½-year-old artist said it was "a pelican kissing a seal." (b) This 11-year-old's drawing is neater and more realistic but also less inventive.

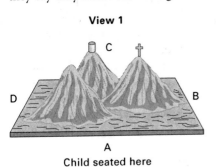

FIGURE 5.2 The Three Mountains Task

View 1 shows the child's perspective from where he or she is sitting. View 2 is an example of the photograph the child would be shown, mixed in with others from different perspectives. To correctly identify this view, the child has to take the perspective of a person sitting at spot *b*. Invariably, a perschool child who thinks in a preoperational way cannot perform this task. When asked what a view of the mountains looks like from position *b*, the child selects a photograph taken from location *a*, the child's view at the time.

intuitive thought substage The second substage of preoperational thought, lasting from about 4 to 7 years of age. Children begin to use primitive reasoning and want to know the answer to all sorts of questions. They seem so sure about their knowledge in this substage but are unaware of how they know what they know.

FIGURE 5.3 Arrays

(a) A random array of objects.
(b) An ordered array of objects.

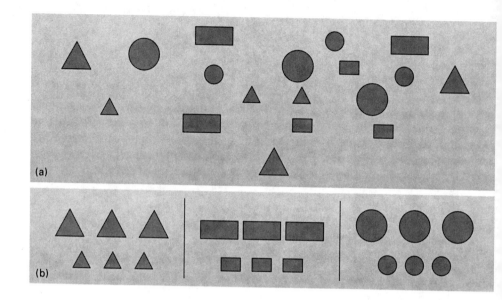

An example of young children's limitation in reasoning ability is the difficulty they have putting things into correct categories. Look at the collection of objects in Figure 5.3a. You would probably respond to the direction "Put the things together that you believe belong together" by grouping the objects by size and shape. Your sorting might look something like that shown in Figure 5.3b. Faced with a similar collection of objects that can be sorted on the basis of two or more properties, preoperational children seldom are capable of using these properties consistently to sort the objects into appropriate groupings. In the social realm, if a 4-year-old girl is given the task of dividing her peers into groups according to whether they are friends and whether they are boys or girls, she is unlikely to arrive at a classification of friendly boys, friendly girls, unfriendly boys, unfriendly girls.

Many of these preoperational examples show a characteristic of thought called **centration,** which involves focusing (or centering) attention on one characteristic to the exclusion of all others. Centration is most clearly present in preoperational children's lack of **conservation,** the idea that some characteristic of an object stays the same even though the object might change in appearance. For example, to adults it is obvious that a certain amount of liquid stays the same regardless of a container's shape. But this is not obvious at all to young children. Rather, they are struck by the height of the liquid in the container. In this type of conservation task (Piaget's most famous), a child is presented with two identical beakers, each filled to the same level with liquid (see Figure 5.4). The child is asked if the beakers have the same amount of liquid. The child usually says yes. Then the liquid from one beaker is poured into a third beaker, which is taller and thinner. The child now is asked if the amount of liquid in the tall, thin beaker is equal to the liquid that remains in the second original beaker. Children younger than 7 or 8 usually say no. They justify their answer by referring to the differing height or width of the beakers. Older children usually answer yes. They justify their answers appropriately: If you poured the liquid back, the amount would still be the same.

In Piaget's view, failing the conservation of liquid task indicates that the child is at the preoperational stage of thinking. Passing the test suggests the child is at the concrete operational stage of thinking.

According to Piaget, preoperational children also cannot perform what he called *operations.* In Piaget's theory, operations are mental representations that are reversible.

centration Focusing, or centering, attention on one characteristic to the exclusion of all others; characteristic of preoperational thinking.

conservation The idea that some characteristic of an object stays the same even though the object might change in appearance; a cognitive ability that develops in the concrete operational stage, according to Piaget.

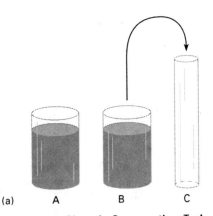
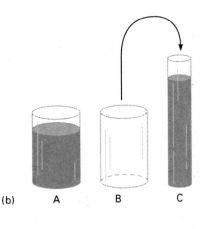

(a) A   B   C   (b) A   B   C

FIGURE 5.4 Piaget's Conservation Task

The beaker test is a well-known Piagetian test to determine whether a child can think operationally—that is, can mentally reverse actions and show conservation of the substance. (a) Two identical beakers are presented to the child. Then, the liquid is poured from B into C, which is taller and thinner than A or B. (b) The child is asked if these beakers (A and C) have the same amount of liquid. The preoperational child says no. When asked to point to the beaker that has more liquid, the preoperational child points to the tall, thin beaker.

As in the beaker task, preschool children have difficulty understanding that reversing an action brings about the original conditions from which the action began. These two examples should further help you understand Piaget's concepts of operations. A young child might know that $4 + 2 = 6$ but not understand that the reverse, $6 - 2 = 4$, is true. Or let's say a preschooler walks to his friend's house each day but always gets a ride home. If asked to walk home from his friend's house, he probably would reply that he didn't know the way because he never had walked home before.

Some developmentalists do not believe Piaget was entirely correct in his estimate of when conservation skills emerge. For example, Rochel Gelman (1969) trained preschool children to attend to relevant aspects of the conservation task. This improved their conservation skills. Gelman also has shown that attentional training on one type of conservation task, such as number, improves young children's performance on another type of conservation task, such as mass. She argues that young children develop conservation skills earlier than Piaget envisioned and that such skills can be improved with attentional training.

Further, children show considerable variation in attaining conservation skills. Researchers have found that 50 percent of children develop conservation of mass at 6 to 9 years of age, 50 percent demonstrate conservation of length at 4 to 9 years of age, 50 percent show conservation of area at 7 to 9 years of age, and 50 percent of children don't attain conservation of weight until 8 to 10 years of age (Horowitz & others, 2005; Sroufe & others, 1992).

Yet another characteristic of preoperational children is that they ask a lot of questions. The barrage begins around age 3. By about 5, they have just about exhausted the adults around them with "Why?" "Why" questions signal the emergence of the child's interest in figuring out why things are the way they are. Following is a sampling of 4- to 6-year-olds' questions (Elkind, 1976):

"What makes you grow up?"

"What makes you stop growing?"

"Who was the mother when everybody was a baby?"

"Why do leaves fall?"

"Why does the sun shine?"

BEST PRACTICES
Strategies for Working with Preoperational Thinkers

1. *To reduce egocentrism, involve children in social interactions.*

2. *Ask children to make comparisons.* These might involve such concepts as bigger, taller, wider, heavier, and longer.

3. *Give children experience in ordering operations.* For example, have children line up in rows from tall to short and vice versa. Bring in various examples of animal and plant life cycles, such as several photographs of butterfly development or the sprouting of beans or kernels of corn. Examples of these natural stages help children's ordering ability.

4. *Have children draw scenes with perspective.* Encourage them to make the objects in their drawings appear to be at the same location as in the scene they are viewing.

For example, if they see a horse at the end of a field, they should place the horse in the same location in the drawing.

5. *Construct an inclined plane or a hill.* Let children roll marbles of various sizes down the plane. Ask them to compare how quickly the different-size marbles reach the bottom. This should help them understand the concept of speed.

6. *Ask children to justify their answers when they draw conclusions.* For example, when they say that pouring a liquid from a short, wide container into a tall, thin container makes the liquid change in volume, ask, "Why do you think so?" or "How could you prove this to one of your friends?"

The Concrete Operational Stage   The **concrete operational stage,** the third Piagetian stage of cognitive development, lasts from about 7 to about 11 years of age. Concrete operational thought involves using operations. Logical reasoning replaces intuitive reasoning, but only in concrete situations. Classification skills are present, but abstract problems go unsolved.

A concrete operation is a reversible mental action pertaining to real, concrete objects. Concrete operations allow the child to coordinate several characteristics rather than focus on a single property of an object. At the concrete operational level, children can do mentally what they previously could do only physically, and they can reverse concrete operations. For example, to test conservation of matter, the child is presented with two identical balls of clay. The experimenter rolls one ball into a long, thin shape. The child is asked if there is more clay in the ball or in the long, thin piece of clay. By the time children are seven or eight years old, most answer that the amount of clay is the same. To answer this problem correctly, children have to imagine that the clay ball can be rolled out into a long, thin strip and then returned to its original round shape. In this example, the preoperational child would have focused either on height or length. The concrete operational child coordinates information about both dimensions.

An important concrete operation is classifying or dividing things into different sets or subsets and considering their interrelationships. Reasoning about a family tree of four generations reveals a child's concrete operational skills (Furth & Wachs, 1975). The family tree shown in Figure 5.5 suggests that the grandfather (A) has three children (B, C, and D), each of whom has two children (E through J), and one of these children (J) has three children (K, L, and M). Concrete operational thinkers understand the classification. For example, they can reason that person J can at the same time be father, brother, and grandson. A preoperational thinker cannot.

Some Piagetian tasks require children to reason about relations between classes. One such task is **seriation,** the concrete operation that involves ordering stimuli along some quantitative dimension (such as length). To see if students can serialize, a teacher might place eight sticks of different lengths in a haphazard way on a table.

concrete operational stage
Piaget's third cognitive developmental stage, occurring between about 7 to 11 years of age. At this stage, the child thinks operationally and logical reasoning replaces intuitive thought but only in concrete situations; classification skills are present but abstract problems present difficulties.

seriation A concrete operation that involves ordering stimuli along some quantitative dimension.

BEST PRACTICES
Strategies for Working with Concrete Operational Thinkers

1. *Encourage students to discover concepts and principles.* Ask relevant questions about what is being studied to help them focus on some aspect of their learning. Refrain from telling students the answers to their questions outright. Try to get them to reach the answers through their own thinking.

2. *Involve children in operational tasks.* These include adding, subtracting, multiplying, dividing, ordering, seriating, and reversing. Use concrete materials for these tasks, possibly introducing math symbols later.

3. *Plan activities in which students practice the concept of ascending and descending classification hierarchies.* Have students list the following in order of size (such as largest to smallest): city of Atlanta, state of Georgia, country of United States, Western Hemisphere, and planet Earth.

4. *Include activities that require conservation of area, weight, and displaced volume.* Realize that there is considerable variation in children's attainment of conservation across different domains.

5. *Create activities in which children order and reverse order.* Many third-graders have difficulty in reversing order, such as going from tall to short rather than short to tall. They also have trouble, after listing the cities they will pass through in taking a trip, reversing the order for coming home.

6. *Continue to ask students to justify their answers when they solve problems.* Help them to check the validity and accuracy of their conclusions.

7. *Encourage children to work in groups and exchange thoughts with each other.* For example, ask a group of children to create a play, sharing their viewpoints with each other.

8. *When trying to teach anything complex, create props and visual aids.* For example, in teaching a social science lesson on what a democracy is, show a video that illustrates the concept. Encourage students to manipulate and experiment in science, use concrete materials in mathematics, create and act out in language arts, and discuss their perspectives with each other and take field trips in social studies.

The teacher then asks the student to order the sticks by length. Many young children end up with two or three small groups of "big" sticks or "little" sticks rather than a correct ordering of all eight sticks. Another mistaken strategy they use is to evenly line up the tops of the sticks but ignore the bottoms. The concrete operational thinker simultaneously understands that each stick must be longer than the one that precedes it and shorter than the one that follows it.

Transitivity involves the ability to reason about and logically combine relationships. If a relation holds between a first object and a second object, and also holds between the second object and a third object, then it also holds between the first and third objects. For example, consider three sticks (A, B, and C) of differing lengths. A is the longest, B is intermediate in length, and C is the shortest. Does the child understand that if A is longer than B, and B is longer than C, then A is longer than C? In Piaget's theory, concrete operational thinkers do; preoperational thinkers do not.

The Formal Operational Stage   The **formal operational stage,** which emerges at about 11 to 15 years of age, is Piaget's fourth and final cognitive stage. At this stage, individuals move beyond reasoning only about concrete experiences and think in more abstract, idealistic, and logical ways.

The abstract quality of formal operational thinking is evident in verbal problem solving. The concrete operational thinker needs to see the concrete elements A, B,

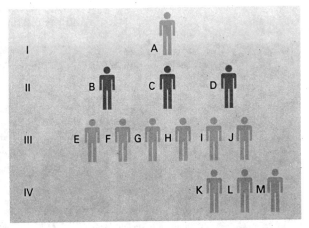

FIGURE 5.5 Classification
Classification is an important ability in concrete operational thought. When shown a family tree of four generations (I to IV), the preoperational child has trouble classifying the members of the four generations; the concrete operational child can classify the members vertically, horizontally, and obliquely (up and down and across).

transitivity The ability to reason and logically combine relationships.

formal operational stage Piaget's fourth cognitive developmental stage, which emerges between about 11 and 15 years of age; thought is more abstract, idealistic, and logical in this stage.

hypothetical-deductive reasoning Piaget's formal operational concept that adolescents can develop hypotheses to solve problems and systematically reach (deduce) a conclusion.

and C to make the logical inference that if A = B and B = C, then A = C. In contrast, the formal operational thinker can solve this problem when it is verbally presented.

Accompanying the abstract nature of formal operational thought are the abilities to idealize and imagine possibilities. At this stage, adolescents engage in extended speculation about the ideal qualities they desire in themselves and others. These idealistic thoughts can merge into fantasy. Many adolescents become impatient with their newfound ideals and the problems of how to live them out.

At the same time as adolescents are thinking more abstractly and idealistically, they also are beginning to think more logically. As formal operational thinkers, they think more like scientists. They devise plans to solve problems and systematically test solutions. Piaget's term **hypothetical-deductive reasoning** embodies the concept that adolescents can develop hypotheses (best hunches) about ways to solve problems and systematically reach a conclusion.

One example of hypothetical-deductive reasoning involves a modification of the familiar game "Twenty Questions." Individuals are shown a set of 42 color pictures displayed in a rectangular array (six rows of seven pictures each) and asked to determine which picture the experimenter has in mind (that is, which is "correct"). The subjects are only allowed to ask questions to which the experimenter can answer yes or no. The object of the game is to select the correct picture by asking as few questions as possible.

Adolescents who are deductive hypothesis testers formulate a plan and test a series of hypotheses, which considerably narrows the field of choices. The most effective plan is a "halving" strategy (*Q:* Is the picture in the right half of the array? *A:* No. *Q:* OK. Is it in the top half? And so on). A correct halving strategy guarantees the answer in seven questions or less. In contrast, the concrete operational thinker might persist with questions that continue to test some of the same possibilities that previous questions could have eliminated. For example, they might ask whether the correct picture is in row 1 and are told that it is not. Later, they ask whether the picture is *X*, which is in row 1.

Thus, formal operational thinkers test their hypotheses with judiciously chosen questions and tests. In contrast, concrete operational thinkers often fail to understand the relation between a hypothesis and a well-chosen test of it, stubbornly clinging to ideas that already have been discounted.

A form of egocentrism also emerges in adolescence (Elkind, 1978). *Adolescent egocentrism* is the heightened self-consciousness reflected in adolescents' beliefs that others are as interested in them as they themselves are. Adolescent egocentrism also includes a sense of personal uniqueness. It involves the desire to be noticed, visible, and "on stage." Consider 12-year-old Tracy, who says, "Oh my gosh! I can't believe it. Help! I can't stand it!" Her mother asks, "What is the matter?" Tracy responds, "Everyone in here is looking at me." The mother queries, "Why?" Tracy says, "This one hair won't stay in place," as she rushes to the rest room to plaster it with hairspray. Perceived uniqueness also is evident in 16-year-old Margaret's feelings after her boyfriend has broken up with her. She tells her mother, "You have no idea how I feel. You have never experienced this kind of pain."

Egocentrism is a normal adolescent occurrence, more common in the middle school than in high school years. However, for some individuals, adolescent egocentrism can contribute to reckless

Might adolescents' ability to reason hypothetically and to evaluate what is ideal versus what is real lead them to engage in demonstrations, such as this protest related to better ethnic relations? What other causes might be attractive to adolescents' newfound cognitive abilities of hypothetical-deductive reasoning and idealistic thinking?

BEST PRACTICES
Strategies for Working with Formal Operational Thinkers

1. *Realize that many adolescents are not full-fledged formal operational thinkers.* Although Piaget believed formal operational thought emerges between 11 and 15 years of age, many students in this age range actually are concrete operational thinkers or are just beginning to use formal operational thought. Thus, many of the teaching strategies discussed earlier regarding the education of concrete operational thinkers still apply to many young adolescents. As discussed next, Jerri Hall, a math teacher at Miller Magnet High School, in Georgia, emphasizes that when a curriculum is too formal and too abstract it will go over students' heads.

THROUGH THE EYES OF TEACHERS
Piaget as a Guide

I use Piaget's developmental theory as a guide in helping children learn math. In the sixth, seventh, and eighth grades, children are moving from the concrete to the abstract stage in their cognitive processes; therefore, when I teach, I try to use different methods to aid my students to understand a concept. For example, I use fraction circles to help students understand how to add, subtract, multiply, and divide fractions, and the students are allowed to use these until they become proficient with the algorithms. I try to incorporate hands-on experiences in which students discover the rules themselves, rather than just teaching the methods and having the students practice them with drill. It is extremely important for students to understand the why behind a mathematical rule so they can better understand the concept.

---

2. *Propose a problem and invite students to form hypotheses about how to solve it.* For example, a teacher might say, "Imagine that a girl has no friends. What should she do?"

3. *Present a problem and suggest several ways it might be approached.* Then ask questions that stimulate students to evaluate the approaches. For example, describe several ways to investigate a robbery and ask students to evaluate which is best.

4. *Select a particular problem that is familiar to the class and ask questions related to it.* For example, the teacher asks, "What factors should be considered if we are going to be able to get the economy back on track?"

5. *Ask students to discuss their prior conclusions.* For example, ask, "What steps did you go through in solving this problem?"

6. *Develop projects and investigations for students to carry out.* Periodically ask them how they are going about collecting and interpreting the data.

7. *Encourage students to create hierarchical outlines when you ask them to write papers.* Make sure they understand how to organize their writing in terms of general and specific points. The abstractness of formal operational thinking also means that teachers with students at this level can encourage them to use metaphors.

8. *Recognize that adolescents are more likely to use formal operational thinking in the areas in which they have the most expertise and experience.* For example, a student who loves English and reads and writes a lot might use formal operational thinking in that area. The same student, however, might not like math and might show concrete operational thinking in that area.

---

behavior, including suicidal thoughts, drug use, and failure to use contraceptives during sexual intercourse. Egocentricity leads some adolescents to think that they are invulnerable.

Evaluating Piaget's Theory What were Piaget's main contributions? Has his theory withstood the test of time?

Contributions Piaget is a giant in the field of developmental psychology. We owe to him the present field of children's cognitive development. We owe to him a long list of masterful concepts including assimilation and accommodation, object permanence, egocentrism, conservation, and hypothetical-deductive reasoning. Along with William James and John Dewey, we also owe Piaget the current vision of children as active,

Many adolescent girls spend long hours in front of the mirror, depleting cans of hairspray, tubes of lipstick, and jars of cosmetics. How might this behavior be related to changes in adolescent cognitive and physical development?

Piaget is shown here with his family. Piaget's careful observations of his three children—Lucienne, Laurent, and Jacqueline—contributed to the development of his cognitive theory.

neo-Piagetians Developmental psychologists who believe that Piaget got some things right but that his theory needs considerable revision; emphasize how to process information through attention, memory, and strategies.

constructive thinkers. And we owe to him the current belief that concepts do not emerge all of a sudden, full-blown, but instead emerge through a series of partial accomplishments that lead to increasingly comprehensive understanding (Haith & Benson, 1998).

Piaget also was a genius when it came to observing children. His careful observations showed us inventive ways to discover how children act on and adapt to their world (Vidal, 2000). Piaget showed us some important things to look for in cognitive development, such as the shift from preoperational to concrete operational thinking. He also showed us how children need to make their experiences fit their schemas (cognitive frameworks) yet simultaneously adapt their schemas to experience. Piaget also revealed how cognitive growth is likely to occur if the context is structured to allow gradual movement to the next higher level.

Criticisms   Piaget's theory has not gone unchallenged. Questions have been raised in the following areas:

- *Estimates of children's competence.* Some cognitive abilities emerge earlier than Piaget thought (Bornstein, Arterberry, & Mash, 2005; Cohen & Cashon, 2006). For example, some aspects of object permanence emerge earlier than he believed. Even 2-year-olds are nonegocentric in some contexts. When they realize that another person will not see an object, they investigate whether the person is blindfolded or looking in a different direction. Conservation of number has been demonstrated as early as age 3, although Piaget did not think it emerged until 7. Young children are not as uniformly "pre-" this and "pre-" that (precausal, preoperational) as Piaget thought (Flavell, Miller, & Miller, 2002).

- Other cognitive abilities can emerge later than Piaget thought. Many adolescents still think in concrete operational ways or are just beginning to master formal operations. Even many adults are not formal operational thinkers. In sum, recent theoretical revisions highlight more cognitive competencies of infants and young children and more cognitive shortcomings of adolescents and adults (Bauer, 2006; Keating, 2004).

- *Stages.* Piaget conceived of stages as unitary structures of thought. Thus, his theory assumes developmental synchrony—that is, various aspects of a stage should emerge at the same time. Some concrete operational concepts, however, do not appear in synchrony. For example, children do not learn to conserve at the same time as they learn to cross-classify. Thus, most contemporary developmentalists agree that children's cognitive development is not as stagelike as Piaget thought (Bjorklund, 2005; Garton, 2004; Horowitz & others, 2005; Kuhn & Franklin, 2006; Siegler, 2006).

- *Training children to reason at a higher level.* Some children who are at one cognitive stage (such as preoperational) can be trained to reason at a higher cognitive stage (such as concrete operational). This poses a problem for Piaget. He argued that such training is only superficial and ineffective, unless the child is at a maturational transition point between the stages (Gelman & Opfer, 2004; Gelman & Williams, 1998).

- *Culture and education.* Culture and education exert stronger influences on children's development than Piaget believed (Greenfield, Suzuki, & Rothstein-Fisch, 2006). The age at which children acquire conservation skills is related to the extent to which their culture provides relevant practice (Cole, 2005, 2006). For example, an outstanding teacher can guide students' learning experiences that will help them move to a higher cognitive stage.

Still, some developmental psychologists believe we should not throw out Piaget altogether (Smith, 2004). These **neo-Piagetians** argue that Piaget got some things right but that his theory needs considerable revision. In their revision of Piaget, neo-Piagetians emphasize how children process information through attention, memory, and strategies (Case, 2000). They especially believe that a more accurate vision of children's thinking requires more knowledge of strategies, how fast and how automatically children process information, the particular cognitive task involved, and the division of cognitive problems into smaller, more precise steps.

Despite such criticisms, Piaget's theory is a very important one, and as we already have seen, information about his stages of development can be applied to teaching children. Here are some more ideas for applying Piaget's theory to children's education.

An outstanding teacher and education in the logic of science and mathematics are important cultural experiences that promote the development of operational thought. Might Piaget have underestimated the roles of culture and schooling in children's cognitive development?

Adolescent Thought

Thought takes interesting turns in early adolescence and carries teenagers places children don't easily go. Adolescents can think about things that don't exist and may never exist. They can think about what is possible as well as what actually is. Thinking becomes highly systematic and logical. This is not to say that adolescents are always logical and that children never are, or that children never consider possibilities as well as realities, or that adolescents always reason in the abstract. It is, rather, that adolescents do so more often and with greater ease. Each of these characteristics of adolescent thought—thinking abstractly, thinking hypothetically, and thinking logically—is discussed in the sections that follow.

Thinking Abstractly

"How is a horse like a goldfish?" If you ask adolescents this question, they are likely to come up with any number of answers. They might say, "Well, a horse and a fish are both animals," or "Both have to eat to live," or "Both take in oxygen and give off carbon dioxide." Children are more likely to stare you down. You can almost hear them think, "That was a stupid question!" In any event, they are not likely to think of any similarities. Why is their response so different from that of adolescents?

Children tend to think of things in terms of their physical properties. With horses and goldfish, this approach doesn't take them very far. If you had asked how a horse was like a dog, they would have had no problem: Both have four legs. They could tell you how a horse is like a cow: Both are large and eat grass. But as long as their thoughts are bound by the physical characteristics of things, fish remain worlds removed from horses. Adolescents can think of things as members of classes and can even think of ways to classify those classes (Drumm & Jackson, 1996). An adolescent can say, for example, "Both are animals, and animals can be either aquatic or terrestrial."

Thinking Hypothetically

Thinking abstractly is related to another characteristic of adolescent thought: hypothetical thinking. Adolescents can turn a problem around in their minds and come up with possible variations it might take (Figure 5.6). Only then do they start to work, testing each possibility to find the one that applies in that situation. Being able to imagine what is possible, instead of thinking only of what is real, allows adolescents to think hypothetically.

Children, in contrast, focus on the actual, perceptible elements of a situation and rarely speculate about possibilities they cannot generate by actually doing something. They are more likely to jump in and do something with no plan of attack. Even if they succeed in solving the problem, they are not likely to have kept a record of what they did. John Flavell, a psychologist at Stanford University who has written widely on cognitive development, remarks that the school child's "speculations about other possibilities—that is, about other potential, as yet undetected realities—occur only with difficulty and as a last resort. An ivory-tower theorist the elementary school child is not" (Flavell, Miller, & Miller, 1993).

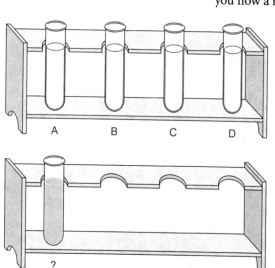

FIGURE 5.6 A Problem Involving Chemical Solutions That Requires Hypothetical Thinking to Solve.
When asked which combination of these four solutions produces a yellow liquid, adolescents think of all the possible combinations and systematically test each one, whereas children combine the solutions in a haphazard way.

Source: Adapted from B. Inhelder & J. Piaget. (1958). *The growth of logical thinking from childhood to adolescence.* New York: Basic Books.

Thinking Logically

As thought becomes abstract, adolescents are able to test different ideas against one another to establish their truth. They become aware of the logical relations that exist among ideas and can use logical consistency to determine whether a statement is true or false. Children check their ideas against hard facts; so do adolescents, but logical consistency is equally compelling for them.

This difference is dramatically illustrated in a simple experiment. Adolescents and children are shown poker chips and asked to judge whether statements about the chips are true or false. Sometimes the chips are hidden in the experimenter's hand; at other times they are clearly visible. The experimenter has just picked up a green chip and holds it in clear view. He says, "The chip in my hand is either green or not green." Both the adolescent and the child agree that the statement is true. Next the experimenter holds up a chip that is hidden in his hand and says, "The chip in my hand is either red or not red." The adolescent knows the statement must be true and agrees. The child says, "I can't tell," and asks to see the chip! Children evaluate statements such as these by comparing them to what they can see, not realizing that they could still evaluate their truth based on logical properties. Adolescents know that thoughts can be checked against themselves for logical consistency (Osherson & Markman, 1975).

One might assume, at this point, that all adolescents think and solve problems alike. But thinking, like every other aspect of development, is highly individual. Tremendous differences exist among early adolescents in the rate at which they acquire new reasoning abilities, and many adolescents do not reason in these ways even by the end of middle school or junior high (Figure 5.7). Instead, thinking improves with age throughout adolescence (Arnett & Taber, 1994).

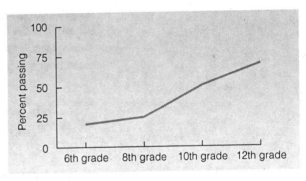

FIGURE 5.7 Adolescents Passing Piaget's Measures of Formal Thought.
Reasoning improves with age throughout adolescence; late adolescents can solve more of Piaget's tasks than early adolescents.

Source: S. C. Martorano. (1977). A developmental analysis of performance on Piaget's formal operations tasks. *Developmental Psychology, 13*, 666–672.

The Self and Gender

"Who in the world am I? Ah, *that's* the great puzzle," said Lewis Carroll's Alice in Wonderland, after her size had abruptly changed—again. Solving Alice's "puzzle" is a lifelong process of getting to know one's self.

An important function of the self is what Piaget called *organization*, the newborn's primary task. Without organization, the world would seem chaotic, a jumble of confusing sights and sounds. The self's attachment to a caregiver enables infants to organize working models of what they can expect in the way of food, nurture, and affection and how to behave in order to get those needs met. Throughout childhood and adolescence, the self *shapes goals*, both immediate and long run, and *monitors and regulates behavior* in comparison with socially approved standards (Harter, 1998).

56 THE I-SELF AND THE ME-SELF: INFANCY AND TODDLERHOOD

William James, in the late nineteenth century, proposed a concept of the self that is widely accepted today. James (1950) described two selves: the *I-self* and the *Me-self*, the knower and the known. The *I-self* is a subjective entity that constructs and seeks to know the Me-self. The *Me-self* is what can objectively be known about the self. It is called the *self-concept*.

The *self-concept* is our image of ourselves. It is what the I-self believes about the Me-self—our total picture of our abilities and traits. The self-concept involves both cognition and emotion. It describes what we (our I-selves) know and feel about ourselves (our me-selves) and guides our actions (Harter, 1996, p. 207). It is also a *social construction*, crafted in the context of relationships with others. Like Evita Duarte, branded with the social stigma of illegitimacy, children incorporate into their self-image the picture that others reflect back to them.

James (1950) divided the Me-self, or self-concept, into three parts, which may sometimes conflict: the *material self* (physical attributes and possessions); the *social self* (the self seen by others, which is different for each "viewer"); and the highest level, the *spiritual self*, an enduring inner core of thoughts, values, dispositions, and the like.

When and how do the two main aspects of the self develop?

Emergence of the I-Self (Birth to 15 months)

Developmental scientists generally agree that the I-self is the first aspect of the self to emerge; that it does so in the context of the infant-caregiver relationship, which profoundly shapes it; and that infants may be biologically disposed to interact with caregivers from birth.* Newborns seem to be able to link isolated experiences (say, one breast-feeding session and another), extracting consistent patterns that become the rudiments of concepts of self and other. Coordinating these patterns leads to the establishment of predictable cycles of feeding, sleep, and arousal. These early experiences are highly emotional. Depending on what kind of care the infant receives and how the infant responds, pleasant or unpleasant emotions become connected with sensorimotor experiences (such as sucking) that play an important part in the growing organization of the self.

---

* The discussion in this section is indebted to Harter, 1998.

self-concept Sense of self; descriptive and evaluative mental picture of one's abilities and traits.

Guidepost 2

When and how do the self and the self-concept develop?

Physical changes can affect the self-image, as Lewis Carroll's Alice discovered.

Between 4 and 10 months, when infants learn to reach, grasp, and make things happen, they may begin to experience a sense of personal *agency* ("I can make the mobile move"), a feature of the I-self. The sense of agency—the realization that one can control external events—is a forerunner of what Bandura (1994) calls ***self-efficacy,*** a sense of being able to master challenges and achieve goals. A related aspect of the I-self is self-coherence, the sense of being a physical whole with boundaries, the place where agency resides.

These developments occur in interaction with caregivers in games such as peeka-boo, in which the infant becomes increasingly aware of the difference between self and other ("I see you!"). It is this awareness that allows attachment to occur—a manifestation of both individuation and connectedness.

Between 10 and 15 months, "infants come to realize that their subjective experiences, their attention, intentions, and affective states can be shared with another" who is also an independent agent (Harter, 1998, p. 561). Emotional expressions are the "language" through which this sharing occurs. When a crawling infant looks at the mother's face to see whether or not it's all right to touch a pretty vase, an emotional communication has occurred between two selves.

Emergence of the Me-Self (15 to 30 months)

Sometime between 15 and 18 months, the Me-self—the knowledge of self—is believed to emerge. Toward the end of this period babies begin to recognize themselves in mirrors or pictures, showing *self-awareness:* awareness of themselves as physically distinct beings. In a classic line of research, investigators dabbed rouge on the noses of 6- to 24-month-olds and sat them in front of a mirror. Three-fourths of 18-month-olds and all 24-month-olds touched their red noses more often than before, whereas babies younger than 15 months never did. This behavior suggests that the older babies knew they didn't normally have red noses and that they recognized the image in the mirror as their own (Lewis, 1997; Lewis & Brooks, 1974).

self-efficacy Sense of capability to master challenges and achieve goals.

What's Your View?

- Given the integral importance of relationships with caregivers to infants' self-development, what kinds of caregiving practices do you think would lead to a healthy sense of self?

Checkpoint

Can you . . .

- List three functions of the self?

- Explain the difference between the I-self and the Me-self, and discuss how they emerge and develop in infancy and toddlerhood?

By 20 to 24 months, toddlers begin to use first-person pronouns, another sign of self-awareness (Lewis, 1997). The use of "I," "me," and "you" enables toddlers to represent and refer to both the self and the other. Once they have a concept of themselves as distinct beings, children begin to apply descriptive terms ("big" or "little"; "straight hair" or "curly hair") and evaluative ones ("good," "pretty," or "strong") to themselves. This normally occurs sometime between 19 and 30 months, as representational ability and vocabulary expand. The rapid development of language during this period makes it possible for children to think and talk about the self and to incorporate parents' verbal descriptions ("You're so smart!" "What a big boy!") into their own emerging self-image (Stipek, Gralinski, & Kopp, 1990).

57 SELF-REPRESENTATIONS IN CHILDHOOD AND ADOLESCENCE

From a neo-Piagetian perspective, the self is one domain of knowledge, and the development of the self-concept is as much related to children's growing cognitive abilities as is their knowledge of any other aspect of the world. The I-self's picture of the Me-self, which comes into focus in toddlerhood, becomes clearer and more compelling as a person gains in cognitive abilities and deals with the developmental tasks of childhood, of adolescence, and then of adulthood.

The Continuous Self

A shift in self-awareness may occur near the age of 4, as autobiographical memory and a more sophisticated theory of mind develop: an awareness that the self is *continuous in time*. When 3½- and 4-year-olds were shown a videotape or photograph, taken a few minutes earlier, of a researcher placing a large sticker on their heads—an act of which they had been unaware—the children instantly reached up to feel and remove the sticker. Two-year-olds and younger 3-year-olds did not do that. Yet when shown the

This toddler shows self-awareness by touching the spot on her face where she sees in the mirror that experimenters have placed a dot of rouge. According to this research, toddlers come to recognize their own image between 18 and 24 months of age.

same thing happening in a mirror, the younger children did seem aware that a sticker was on their heads.

Does this mean that these children recognized themselves in a mirror but not in a photograph or videotape? That does not seem likely. Nor does it seem likely that they did not remember participating in a photograph session a few minutes earlier. A likelier explanation is that because younger children's memories are generic and not yet autobiographical, they may not think of the events in the videotape or photograph as having happened to *them* (Povinelli, Landau, & Perillous, 1996).

Self-Definition in Early Childhood

self-definition Cluster of characteristics used to describe oneself.

By age 4, Jason's attempts at ***self-definition*** are becoming more comprehensive as he begins to identify a cluster of characteristics to describe himself:

> My name is Jason and I live in a big house with my mother and father and sister, Lisa. I have a kitty that's orange and a television set in my own room. . . . I like pizza and I have a nice teacher. I can count up to 100, want to hear me? I love my dog, Skipper. I can climb to the top of the jungle gym, I'm not scared! Just happy. You can't be happy and scared, no way! I have brown hair, and I go to preschool. I'm really strong. I can lift this chair, watch me! (Harter, 1996, p. 208)

The way Jason describes himself is typical of children his age. He talks mostly about concrete, observable behaviors; external characteristics, such as physical features; preferences; possessions; and members of his household. He mentions particular skills (running and climbing) rather than general abilities (being athletic). His self-descriptions are unrealistically positive, and they frequently spill over into demonstrations; what he *thinks* about himself is almost inseparable from what he *does*. Not until middle childhood (around age 7) will he describe himself in terms of generalized traits, such as *popular, smart,* or *dumb;* recognize that he can have conflicting emotions; and be self-critical while holding a positive overall self-concept.

During the past twenty-five years, researchers have become interested in pinpointing the intermediate changes that make up this "age 5 to 7 shift." An analysis based on neo-Piagetian theory (Case, 1985, 1992a; Fischer, 1980) describes the 5 to 7 shift as occurring

This girl watching a video taken of herself, taken a few minutes earlier, seems unaware of the sticker the researcher had unobtrusively placed on her head, even though the sticker is clearly visible on the screen. By 3½ or 4, children tend to reach for the sticker, showing that they understand that the self is continuous in time.

self-definition Cluster of characteristics used to describe oneself.

single representations In neo-Piagetian terminology, first stage in development of self-definition, in which children describe themselves in terms of individual, unconnected characteristics and in all-or-nothing terms.

real self The self one actually is.

ideal self The self one would like to be.

representational mappings In neo-Piagetian terminology, the second stage in development of self-definition, in which a child makes logical connections between aspects of the self but still sees these characteristics in all-or-nothing terms.

What's Your View?

- Can you think of ways in which all-or-nothing thinking may affect a preschooler's behavior? How can knowledge of this characteristic of young children's thought help parents and teachers?

representational systems In neo-Piagetian terminology, the third stage in development of self-definition, characterized by breadth, balance, and the integration and assessment of various aspects of the self.

Checkpoint

Can you . . .

- From a neo-Piagetian perspective, tell how the self-concept develops in early and middle childhood?

Guidepost 3

How do children develop self-esteem, and what influences whether it is high or low?

in three steps, which actually form a continuous progression.* At 4, Jason is at the first step: his statements about himself are *single representations*—isolated, one-dimensional items. His thinking jumps from particular to particular, without logical connections. At this stage he cannot imagine having two emotions at once ("You can't be happy *and* scared"). He cannot decenter, in part because of his limited working memory capacity, and so he cannot consider different aspects of himself at the same time. His thinking is all-or-nothing. He cannot acknowledge that his *real self,* the person he actually is, is not the same as his *ideal self,* the person he would like to be. So he describes himself as a paragon of virtue and ability.

At about age 5 or 6, Jason moves up to the second step, as he begins to link one aspect of himself to another: "I can run fast, and I can climb high. I'm also strong. I can throw a ball real far, I'm going to be on a team some day!" (Harter, 1996, p. 215). However, these *representational mappings*—logical connections between parts of his image of himself—are still expressed in completely positive, all-or-nothing terms. Since good and bad are opposites, he cannot see how he might be good at some things and not at others. As all-or-nothing thinking declines in middle childhood, Jason's self-descriptions will become more balanced ("I'm good at hockey but bad at arithmetic").

Self-Definition in Middle Childhood

The third step takes place around age 7 or 8, when children begin to form *representational systems:* broad, inclusive, multidimensional self-concepts that integrate specific aspects of the self. Judgments about the self now become more realistic, more balanced, more comprehensive, and more consciously expressed.

"At school I'm feeling pretty smart in certain subjects, Language Arts and Social Studies," says 8-year-old Lisa. "I got A's in these subjects on my last report card and was really proud of myself. But I'm feeling really dumb in Arithmetic and Science, particularly when I see how well the other kids are doing. . . . I still like myself as a person, because Arithmetic and Science just aren't that important to me. How I look and how popular I am are more important" (Harter, 1996, p. 208).

Lisa's self-description shows that she can focus on more than one dimension of herself. She has outgrown an all-or-nothing, black-or-white self-definition; she recognizes that she can be "smart" in certain subjects and "dumb" in others. Her self-descriptions are more balanced; she can verbalize her self-concept better, and she can weigh different aspects of it ("How I look and how popular I am are more important."). She can compare her *real self* with her *ideal self* and can judge how well she measures up to social standards in comparison with others. All of these changes contribute to the development of self-esteem, her assessment of her *global self-worth* ("I like myself as a person").

58 SELF-ESTEEM

Self-esteem is the self-evaluative part of the self-concept, the judgment children make about their overall worth. From a neo-Piagetian perspective, then, self-esteem is based on children's growing cognitive ability to describe and define themselves. Erikson, on the other hand, saw self-esteem as a psychosocial development, the outcome of the stage of industry versus inferiority.

When does self-esteem emerge? What contributes to it, and how accurate is it? Does it remain stable or change? Although individual differences exist, researchers have observed certain developmental patterns.

---

* This discussion of children's developing understanding of themselves is indebted to Harter (1990, 1993, 1996, 1998).

Developmental Changes in Self-Esteem

Children do not generally articulate a concept of self-worth until about age 8, but they show by their behavior that they have one. Recent attempts to measure young children's self-esteem often incorporate teacher and parent reports (Davis-Kean & Sandler, 2001) or puppets and doll play (Measelle, Ablow, Cowan, & Cowan, 1998) in addition to self-reports.

In a study in Belgium (Verschueren, Buyck, & Marcoen, 2001), researchers measured 5-year-olds' self-representations, using two measures: (1) the Harter (1985b) Self-Perception Profile for Children (SPPC), which covers overall (global) self-worth, as well as specific perceptions about physical appearance, scholastic and athletic competence, social acceptance, and behavioral conduct; and (2) the Puppet Interview (Cassidy, 1988; Verschueren, Marcoen, & Schoefs, 1996), in which puppets are used to reveal a child's perception of what another person thinks of him or her. Children's positive or negative self-perceptions at age 5 tended to predict their self-perceptions and socioemotional functioning (as reported by teachers) at age 8.

Still, before the 5 to 7 shift, young children's self-esteem is not necessarily based on a realistic appraisal. Although they can make judgments about their competence at various activities, they are not yet able to rank them in importance. They tend to accept the judgments of adults, who often give positive, uncritical feedback, and thus may overrate their abilities (Harter, 1990, 1993, 1996, 1998).

Self-esteem in early childhood tends to be all-or-none: "I am good" or "I am bad" (Harter, 1996, 1998). Not until middle childhood do personal evaluations of competence and adequacy (based on internalization of parental and societal standards) normally become critical in shaping and maintaining a sense of self-worth (Harter, 1990, 1996, 1998).

Self-evaluations tend to become less positive in middle childhood, as children develop a more objective perspective, get more accurate social feedback, engage in more comparisons with others, and become more inclined to self-reflection. As they develop a more realistic picture of their characteristics and abilities, they take into account how much effort they must put in to achieve their goals (Harter, 1998).

A further decline in self-esteem may occur in early adolescence, around ages 11 to 13, as children move into school environments that put more emphasis on competition, grading, and strict teacher control. The dramatic physical, cognitive, emotional, and social changes connected with puberty may temporarily threaten the continuity of the sense of self and undermine self-esteem. Typically self-esteem rebounds in middle or later adolescence. However, young people, especially early-maturing girls, who experience the stress of school transitions at the same time they enter puberty, tend to show greater losses in self-esteem and may not recover as easily (Harter, 1998).

Some research suggests that adolescent girls have lower self-esteem than adolescent boys (Chubb, Fertman, & Ross, 1997). Highly publicized studies during the early 1990s found that girls' self-confidence and self-esteem stay fairly high until age 11 or 12 and then tend to falter (American Association of University Women [AAUW] Educational Foundation, 1992; L. M. Brown & Gilligan, 1990). A recent analysis of hundreds of studies involving nearly 150,000 respondents concluded that boys and men do have higher self-esteem than girls and women, especially in late adolescence, but the difference is small. Contrary to an earlier finding, both males and females seem to gain in self-esteem with age (Kling, Hyde, Showers, & Buswell, 1999).

William James (1950) suggested that there are *two* self-concepts: a core, or *baseline*, self-image that remains fairly consistent and a *barometric* self-image that varies in different situations. This is especially true of adolescents; they tend to think more of themselves or less, depending on the people they are with (Harter, 1998).

self-esteem The judgment a person makes about his or her self-worth.

Middle childhood, according to Erikson, is a time for learning the skills one's culture considers important. In driving geese to market, this Vietnamese girl is developing a sense of competence and gaining self-esteem.

Overall, most adolescents around the world have positive self-images. Daniel Offer and his colleagues (Offer et al., 1988) administered the Offer Self-Image Questionnaire to varied samples totaling 5,938 adolescents in schools in ten countries: Australia, Bangladesh, Hungary, Israel, Italy, Japan, Taiwan, Turkey, the United States, and West Germany. In general, these "universal adolescents" described themselves as happy; felt able to cope with life, make decisions, and use self-control; cared about others and liked being with and learning from them; enjoyed a job well done; were confident about their sexuality; did not harbor grudges against their parents; saw their mothers and fathers as getting along well most of the time; and expected to be able to take responsibility for themselves as they grew older. All in all, the researchers judged at least 73 percent of the total sample to have "a healthy adolescent self-image."

Sources of Self-Esteem

According to Erikson (1982), a major determinant of self-esteem is children's view of their capacity for productive work. Perhaps because younger children do not talk about self-esteem, Erikson identified middle childhood as the critical time for its development. The issue to be resolved in middle childhood, according to Erikson, is *industry versus inferiority*. The "virtue" that develops with successful resolution of this conflict is *competence*, a view of the self as able to master skills and complete tasks.

industry versus inferiority Erikson's fourth stage of psychosocial development, in which children must learn the productive skills their culture requires or else face feelings of inferiority.

Children have to learn skills valued in their society. Arapesh boys in New Guinea learn to make bows and arrows and to lay traps for rats; Arapesh girls learn to plant, weed, and harvest. Inuit children of Alaska learn to hunt and fish. Children in industrialized countries learn to read, write, count, and use computers. Most children around the world learn household skills, run errands, and help out with odd jobs. Children compare their abilities with those of their peers; if they feel inadequate, they may retreat to the protective embrace of the family. If, on the other hand, they become too industrious, they may neglect social relationships and turn into "workaholics."

A different view of sources of self-worth comes from research by Susan Harter (1985a, 1990, 1993, 1998). Using the SPPC, Harter (1985a) asked 8- to 12-year olds to rate their appearance, behavior, school performance, athletic ability, and acceptance by other children and to assess how much each of these areas affected their opinion of themselves. The children rated physical appearance most important. Social acceptance came next. Less critical were schoolwork, conduct, and athletics.

In contrast, then, to the high value Erikson placed on mastery of skills, Harter suggests that today's school-age children, at least in North America, judge themselves more by good looks and popularity. Indeed, in many studies, physical appearance consistently tops the list of contributors to self-esteem from early childhood to adulthood (Harter, 1998).

Concern with *body image*—how one believes one looks—begins to be important toward the end of middle childhood. Teenagers of both sexes worry about their weight, their complexion, and their facial features. Girls tend to be unhappier about their looks than boys of the same age, reflecting the greater cultural emphasis on women's physical attributes. Girls, especially those who are advanced in pubertal development, tend to think they are too fat even when they are not. This negative body image can lead to depression (Stice & Bearman, 2001) and to eating disorders, which, if untreated, can impair fertility and even become life threatening (Richards et al., 1990).

The hormonal changes of puberty apparently reinforce feelings of competence in certain areas that have different social value for boys and girls. Among fifty-six adolescents with delayed puberty, testosterone treatments tended to improve boys' perception of their athletic ability, according to the Harter Self-Perception Profile for Adolescents (an extension of the SPPC), and estrogen increased girls' ratings of their romantic appeal and the intimacy of their friendships. For both sexes, the hormone treatments positively affected perceived job competence (Schwab et al., 2001). Of course, this does not mean that hormones alone account for these perceptions.

Self-esteem during adolescence develops largely in the context of relationships with peers, particularly those of the same sex. Male self-esteem seems to be linked with striving for individual achievement, whereas female self-esteem depends more on connections with others. In one longitudinal study, eighty-four mostly white, socioeconomically diverse young adults, whose self-esteem had been measured at ages 14 and 18, described memories about important experiences with others. Men who had had high self-esteem during adolescence tended to recall wanting to assert themselves with male friends, whereas women who had had high self-esteem recalled efforts to help female friends—efforts that involved asserting themselves in a collaborative rather than a competitive way (Thorne & Michaelieu, 1996).

Contingent Self-Esteem: The "Helpless" Pattern

When self-esteem is high, a child is motivated to achieve. However, if self-esteem is *contingent* on success, children may view failure or criticism as an indictment of their worth and may feel helpless to do better. About one-third to one-half of preschoolers, kindergartners, and first-graders show elements of this "helpless" pattern: self-denigration or self-blame, negative emotion, lack of persistence, and lowered expectations for themselves (Burhans & Dweck, 1995; Ruble & Dweck, 1995). Instead of trying a different way to complete a puzzle, as a child with unconditional self-esteem might do, "helpless" children feel ashamed and give up, or go back to an easier puzzle they have already done. They do not expect to succeed, and so they do not try. Whereas older children who fail may conclude that they are dumb, preschoolers interpret poor performance as a sign of being "bad." Furthermore, they believe that "badness" is permanent. This sense of being a bad person may persist into middle childhood and on into adulthood.

body image Descriptive and evaluative beliefs about one's appearance.

Checkpoint

Can you . . .

- Tell how young children's self-esteem differs from that of school-age children and adolescents?

- Compare Erikson's and Harter's views on sources of self-esteem?

- Discuss how self-esteem changes in adolescence?

Individual differences in self-esteem may hinge on whether children think their traits and attributes are fixed or can be changed (Harter, 1998). Children who believe their attributes are permanent tend to become demoralized when, say, they fail a test, believing there is nothing they can do to improve. Often these children attribute poor performance or social rejection to their own personality deficiencies, which they believe they are helpless to change. Rather than trying new ways to gain approval, they repeat unsuccessful strategies or just give up. Children with high self-esteem, by contrast, tend to attribute failure or disappointment to factors outside themselves or to the need to try harder. Like Eva Perón, who overcame several setbacks in her climb to power, if initially unsuccessful or rejected they persevere, trying new strategies until they find one that works (Erdley, Cain, Loomis, Dumas-Hines, & Dweck, 1997; Pomerantz & Saxon, 2001). Children with high self-esteem tend to have parents and teachers who give specific, focused feedback rather than criticizing the child as a person ("Look, the tag on your shirt is showing in front," not "Can't you see your shirt is on backwards? When are you going to learn to dress yourself?").

59 GENDER

Being male or female affects how people look, how they move their bodies, and how they work, play, and dress. It influences what they think about themselves and what others think of them. All those characteristics—and more—are included in the word *gender:* what it means to be male or female. Gender is a much broader concept than *sex*, which refers only to biological structure and functioning. Gender refers to degrees of masculinity and femininity, which often are culturally influenced.

Gender identity, awareness of one's femaleness or maleness and what it implies in a particular society, is an important aspect of the developing self-concept. Eva Perón's strong awareness of herself as a female dependent on a man's favor—so central to the way she thought of herself and the way she acted as an adult—went back to her early years as the daughter of a "kept woman" on the Argentinian *pampas.* Gender identity tends to be strong and stable by the middle school years (Egan & Perry, 2001).

How different are young boys and girls? What causes those differences? How do children develop gender identity, and how does it affect their attitudes and behavior? *Gender differences* are psychological or behavioral differences between the sexes. How pronounced are these differences?

60 GENDER DIFFERENCES

Measurable differences between baby boys and girls are few. The two sexes are equally sensitive to touch and tend to teethe, sit up, and walk at about the same ages (Maccoby, 1980). Girls do seem to have a *biological* advantage; they are less vulnerable than boys from conception on, develop faster, are less reactive to stress, and are more likely to survive infancy (Keenan & Shaw, 1997). On the other hand, baby boys are a bit longer and heavier than baby girls and may be slightly stronger. An analysis of a large number of studies found baby boys more active than baby girls, though this difference is not consistently documented (Eaton & Enns, 1986).

One of the earliest *behavioral* differences, appearing as early as age 2, is in the choice of toys and play activities and of playmates of the same sex (Turner & Gervai, 1995). While some gender differences become more pronounced after age 3, boys and girls on average remain more alike than different. The clearest difference is that boys, from preschool age on, act more aggressively than girls, both physically and verbally (Coie & Dodge,

Checkpoint

Can you . . .

• Describe how the "helpless pattern" arises and how it can affect children's reactions to social rejection?

What's Your View?

• As a parent or preschool teacher, how could you help a child who shows the helpless pattern to develop higher self-esteem?

Guidepost 4

How do boys and girls become aware of the meaning of gender, and what explains differences in behavior between the sexes?

gender identity Awareness, developed in early childhood, that one is male or female.

1998; Turner & Gervai, 1995). Most studies find that girls are more empathic and prosocial (Keenan & Shaw, 1997), and some find that girls are more compliant and cooperative with parents and seek adult approval more than boys do (N. Eisenberg, Fabes, Schaller, & Miller, 1989; M. L. Hoffman, 1977; Maccoby, 1980; Turner & Gervai, 1995).

Intelligence test scores show no overall gender differences (Keenan & Shaw, 1997). This is not surprising, since the most widely used tests are designed to eliminate gender bias (Neisser et al., 1996). However, there are differences in scores on specific abilities. Females tend to do better at verbal tasks (but not analogies), at mathematical computation, and at tasks requiring fine motor and perceptual skills, while males excel in most spatial abilities and in abstract mathematical and scientific reasoning (Halpern, 1997).

Some of these cognitive differences, which seem to exist across cultures, begin quite early in life. Girls' superiority in perceptual speed and verbal fluency appears during infancy and toddlerhood, and boys' greater ability to mentally manipulate figures and shapes and solve mazes becomes evident early in the preschool years. Other differences do not become apparent in children of average ability until preadolescence or beyond (Halpern, 1997; Levine et al., 1999).

As toddlers, boys and girls are equally likely to hit, bite, and throw temper tantrums, and they are just as likely to show "difficult" temperaments. Around age 4, however, problem behavior diminishes in girls, whereas boys tend to get in trouble or "act up." This absence of problem behavior among girls persists until adolescence, when they become more prone to anxiety and depression (Keenan & Shaw, 1997).

Possible reasons for this divergence may lie in the biological and cognitive differences just discussed. Lower reactivity to stress may enable girls to deal with frustration or anger in a more controlled way, and girls' greater facility with language may enable them to communicate their feelings in healthier ways. Another reason may be a difference in the way boys and girls are socialized. Girls, more than boys, are taught to control themselves, to share toys, and to think about how their actions affect others; and their greater empathic ability may help them internalize social standards (Keenan & Shaw, 1997). Girls talk about their experiences in more detail than boys do, and they tend to talk more about feelings, people, and relationships (Buckner & Fivush, 1998).

We need to remember, of course, that gender differences are valid for large groups of boys and girls but not necessarily for individuals. By knowing a child's sex, we cannot predict whether that *particular* boy or girl will be faster, stronger, smarter, more obedient, or more assertive than another child.

61 PERSPECTIVES ON GENDER DEVELOPMENT: NATURE AND NURTURE

What accounts for gender differences, and why do some of them emerge with age? The most influential explanations, until recently, centered on the differing experiences and social expectations that boys and girls meet almost from birth (Halpern, 1997; Neisser et al., 1996). These experiences and expectations concern three related aspects of gender identity: *gender roles, gender-typing,* and *gender stereotypes.*

Gender roles are the behaviors, interests, attitudes, skills, and personality traits that a culture considers appropriate for males or females. All societies have gender roles. Historically, in most cultures, women have been expected to devote most of their time to caring for the household and children, while men were providers and protectors. Women were expected to be compliant and nurturant; men, to be active, aggressive, and competitive. In Eva Perón's Argentina, an ambitious woman with leadership qualities could rise to the highest echelons—but only on the arm of a man. Today, gender roles in western cultures have become more diverse and more flexible.

TABLE 5-1 Four Perspectives on Gender Development

Theories	Major Theorists	Key Processes	Basic Beliefs
Biological Approach		Genetic, neurological, and hormonal activity	Many or most behavioral differences between the sexes can be traced to biological differences.
Psychoanalytic Approach			
Psychosexual theory	Sigmund Freud	Resolution of unconscious emotional conflict	Gender identity occurs when child identifies with same-sex parent.
Cognitive Approach			
Cognitive-developmental theory	Lawrence Kohlberg	Self-categorization	Once a child learns she is a girl or he is a boy, child sorts information about behavior by gender and acts accordingly.
Gender-schema theory	Sandra Bem, Carol Lynn Martin, & Charles F. Halverson	Self-categorization based on processing of cultural information	Child organizes information about what is considered appropriate for a boy or a girl on the basis of what a particular culture dictates, and behaves accordingly. Child sorts by gender because the culture dictates that gender is an important schema.
Socialization Approach			
Social cognitive theory	Albert Bandura	Modeling, reinforcement, and teaching	Gender-typing is a result of interpretation, evaluation, and internalization of socially transmitted standards.

Gender-typing, the process by which children learn and acquire gender roles, takes place early in childhood, but children vary in the degree to which they become gender-typed. *Gender stereotypes* are preconceived generalizations about male or female behavior ("All females are passive and dependent; all males are aggressive and independent"). Gender stereotypes pervade many cultures. They are seen to some degree in children as young as 2½ or 3, increase during the preschool years, and reach a peak at age 5 (Haugh, Hoffman, & Cowan, 1980; Ruble & Martin, 1998; J. E. Williams & Best, 1982). Preschoolers—and even much older children—often attribute positive qualities to their own sex and negative qualities to the other sex (Egan & Perry, 2001; Ruble & Martin, 1998; Underwood, Schockner, & Hurley, 2001). Still, among preschoolers, *both* boys and girls call boys strong, fast, and cruel, and girls fearful and helpless (Ruble & Martin, 1998).

How do children acquire gender roles, and why do they adopt gender stereotypes? Are these purely social constructs, or do they reflect underlying biological differences between males and females? Do social and cultural influences create gender differences, or merely accentuate them?

Today investigators are uncovering evidence of biological explanations for gender differences: genetic, hormonal, and neurological. These explanations are not either-or. Both nature and nurture probably play important parts in what it means to be male or female. Biological influences are not necessarily universal, inevitable, or unchangeable; nor are social and cultural influences easily overcome.

Let's look, then, at four perspectives on gender development (summarized in Table 5-1): *biological, psychoanalytic, cognitive,* and *socialization-based* approaches. Each of these perspectives can contribute to our understanding; none fully explains why boys and girls turn out differently in some respects and not in others.

Biological Approach

The existence of similar gender roles in many cultures suggests that some gender differences may be biologically based. How do biological differences affect behavior?

By age 5, when the brain reaches approximate adult size, boys' brains are about 10 percent larger than girls' brains, mostly because boys have more gray matter in the cerebral cortex, whereas girls have greater neuronal density. What these findings may tell us about brain organization and functioning is unknown (Reiss, Abrams, Singer, Ross, & Denckla, 1996).

We do have evidence that size differences in the *corpus callosum,* the band of tissue joining the right and left cortical hemispheres, are correlated with verbal fluency (Hines et al., 1992). Since girls have a larger corpus callosum, better coordination between the two hemispheres may help explain girls' superior verbal abilities (Halpern, 1997).

Hormones in the bloodstream before or about the time of birth may affect the developing brain and influence gender differences. The male hormone testosterone, along with low levels of the neurotransmitter serotonin, seems related to aggressiveness, competitiveness, and dominance, perhaps through action on certain brain structures, such as the hypothalamus and amygdala (Bernhardt, 1997). Attempts also have been made to link prenatal hormonal activity with other aspects of brain functioning, such as those involved in spatial and verbal skills (Neisser et al., 1996), but this research is controversial (Ruble & Martin, 1998).

Other research focuses on children with unusual hormonal histories. Girls with a disorder called congenital adrenal hyperplasia (CAH) have unusually high prenatal levels of *androgens* (male sex hormones). Although raised as girls, they tend to develop into "tomboys," showing preferences for "boys' toys," rough play, and male playmates, as well as strong spatial skills. *Estrogens* (female hormones), on the other hand, seem to have less influence on boys' gender-typed behavior. Since these studies are natural experiments, they cannot establish cause and effect; other factors besides hormonal differences, such as early interactions with parents, may play a role. Also, hormonal differences may themselves be affected by environmental or other factors. In any case, such atypical patterns of behavior have not been found in children with normal hormonal variations (Ruble & Martin, 1998).

Perhaps the most dramatic examples of biologically based research have to do with infants born with ambiguous sexual organs (part male and part female). John Money and his colleagues (Money, Hampson, & Hampson, 1955) developed guidelines for such cases, recommending that the child be assigned as early as possible to the gender that holds the potential for the most nearly normal functioning and for stable gender identity. These guidelines have also been applied when sexual organs were accidentally damaged.

In the case of a 7-month-old boy whose penis was accidentally cut off during circumcision, the decision was made at 17 months to rear the child as a girl, and four months later doctors performed surgical reconstruction (Money & Ehrhardt, 1972). Although initially described as developing into a normal female, the child later rejected female identity and, at puberty, switched to living as a male. After a second surgical reconstruction, he married a woman and adopted her children. The implicit lesson was that gender identity may be rooted in chromosomal structure or prenatal development and cannot easily be changed (Diamond & Sigmundson, 1997).

Another case of this kind had a different outcome. This time, the accident occurred at 2 months, and penile removal and sexual reassignment took place by 7 months. When interviewed at ages 16 and 26, the patient identified as a female, was living as a woman, and had had sexual relationships with both men and women—suggesting that assignment of gender, at least during early infancy, may have some flexibility after all (Bradley, Oliver, Chernick, & Zucker, 1998). But a recent study of twenty-seven male

Checkpoint

Can you . . .

• Assess evidence for biological explanations of gender differences?

identification In Freudian theory, the process by which a young child adopts characteristics, beliefs, attitudes, values, and behaviors of the parent of the same sex.

gender constancy Awareness that one will always be male or female. Also called *sex-category constancy*.

children born without penises went the other way. Although twenty-five of these infants were raised as girls, in childhood they considered themselves boys and engaged in rough-and-tumble play, suggesting that hormones do play a powerful role in gender identity (Reiner, 2000).

The evidence as to biological bases of behavior, then, is still inconclusive. But the limited experience with sex reassignment raises warning flags as to the advisability of ignoring biology altogether.

Psychoanalytic Approach

"Dad, where will you live when I grow up and marry Mommy?" asks Timmy, age 4. From the psychoanalytic perspective, Timmy's question is part of his acquisition of gender identity. That process, according to Freud, is one of *identification,* the adoption of characteristics, beliefs, attitudes, values, and behaviors of the parent of the same sex. Freud and other classical psychoanalytic theorists considered identification an important personality development of early childhood. Some social learning theorists also have used the term.

According to classical Freudian theory, identification will occur for Timmy when he represses or gives up the wish to possess the parent of the other sex (his mother) and identifies with the parent of the same sex (his father). Although this explanation for gender development has been influential, it has been difficult to test. Despite some evidence that preschoolers tend to act more affectionately toward the opposite-sex parent and more aggressively toward the same-sex parent (Westen, 1998), the theory has little research support (Maccoby, 1992). Most developmental psychologists today favor other explanations.

Cognitive Approach

Sarah figures out she is a girl because people call her a girl. She figures out that she will always be a girl. She comes to understand gender the same way she comes to understand everything else: by actively thinking about and constructing her own gender-typing. This is the heart of Lawrence Kohlberg's (1966) cognitive-developmental theory.

According to Kohlberg, children classify themselves as male or female and then organize their behavior around that classification. They do this by adopting behaviors they perceive as consistent with their gender. Thus, Sarah prefers dolls to trucks because she views playing with dolls as consistent with her idea of herself as a girl. According to Kohlberg, *gender constancy,* more recently called *sex-category constancy*—a child's realization that his or her sex will always be the same—leads to the acquisition of gender roles. Once children realize they are permanently male or female, they adopt what they see as gender-appropriate behaviors.

Development of gender constancy seems to occur in three stages (Ruble & Martin, 1998; Szkrybalo & Ruble, 1999). First, children become aware of their own gender and that of others. Next, a girl realizes that she will grow up to be a woman, and a boy that he will grow up to be a man—in other words, that gender remains the same across time. Children at this stage may base judgments about gender on superficial external appearances and stereotyped behaviors. Finally comes the realization that a girl remains a girl even if she has a short haircut and wears pants, and a boy remains a boy even if he has long hair and earrings.

When does this final stage occur? Answers vary from ages 3 to 7, or even later. This wide range in findings may be due to the kinds of questions asked, to differing criteria, to differences in children's reasoning at different ages, or to methodological differences (Ruble & Martin, 1998; Szkrybalo & Ruble, 1999).

In any case, there is little evidence for Kohlberg's view that gender constancy is the key to gender-typing. Long before children attain the final stage of gender constancy, they show gender-typed preferences (Bussey & Bandura, 1992; Ruble & Martin, 1998). They categorize activities and objects by gender, know a lot about what males and females do, and often acquire gender-appropriate behaviors (G. D. Levy & Carter, 1989; Luecke-Aleksa, Anderson, Collins, & Schmitt, 1995). Even at 2½, girls show more interest in dolls and boys in cars, and both begin to prefer being with children of their own sex (Ruble & Martin, 1998).

It is possible that gender constancy, once achieved, may further sensitize children to gender-related information (Ruble & Martin, 1998). Five-year-old boys who have reached or are on the brink of gender constancy pay more attention to male characters on television and watch more sports and action programs than other boys their age (Luecke-Aleksa et al., 1995). Later, children develop more complex beliefs about gender and become more flexible in their views about gender roles (Ruble & Martin, 1998; M. G. Taylor, 1996).

MR